In Defense of

SIN

In Defense of

SIN

Edited by
John Portmann

palgrave

for St. Martin's Press

IN DEFENSE OF SIN
© John Portmann, 2001

First published 2001 by
PALGRAVE
175 Fifth Avenue, New York, N.Y.10010.
Companies and representatives throughout the world

PALGRAVE is the new global publishing imprint of St. Martin's Press LLC Scholarly and Reference Division and Palgrave Publishers Ltd (formerly Macmillan Press Ltd).

ISBN 0-312-23986-6 (hardback)

Library of Congress Cataloging-in-Publication Data

In defense of sin / edited by John Portmann.
    p. cm.
    Includes bibliographical references and index.
    ISBN 0-312-23986-6
1. Christian ethics. 2. Ethics, Jewish. 3. Sin. I. Portmann, John
BJ1275 .I52 2001
170—dc21
2001021829

Design by planettheo.com.

First edition: September 2001
10 9 8 7 6 5 4 3 2 1

Printed in the United States of America.

PERMISSIONS

CONTENTS

ACKNOWLEDGMENTS

Gayatri Patnaik tops the list of people to whom I am grateful: It is good fortune to land so able an editor. Her assistant Kasy Moon deftly shepherded this manuscript, which Sonia Wilson then polished. Alan Bradshaw saved me from numerous errors.

Cora Diamond, Virginia Germino, Susannah Rutherglen, and Cassandra Fraser kindly read over the introduction. Merlin Holland patiently explained to me the intricacies of copyright law as they apply to the works of his grandfather, Oscar Wilde. Cheshire Calhoun advised me on a much earlier version of the table of contents.

Daniel Ortiz and Cynthia Read encouraged me as few others could.

The volume is dedicated to all who have suffered monstrous punishment for their sins and particularly to children who are abandoned or unloved.

"You are all sinners in the hands of an angry God."

—Jonathan Edwards

The
HALF-LIFE
OF SIN

The sky is falling, it seems. Wildly diverse people who cannot see eye to eye on much of anything seem to agree that morality suffers from terrible public neglect. Indifference and outright hostility have conspired to erode the importance of doing the right thing, they protest. Does anyone care about morality anymore?

Gone are the days when people heroically struggle with their consciences and emerge confident they have chosen the virtuous path. Gone, apparently, are the days when people suffer because of sin. College students today may puzzle over this climactic passage from Evelyn Waugh's *Brideshead Revisited* (1945), in which the stunningly beautiful and fabulously wealthy Julia cries to her lover:

> "There you've got it, in black and white.
>
> "All in one word, too, one little, flat, deadly word that covers a lifetime.

"'Living in sin'; not just doing wrong . . . doing wrong, knowing it is wrong, stopping doing it, forgetting. That's not what they mean. That's not [her virtuous brother's] pennyworth. He means just what it says in black and white.

"*Living in sin*, with sin, by sin, for sin, every hour, every day, year in, year out. Waking up with sin in the morning, seeing the curtains drawn on sin, bathing it, dressing it, clipping diamonds to it, feeding it, showing it round, giving it a good time, putting it to sleep at night with a tablet of [aspirin] if it's fretful."

In revealing to her lover such anguish, she dooms her future with him:

"Past and future . . . putting [her first husband] away, forgetting him, finding you, the past two years with you, all the future with you, all the future with or without you, war coming, world ending—sin."[1]

Why does sin torture Julia? The image of a divorced Catholic woman surreptitiously carrying on an affair with a Protestant man will hardly strike contemporary readers as shocking, if at all sinful. The account of Julia's conscience has more to do with psychological problems, we may think, than with moral impulses striving to guide a course of action. If anything about this passage surprises us, it might be the very idea that sin used to lead to gnawing regret, even ruined some lives.

Those who throw up their arms and ask whether anyone cares about morality anymore must feel as Julia does. They must see in sin something lost on the rest of the world. What could that be? Quite a few people have gone on record over the course of the last two thousand years as feeling frightened by the moral decay they perceived around them. If the sky is indeed falling, it is taking a long time to reach the ground. The world keeps turning.

If only to understand how it can hurt us, morality deserves our attention. Knowing right from wrong doesn't require familiarity with sophisticated theories; morality often will confront us at our parents' knees, in the classroom, at the office, and on the television shows we watch. Other people will surely appeal to it at one time or another to rebuke us; we will likely return the favor, all in the name of making the world a better place.

Morality seems to get more confusing as the world gets smaller. At the dawn of a new century, celebration of ethnic diversity seems to many one of the best ways to improve our "global village." Our teachers strive to show us that we are all different yet basically the same. The reasons foreigners give for what they do may baffle and even enrage us, however. Ethnic and moral diversity are two very different things, and we still struggle to accept the second.

If anything can morally unite Jews and Christians and Muslims at the dawn of a new century, the Decalogue, or "Ten Commandments," must be it. Even secular people in the West who have bowed out of or run from one of these religious traditions usually point to the Ten Commandments as the bedrock of morality (to the extent that there can be said to be one at all). Beyond the Ten Commandments, the seven deadly sins can also evoke moral consensus as to their unacceptability.

Perhaps more so than the Ten Commandments, the seven deadly sins (pride, anger, envy, greed, gluttony, lust, and sloth) target day-to-day life. Each of the seven deadly sins in some real way reveals what we have in common with others, and what we need to overcome in order to live harmoniously in groups. Because the word "sin" harbors strong religious connotations, atheists might think that the seven deadly sins have to deal only with people bent on pleasing some divine spirit. But the word "sin" has almost invariably indicated an act or attitude that offends not only God but also the people around us. We might not be able to change God's mind, but we can and do change the way people around us think. If God didn't exist and the people around us began to approve of the seven deadly sins, would we have conquered sin? This is a ponderous question and the springboard for this book.

Not everyone believes in God, we know. Some may still wonder why an atheist would decide to follow God's laws. Most atheists want to be good people, and their notion of what it is to live a moral life conveniently coincides with most of the commandments. You don't have to think of the commandments as unchanging, eternal verities to embrace them. Viewing them simply as good ideas is reason enough.

But is it really obvious that the Ten Commandments are good ideas? Second thoughts about the commandments—some playful, some quite serious—continue to accumulate in the public realm. Collected together, these reservations raise the question of whether sin actually can be defended.

Sin and vice can become quite legalistic, but the defenses of sin collected here focus on basic moral wrongdoing. Sin (which denotes an offense against God) technically differs from vice (which denotes a general moral shortcoming). In an increasingly secular age, however, sin and vice are often seen as the same thing. This convergence between sin and vice might highlight a parallel convergence between believers and pagans.

In the pagan world, hubris, the excessive pride that led a person to think of himself as equal to the gods, offended and alarmed the ancient Greeks as few other faults could. As Jerome Neu shows in chapter 10, Christians embraced this pagan sensibility and declared pride the worst sin of all. Today we hear endlessly that hearty self-esteem, a kind of pride, is the key to getting what we want from life. In chapter 9, David Novitz explains that forgiving others for the bad things they do to us comes at a cost: We may sacrifice some of our self-respect. To compete in today's world, we can't even get off the blocks without pride. What has happened to humility? And how can you bolster your self-esteem while meditating on your sinfulness? Sin, like humility, just gets in the way.

We are increasingly inclined to disregard the fears of our forebears. It seems that sins, like radioactive substances, have half-lives, some of which last longer than others. The most lethal chemicals require the most time to lose their sting, and the same is true of sin. Those sins with the longest half-lives will take the most time to recede from our consciousness. The biggest sins are those targeted in the Ten Commandments.

These laws, found in two places in the Bible (Exodus 20 and Deuteronomy 5), have come down to us principally in the following order:

1. Prohibition of false or foreign gods (idolatry)
2. Prohibition of images
3. Prohibition of the vain use of the divine name (blasphemy)
4. Keeping holy the Sabbath
5. Honoring one's father and mother
6. Prohibition of murder
7. Prohibition of adultery
8. Prohibition of theft
9. Prohibition of false witness against one's neighbor (lying)
10. Prohibition against coveting a neighbor's house, wife, slaves, or possessions (greed).

The first five commandments cover duties to God (parents, who give us life, are considered representatives of God); the last five convey duties to other human beings. It is often thought that these truths are etched in stone, but that is not clearly the case. In the New Testament, for example, a young man asks Jesus how to become perfect. Referring presumably to what we now take to be the Ten Commandments, Jesus cites some but not all of the laws and not in the order in which we think of them (Matthew 9:18–19; Mark 10:19; Luke 18:20). Jesus famously condenses the last six laws into "the Golden Rule." Freud's stinging criticism of the Golden Rule, reproduced here in part, continues to pain some Christians today.

Ancient Hebrews generally viewed sin as the failing of a group, whereas early Christians tied sin to individuals. Everyone agreed that sin was very real and very dangerous. Of course Jews, Christians, and Muslims base moral thinking on more than just the commandments (specifically, on the Torah, the New Testament, and the Koran respectively), and culture filters the ways in which people understand them. The Ten Commandments say nothing about homosexuality, for example, yet each of these traditions has expressed moral revulsion to the idea.

The really big sins may confuse us as much as they frighten us. Take lying, which, in principle, is plainly wrong. Aristotle, the guiding star of early Roman Catholic theologians, says in the *Nichomachean Ethics*, "a lie is of itself mean and something to be avoided, while the truth is good and praiseworthy."[2] Roughly a thousand years later Augustine insists in *Against Lying* that "every lie is a sin" and the great Protestant moralist Kant follows suit in the eighteenth century.[3] And yet Pope John XXIII, the most admired pontiff of the twentieth century, freely distributed thousands of blank birth certificates so that Jews could falsely claim Christian birth and thereby escape Nazi territories. Today Jews and Roman Catholics both eagerly anticipate the day this liar will be canonized a saint.

Other sins also seem to turn on context. St. Thomas Aquinas writes in the *Summa Theologiae* that poor people may morally steal from the wealthy in times of shortage.[4] Aquinas defies one of the commandments in the name of lessening human suffering. If poverty justifies theft, why not prostitution? Or selling a family member into slavery (as in Thomas Hardy's novel *The Mayor of Casterbridge*)? To the shock of many moderns, Aristotle,[5] and several influential Catholic theologians following his example, considered slavery perfectly moral. Well into the nineteenth century, substantial parts of the world accepted slavery—morally and legally. Today, a great many working-class people and members of racial and sexual minorities owe whatever privileges they currently enjoy to repeated and quite deliberate criminal acts, acts now considered heroic civil disobedience. Sin changes with the times.

That notions of it change does not defeat sin, which has a long history of expanding and contracting. Think of the Hebrew Bible, called the Old Testament by Christians. First Abraham brought us two laws. Then Noah brought us a few more. Then Moses brought us many, many more (for a grand total of 613). In the New Testament, St. Paul significantly reduced the number of laws good people were expected to follow. He held that the Hebrew laws could be adhered to if useful or discarded if burdensome. St. Paul revolutionized moral thinking, even as he deepened support for the commandments.

Sins come and go. No one thinks it sinful now for a Catholic woman to enter her church bareheaded. Few Jews think it sinful for a woman who has recently menstruated to enter a synagogue without first visiting the mikvah (ritual purification bath). And hardly anyone thinks it sinful to get tattooed or to wear clothes made of both cotton and polyester. (Here it should be said that Hebrew conceptions of wrongdoing often centered on rules about ritual purity, infractions of which only ambiguously qualify as sins in the Christian sense.) Many acts or states technically sinful now pass unnoticed. Some of their half-lives have faded.

The eighteenth-century Irish statesman Edmund Burke tied sinfulness to social status. The world was becoming more democratic, Burke observed, and simultaneously less refined. Under the system of aristocratic manners, "vice itself lost half its evil by losing all its grossness," he observed in *Reflections on the Revolution in France* (1790). This insight rings true today, for the sins of the great unwashed generally strike us as dirtier than the sins of Hollywood stars and corporate moguls. Whenever Princess Diana went astray, the world sympathetically looked the other way.

And so measuring sins, like classifying them, presents certain difficulties. There is, no doubt, the slippery factor of culture to reckon with, as I have said. Even different communities within the same religious tradition may embrace distinct moral sensibilities. Consider the difference between the French (largely Roman Catholic) and the English (largely Protestant). A century ago the French writer Guy de Maupassant memorably described Victorian women as "those fanatical women of principle, . . . the sort England produces in large numbers . . . those straight-backed unbearable old maids who are seen in the dining-rooms of hotels throughout Europe . . . and wherever they go import their peculiar fads, the morals of fossilised virgins, ghastly clothes, and that faint odour of rubber which makes you suspect that at night they are put away in a box."[6] Moving from country to country, a Christian, a Jew, or a Muslim may feel a stranger even among people who profess his own faith.

Simply arguing for relativism or mitigating circumstances is much less interesting than actually defending sin. Over the course of the last three centuries, skepticism and misgivings about morality have blossomed. In *An Enquiry Concerning the Principles of Morals* (1751), the eighteenth-century philosopher David Hume made fun of "monkish virtues." Moral excesses may ruin our chances for joy. Indeed, the word "moral" is sometimes taken to imply a perverse masochistic (and/or sadistic) denial of pleasure. Lady Sneerwell chides another character in Richard Sheridan's popular play *School for Scandal* (1777): ". . . you are going to be moral and forget you are among friends."[7] With increasing frequency in the nineteenth and twentieth centuries, writers and philosophers called into question whether morality serves to further the interests of ruling groups or persons. In the play *An Ideal Husband* (1895), Oscar Wilde's protagonist states that morality is just an attitude we hold toward people we dislike. Harvard philosopher Alfred North Whitehead asked a few decades later, "What is morality in any given time or place? It is what the majority then and there happen to like, and immorality is what they dislike."[8] I do not share this skepticism completely, but I do take seriously philosophical objections to even the most basic moral principles.

Our thinking about sin has grown more sophisticated in the thousands of years since Moses handed down the Ten Commandments. No one seems to have noticed this formally in the way that this volume does. In the past, moral thinkers tended to portray moral goodness as a function of rationality and moral depravity as a function of irrationality. The essays collected here look sin in the eye and find that it holds much more than merely sensual appeal. These are serious pieces, not merely daring pirouettes. The point is not to stretch an elastic morality to fit nicely over, and thereby justify, anything at all we would like to do. To the contrary: These essays grant moral principles the seriousness and probing analysis sin deserves. Collectively, the defenses raise the question of the limits of morality.

A disappointing but wildly popular book by William J. Bennett, the former United States Secretary of Education, dismisses sin as transparent and obviously wrong. *The Book of Virtues* (1997) rallies the troops to lift the flag of morality ever higher. *In Defense of Sin* takes wrongdoing more seriously and begins from the premise that we cannot really appreciate moral excellence until we have understood sin. The American philosopher Richard Rorty writes in *Achieving Our Country* (1998) that when our culture overcomes the notion of sin, we will have pushed back our sense of personal limitation and improved human life. I, for my part, want to hold on to our sense of sin, to refine it, and to ponder how it distorts human life. If nothing else, sin can rightfully claim to be a great deal more interesting than virtue.

I do not attempt to offer definitive moral answers here, only to suggest that some questions of right and wrong are more complicated than thinkers like Bennett may allow. I do not cover all the commandments. I include four essays on sex for the simple reason that carnal sins are among the most common. No doubt they are also among the most captivating. I consciously avoid what are by now the well-exposed "sins" of abortion, just war, euthanasia, and homosexuality.

The moral stakes in defending sin loom quite high. In the gospel of Matthew, Jesus warns: "Do not think that I have come to abolish the law or the prophets; I have come not to abolish but to fulfill. For truly I tell you, until heaven and earth pass away, not one letter, not one stroke of a letter, will pass from the law until all is accomplished. Therefore, whoever breaks one of the least of these commandments, and teaches others to do the same, will be called least in the kingdom of heaven; but whoever does them and teaches them will be called great in the kingdom of heaven" (Matthew 5: 17–19). It is fair to say that the moral stakes of understanding sin properly are equally high in Judaism and Islam. In any event, even Jews and Muslims may find interesting what Jesus asserts here: The sky will indeed fall one day. It appears the sky may have a half-life as well.

Hating sin, we may deplore the softening influences of time and context. Religious fundamentalists guard the boundary line between virtue and vice and refuse to negotiate. Today moralists and politicians alike will occasionally beseech us to get tougher on sin. This volume raises anew the old question of whether faith can ever greet reason as anything other than an enemy. This collection of essays may sadden and worry religious people who view consciousness of sin as the best way of steering society back to God. By no means do I seek to encourage readers to throw over the Ten Commandments or the very notion of a common morality per se. On the contrary, I urge them to take it seriously. These essays focus our attention on the very difficult question of why sin affronts (or should affront) our moral sensibility. Is sin bad simply because God says it is, or does God say that sin is bad because it is intrinsically perverse?

If sins are truly wrong, their wrongness should emerge from, rather than die on, the examination table. There is no need to cower behind tradition. In his highly influential essay *On Liberty* (1859), the English philosopher John Stuart Mill takes up the "mental slavery" that creeps into minds afraid of criticism. Mill asserts that even the truth can become a kind of superstition when it is held as a prejudice against argument. We owe it to ourselves to evaluate our beliefs and, moreover, to examine our consciences for hypocrisy and self-deception.

Readers will decide for themselves whether these essays reflect moral progress or decay. I believe that we moderns can legitimately congratulate ourselves on our softer response to sin. Our forebears took sin seriously indeed, just as they did the punishment they attached to it. Whereas Jesus instructs his followers to think twice before casting the first stone at a woman caught in adultery, for centuries his followers subjected adulterers and other sinners to horrible spectacles of public humiliation. The French philosopher Michel Foucault detailed the barbaric underside of punishment in his celebrated work *Discipline and Punish* (1975) and the late Muslim leader Ayatollah Khomeini focused global attention on such revenge in 1989, when he publicly called for the death of Salman Rushdie, whose novel *The Satanic Verses* was judged blasphemous. To the extent that we no longer seek to torture or destroy sinners, our age has indeed progressed.

Sin wouldn't frustrate us if it didn't stand in the way of something we really would like to do. Now, as ever, the power of sin is to reduce the dominion of pleasure. Not surprisingly, clever people with social consciences may strive to find a way to have both—the private pleasures they crave and the social respectability they cultivate. Can philosophers honestly proclaim this moral sophistication? Again, readers will judge for themselves. In any event, to defend sin, hastening the end of its life, is not necessarily to champion pleasure. Rather, defending sin may bring to light certain limits to morality, limits whose recognition can improve the human condition.

For better or for worse, sin does seem to be losing its power to frighten us and therefore to steer our lives. We can argue whether this is the result of a healthy exercise of human reason or of outrageous hubris. Meanwhile, the race between the half-life of sin and human expansion continues, with human expansion taking a clear lead. If the sky does one day fall, it will likely land on a world surprised by sin.

NOTES

1. Evelyn Waugh, *Brideshead Revisited: The Sacred and Profane Memories of Captain Charles Ryder: A Novel* (Boston: Little, Brown, 1973), pp. 286–287.
2. Aristotle, *Nicomachean Ethics,* in *The Basic Works of Aristotle,* trans. Richard McKeon (New York: Random House, 1941), IV, 7, 1127a28.
3. Augustine, *Against Lying.*
4. Thomas Aquinas, *Summa Theologiae,* (New York: McGraw-Hill; Cambridge, England: Blackfriars, 1964–1976), I-II, 3, c, reply to Obj. 4.
5. Aristotle, *Politics* 1.5, in *The Basic Works of Aristotle.*
6. Quoted in Brian Moynahan, *The British Century* (New York: Random House, 1997), p. 10.
7. Richard Sheridan, *School for Scandal and Other Plays,* Eric Rump, ed. (New York: Viking Penguin, 1988), p. 194.
8. Lucien Price, *The Dialogues of Alfred North Whitehead* (Boston: Little, Brown and Company, 1954), p. 177.

CHAPTER ONE

In Defense of
Idolatry

*O*ften considered synonymous with paganism, idolatry signifies worship of physical representations of gods. Whereas paganism always had room for one more god, the ancient Hebrews followed a new religion, one in which there was really only one God. Monotheism was a radically new idea.

Idolatry offends God as few other sins can. According to Jewish tradition, for example, all the laws of the Torah save three—murder, idolatry, and adultery—may be broken in order to save a human life.

Ever since Abraham revolted against his idolatrous father, monotheism has represented steadfast opposition to idol worship. Ludwig Feuerbach turns this opposition on its head and argues that, without realizing it, all practice idolatry. Unwittingly, he claims, religious believers violate the very rule against idolatry they themselves devised.

In this excerpt from 1841, Feuerbach asserts that God is a creation of the human imagination. Feuerbach applauds humanity for having used its imagination so creatively. God is the highest achievement of human art, Feuerbach insists, and man is himself God. Feuerbach defends idolatry (or Christianity—for he saw them as one and the same) because it amounts to worshiping humanity.

Feuerbach wondered why religion was universal and why so many religions instructed people to humble themselves before a greater power. Each culture uses its religion to project its highest ideals into the sky, he concluded. The problem, according to Feuerbach, was that we consequently view ourselves as sinful, fallen creatures instead of congratulating ourselves for having come up with such a wonderful idea.

According to Feuerbach, we cannot get to know ourselves unless we get to know God, who is our own reflection. Although he insisted he was not an atheist, Feuerbach's philosophy unsettled people widely. His famous cry, "To enrich man, one must impoverish God," may not exactly shock twenty-first century believers, but it can hardly fail to bother them at some level. For liberating ourselves from the idea of sin comes at the cost of diminishing God. This trade-off between man and God sets the stage for defending sin and is the theme of this book.

∾

LUDWIG FEUERBACH (1804–1872) made a great splash in Europe upon the publication of *The Essence of Christianity* (1841). His argument that God is merely the outward projection of man's inward essence scandalized contemporary society. Born in Bavaria, he traveled to Berlin to study under Hegel, an eminent philosopher. Although Feuerbach never managed to surpass his first work, he inspired another influential thinker: Karl Marx.

from

THE ESSENCE
OF CHRISTIANITY

Ludwig Feuerbach

translated by George Eliot

. . . Now, when it is shown that what the subject is lies entirely in the attributes of the subject; that is, that the predicate is the true subject; it is also proved that if the divine predicates are attributes of the human nature, the subject of those predicates is also of the human nature. But the divine predicates are partly general, partly personal. The general predicates are the metaphysical, but these serve only as external points of support to religion; they are not the characteristic definitions of religion. It is the personal predicates alone which constitute the essence of religion—in which the Divine Being is the object of religion. Such are, for example, that God is a Person, that he is the moral Lawgiver, the Father of mankind, the Holy One, the Just, the Good, the Merciful. It is, however, at once clear, or it will at least be clear in the sequel, with regard to these and other definitions, that, especially as applied to a personality, they are purely human definitions, and that consequently man in religion—in his relation to God—is in relation to his own nature;

for to the religious sentiment these predicates are not mere conceptions, mere images, which man forms of God, to be distinguished from that which God is in himself, but truths, facts, realities. Religion knows nothing of anthropomorphisms; to it they are not anthropomorphisms. It is the very essence of religion, that to it these definitions express the nature of God. They are pronounced to be images only by the under-standing, which reflects on religion, and which while defending them yet before its own tribunal denies them. But to the religious sentiment God is a real Father, real Love and Mercy; for to it he is a real, living, personal being, and therefore his attributes are also living and personal. Nay, the definitions which are the most sufficing to the religious sentiment are precisely those which give the most offence to the understanding, and which in the process of reflection on religion it denies. Religion is essentially emotion; hence, objectively also, emotion is to it necessarily of a divine nature. Even anger appears to it an emotion not unworthy of God, provided only there be a religious motive at the foundation of this anger.

But here it is also essential to observe, and this phenomenon is an extremely remarkable one, characterising the very core of religion, that in proportion as the divine subject is in reality human, the greater is the apparent difference between God and man; that is, the more by reflection on religion, by theology, is the identity of the divine and human denied, and the human, considered as such, is depreciated.[1] The reason of this is, that as what is positive in the conception of the divine being can only be human, the conception of man, as an object of consciousness, can only be negative. To enrich God, man must become poor; that God may be all, man must be nothing. But he desires to be nothing in himself, because what he takes from himself is not lost to him, since it is preserved in God. Man has his being in God; why then should he have it in himself? Where is the necessity of positing the same thing twice, of having it twice? What man withdraws from himself, what he renounces in himself, he only enjoys in an incomparably higher and fuller measure in God.

The monks made a vow of chastity to God; they mortified the sexual passion in themselves, but therefore they had in heaven, in the Virgin

Mary, the image of woman—an image of love. They could the more easily dispense with real woman in proportion as an ideal woman was an object of love to them. The greater the importance they attached to the denial of sensuality, the greater the importance of the heavenly virgin for them: she was to them in the place of Christ, in the stead of God. The more the sensual tendencies are renounced, the more sensual is the God to whom they are sacrificed. For whatever is made an offering to God has an especial value attached to it; in it God is supposed to have especial pleasure. That which is the highest in the estimation of man is naturally the highest in the estimation of his God; what pleases man pleases God also. The Hebrews did not offer to Jehovah unclean, ill-conditioned animals; on the contrary, those which they most highly prized, which they themselves ate, were also the food of God (*Cibus Dei*, Lev. iii.2).

Wherever, therefore, the denial of the sensual delights is made a special offering, a sacrifice well-pleasing to God, there the highest value is attached to the senses, and the sensuality which has been renounced is unconsciously restored, in the fact that God takes the place of the material delights which have been renounced. The nun weds herself to God; she has a heavenly bridegroom, the monk a heavenly bride. But the heavenly virgin is only a sensible presentation of a general truth, having relation to the essence of religion. Man denies as to himself only what he attributes to God. Religion abstracts from man, from the world; but it can only abstract from the limitations, from the phenomena; in short, from the negative, not from the essence, the positive, of the world and humanity: hence, in the very abstraction and negation it must recover that from which it abstracts, or believes itself to abstract. And thus, in reality, whatever religion consciously denies—always supposing that what is denied by it is something essential, true, and consequently incapable of being ultimately denied—it unconsciously restores in God. Thus, in religion man denies his reason; of himself he knows nothing of God, his thoughts are only worldly, earthly; he can only believe what God reveals to him. But on this account the thoughts of God are human, earthly thoughts: like man, he has plans in his mind, he accommodates himself to circumstances and grades of intelligence, like a tutor with his pupils; he calculates closely the effect of his gifts and revelations; he observes man in all his doings; he knows all things, even the most earthly, the commonest, the most trivial. In brief, man in relation to God denies his own knowledge, his own thoughts, that he may place them in God. Man gives up his personality; but in return, God, the Almighty, infinite, unlimited being, is a person; he denies human dignity, the human *ego;* but in return God is to him a selfish, egoistical being, who in all things seeks only himself, his own honour, his own ends; he represents God as simply seeking the satisfaction of his own selfishness, while yet he frowns on that of every other being; his God is the very luxury of egoism.[2] Religion further denies goodness as a quality of human nature; man is wicked, corrupt, incapable of good; but, on the other hand, God is only good—the Good Being. Man's nature demands as an object goodness, personified as God; but is it not hereby declared that goodness is an essential tendency of man? If my heart is wicked, my understanding perverted, how can I perceive and feel the holy to be holy, the good to be good? Could I perceive the beauty of a fine picture if my mind were aesthetically an absolute piece of perversion? Though I may not be a painter, though I may not have the power of producing what is beautiful myself, I must yet have æsthetic feeling, æsthetic comprehension, since I perceive the beauty that is presented to me externally. Either goodness does not exist at all for man, or, if it does exist, therein is revealed to the individual man the holiness and goodness of human nature. That which is absolutely opposed to my nature, to which I am united by no bond of sympathy, is not even conceivable or perceptible by me. The holy is in opposition to me only as regards the modifications of my personality, but as regards my fundamental nature it is in unity with me. The holy is a reproach to my sinfulness; in it I recognise myself as a sinner; but in so doing, while I blame myself, I acknowledge what I am not, but ought to be, and what, for that very reason, I, according to my destination, can be; for an "ought" which has no corresponding capability does not affect me, is a ludicrous chimæra without any true relation to my mental constitution. But when I acknowledge goodness as my destination, as my law, I acknowledge it, whether consciously or unconsciously, as my own nature. Another nature than my own, one different in quality, cannot touch me. I can perceive sin as sin, only when I perceive it to be a contradiction of myself with myself—that is, of my personality with my fundamental nature. As a contradiction of the absolute, considered as another being, the feeling of sin is inexplicable, unmeaning.

The distinction between Augustinianism and Pelagianism consists only in this, that the former expresses after the manner of religion what the latter expresses after the manner of Rationalism. Both say the same thing, both vindicate the goodness of man; but Pelagianism does it directly, in a rationalistic and moral form; Augustinianism indirectly, in a mystical, that is, a religious form.[3] For that which is given to man's God is in truth given to man himself; what a man declares concerning God, he in truth declares concerning himself. Augustinianism would be a truth, and a truth opposed to Pelagianism, only if man had the devil for his God, and, with the consciousness that he was the devil, honoured, reverenced, and worshipped him as the highest being. But so long as man adores a good being as his God, so long does he contemplate in God the goodness of his own nature.

As with the doctrine of the radical corruption of human nature, so is it with the identical doctrine, that man can do nothing good, *i.e.,* in truth, nothing of himself—by his own strength. For the denial of human strength and spontaneous moral activity to be true, the moral activity of God must also be denied; and we must say, with the Oriental nihilist or pantheist: the Divine being is absolutely without will or action, indifferent, knowing nothing of the discrimination between evil and good. But he who defines God as an active being, and not only so, but as morally active and morally critical,—as a being who lives, works, and rewards good, punishes, rejects, and condemns evil,—he who thus defines God only in appearance denies human activity, in fact, making it the highest, the most real activity. He who makes God act humanly, declares human activity to be divine; he says: A god who is not active, and not morally or humanly active, is no god; and thus he makes the idea of the Godhead dependent on the idea of activity, that is, of human activity, for a higher [being] he knows not.

Man—this is the mystery of religion—projects his being into objectivity,[4] and then again makes himself an object to this projected image of himself thus converted into a subject; he thinks of himself [not a]s an object to himself, but as the object of an object, of another being than himself. Thus here. Man is an object to God. That man is good or evil is not indifferent to God; no! He has a lively, profound interest in man's being good; he wills that man should be good, happy—for without goodness there is no happiness. Thus the religious man virtually retracts the nothingness of human activity, by making his dispositions and actions an object to God, by making man the end of God—for that which is an object to the mind is an end in action; by making the divine activity a means of human salvation. God acts, that man may be good and happy. Thus man, while he is apparently humiliated to the lowest degree, is in truth exalted to the highest. Thus, in and through God, man has in view himself alone. It is true that man places the aim of his action in God, but God has no other aim of action than the moral and eternal salvation of man: thus man has in fact no other aim than himself. The divine activity is not distinct from the human.

How could the divine activity work on me as its object, nay, work in me, if it were essentially different from me; how could it have a human aim, the aim of ameliorating and blessing man, if it were not itself human? Does not the purpose determine the nature of the act? When man makes his moral improvement an aim to himself, he has divine resolutions, divine projects; but also, when God seeks the salvation of man, he has human ends and a human mode of activity corresponding to these ends. Thus in God man has only his own activity as an object. But for the very reason that he regards his own activity as objective, goodness only as an object, he necessarily receives the impulse, the motive not from himself, but from this object. He contemplates his nature as external to himself, and this nature as goodness; thus it is self-evident, it is mere tautology to say that the impulse to good comes only from thence where he places the good.

God is the highest subjectivity of man abstracted from himself; hence man can do nothing of himself, all goodness comes from God.

The more subjective God is, the more completely does man divest himself of his subjectivity, because God is, *per se,* his relinquished self, the possession of which he however again vindicates to himself. As the action of the arteries drives the blood into the extremities, and the action of the veins brings it back again, as life in general consists in a perpetual systole and diastole; so is it in religion. In the religious systole man propels his own nature from himself, he throws himself outward; in the religious diastole he receives the rejected nature into his heart again. God alone is the being who acts of himself,—this is the force of repulsion in religion; God is the being who acts in me, with me, through me, upon me, for me, is the principle of my salvation, of my good dispositions and actions, consequently my own good principle and nature,—this is the force of attraction in religion.

The course of religious development which has been generally indicated consists specifically in this, that man abstracts more and more from God, and attributes more and more to himself. This is especially apparent in the belief in revelation. That which to a later age or a cultured people is given by nature or reason, is to an earlier age, or to a yet uncultured people, given by God. Every tendency of man, however natural—even the impulse to cleanliness, was conceived by the Israelites as a positive divine ordinance. From this example we again see that God is lowered, is conceived more entirely on the type of ordinary humanity, in proportion as man detracts from himself. How can the self-humiliation of man go further than when he disclaims the capability of fulfilling spontaneously the requirements of common decency?[5] The Christian religion, on the other hand, distinguished the impulses and passions of man according to their quality, their character; it represented only good emotions, good dispositions, good thoughts, as revelations, operations— that is, as dispositions, feelings, thoughts,—of God; for what God reveals is a quality of God himself: that of which the heart is full overflows the lips; as is the effect such is the cause; as the revelation, such the being who reveals himself. A God who reveals himself in good dispositions is a God whose essential attribute is only moral perfection. The Christian religion distinguishes inward moral purity from external physical purity;

the Israelites identified the two.[6] In relation to the Israelitish religion, the Christian religion is one of criticism and freedom. The Israelite trusted himself to do nothing except what was commanded by God; he was without will even in external things; the authority of religion extended itself even to his food. The Christian religion, on the other hand, in all these external things made man dependent on himself, *i.e.*, placed in man what the Israelite placed out of himself in God. Israel is the most complete presentation of Positivism in religion. In relation to the Israelite, the Christian is an *esprit fort*, a free-thinker. Thus do things change. What yesterday was still religion is no longer such to-day; and what to-day is atheism, tomorrow will be religion.

NOTES

1. Inter creatorem et creaturam non potest tanta similitudo notari, quin inter eos major sit dissimilitudo notanda.—Later. Conc. can. 2. (Summa Omn. Conc. Carranza. Antw. 1559. p. 326.) The last distinction between man and God, between the finite and infinite nature, to which the religious speculative imagination soars, is the distinction between Something and Nothing, Ens and Non-Ens; for only in Nothing is all community with other beings abolished.

2. Gloriam suam plus amat Deus quam omnes creaturas. "God can only love himself, can only think of himself, can only work for himself. In creating man, God seeks his own ends, his own glory," &c.—Vide P. Bayle, Ein Beitrag zur Geschichte der Philos. u. Menschh., pp. 104–107.

3. Pelagianism denies God, religion—isti tantam tribuunt potestatem voluntati, ut pietati auferant orationem. (August de Nat. et Grat. cont. Pelagium, c. 58.) It has only the Creator, i.e., Nature, as a basis, not the Saviour, the true God of the religious sentiment—in a word, it denies God; but, as a consequence of this, it elevates man into a God, since it makes him a being not needing God, self-sufficing, independent. (See on this subject Luther against Erasmus and Augustine, 1. c. c. 33.) Augustinianism denies man; but, as a consequence of this, it reduces God to the level of man, even to the ignominy of the cross, for the sake of man. The former puts man in the place of God, the latter puts God in the place of man; both lead to the same result—the distinction is only apparent, a pious illusion. Augustinianism is only an inverted Pelagianism; what to the latter is a subject, is to the former an object.

4. The religious, the original mode in which man becomes objective to himself, is (as is clearly enough explained in this work) to be distinguished from the mode in which this occurs in reflection and speculation; the latter is voluntary, the former involuntary, necessary—as necessary as art, as speech. With the progress of time, it is true, theology coincides with religion.

5. Deut. xxiii. 12, 13.

6. See, for example, Gen. xxxv. 2; Levit. xi. 44; xx. 26; and the Commentary of Le Clerc on these passages.

CHAPTER TWO

In Defense of
Blasphemy

*B*lasphemy, or sacrilege, seeps from acts of irreverence directed at God. Although we don't like to discuss this, most religions amount to a denial of other religions: Judaism, Christianity, and Islam in a very real sense denounce each others' claims to truth. Even within Christianity, Protestant churches in a concrete way deny Roman Catholicism (just as Orthodox Judaism contests Reform Judaism). Isn't this blasphemy? It all depends on who gets to answer the question.

It is one thing for believers of one sort to offend believers of another sort. It is another thing entirely to deny God altogether. Of all the blasphemers who have scoffed at God, perhaps none is more jubilant than Friedrich Nietzsche. Being alive is an occasion for celebration, Nietzsche proclaimed, and we shouldn't allow God to rain on the parade. The influential German philosopher, a modern-day Prometheus, devoted his academic life to the attempt to "cure" Europe of its resistance to life. Far from celebrating life, he said, Judaism and Christianity slow it down, eviscerate it.

Take pity, for example: In the experience of pity, we live less. Christianity (which for Nietzsche amounted to essentially the very same thing as Judaism) elevates pity to a supreme virtue and, in so doing, opposes life. Christianity ruins people by increasing their unhappiness, indeed by giving them new reasons to be sad. Questioning whether it is a good idea to forego our own joy and instead join the sadness of others amounts to blasphemy, Nietzsche reasons, in the vile, Christian way of understanding humanity.

"Doubt is thus a sin from the start," Nietzsche explains.

A number of Nietzsche's points are already clearly in evidence in *The Essence of Christianity,* by Ludwig Feuerbach. Nietzsche refines and deepens these insights. His critique strikes at the very heart of Judeo-Christian values and stands as a prime example of what religious believers would properly judge blasphemy.

Blasphemy liberates us from our chains, Nietzsche asserts, and cultivates our imagination. The point of blasphemy is to overcome a hurdle that shouldn't be there in the first place. In *Thus Spake Zarathustra* Nietzsche wrote: "Behold I teach you the superman. The superman is the meaning of the earth . . . Once the sin against God was the greatest sin; but God died, and these sinners died with him. To sin against the earth is now the most dreadful thing." Nietzsche wanted us to work on improving this world, as opposed to attaining heaven in the next.

FRIEDRICH NIETZSCHE (1844–1900), a German, grew up the son of a Lutheran minister. While astonishingly young, he accepted the chair of Classical Philology at the University of Basel. He determined to give his age new values, Schopenhauer's "will to power" serving as the guiding principle. For Nietzsche the will to power held ethical primacy and properly represented the noble man's ultimate objective. Nietzsche denounced Christianity for resenting this world and for consigning all whom it hates to hell. In his major work, *Thus Spake Zarathustra* (1884), he introduces his ideal, a man he called *Uebermensch,* or "superman." Humanity should recognize, Nietzsche insisted, that certain "supermen," by virtue of their native superiority, simply cannot be expected to follow by the rules of the hoi polloi. Ultimately, he went insane and had to be cared for by his rebarbative sister Elisabeth.

from

THE ANTI-CHRIST

by Friedrich Nietzsche
translated by H. L. Mencken

What is good?—Whatever augments the feeling of power, the will to power, power itself, in man.

What is evil?—Whatever springs from weakness.

What is happiness?—The feeling that power *increases*—that resistance is overcome.

Not contentment, but more power; *not* peace at any price, but war; *not* virtue, but efficiency (virtue in the Renaissance sense, *virtu,* virtue free of moral acid).

The weak and the botched shall perish: first principle of *our* charity. And one should help them to it.

What is more harmful than any vice?—Practical sympathy for the botched and the weak—Christianity. . . .

The problem that I set here is not what shall replace mankind in the order of living creatures (—man is an end—): but what type of man must be *bred,* must be *willed,* as being the most valuable, the most worthy of life, the most secure guarantee of the future.

This more valuable type has appeared often enough in the past: but always as a happy accident, as an exception, never as deliberately *willed*. Very often it has been precisely the most feared; hitherto it has been almost *the* terror of terrors;—and out of that terror the contrary type has been willed, cultivated and *attained*: the domestic animal, the herd animal, the sick brute-man—the Christian. . . .

Christianity has waged a war to the death against this *higher* type of man, it has put all the deepest instincts of this type under its ban, it has developed its concept of evil, of the Evil One himself, out of these instincts—the strong man as the typical reprobate, the "outcast among men." Christianity has taken the part of all the weak, the low, the botched; it has made an ideal out of *antagonism* to all the self-preservative instincts of sound life; it has corrupted even the faculties of those natures that are intellectually most vigorous, by representing the highest intellectual values as sinful, as misleading, as full of temptation. . . .

I call an animal, a species, an individual corrupt, when it loses its instincts, when it chooses, when it *prefers*, what is injurious to it. A history of the "higher feelings," the "ideals of humanity" would almost explain why man is so degenerate. Life itself appears to me as an instinct for growth, for survival, for the accumulation of forces, for *power*: whenever the will to power fails there is disaster. My contention is that all the highest values of humanity have been emptied of this will—that the values of *décadence*, of *nihilism*, now prevail under the holiest names.

Christianity is called the religion of *pity*.—Pity stands in opposition to all the tonic passions that augment the energy of the feeling of aliveness: it is a depressant. Suffering is made contagious by pity; under certain circumstances it may lead to a total sacrifice of life and living energy—a loss out of all proportion to the magnitude of the cause (–the case of the death of the Nazarene). This is the first view of it; there is, however, a still more important one. If one measures the effects of pity by the gravity of the reactions it sets up, its character as a menace to life appears in a much clearer light. Pity thwarts the whole law of evolution, which is the law of natural selection. It preserves whatever is ripe for destruction; it fights on the side of those disinherited and condemned by life; by maintaining life in so many of the botched of all kinds, it gives life itself a gloomy and dubious aspect. This depressing and contagious instinct stands against all those instincts which work for the preservation and enhancement of life: in the rôle of *protector* of the miserable, it is a prime agent in the promotion of *décadence*—pity persuades to extinction. . . . Of course, one doesn't say "extinction," one says "the other world," or "God," or "the *true* life," or Nirvana, salvation, blessedness. . . . This innocent rhetoric, from the realm of religious-ethical balderdash, appears *a good deal less innocent* when one reflects upon the tendency that it conceals beneath sublime words: the tendency to *destroy life*. . . . Nothing is more unhealthy, amid all our unhealthy modernism, than Christian pity. To be the doctors *here*, to be unmerciful *here*, to wield the knife *here*—all this is *our* business, all this is *our* sort of humanity, by this sign we are philosophers.

The poisoning goes a great deal further than most people think: I find the arrogant habit of the theologian among all who regard themselves as "idealists"—among all who, by virtue of a higher point of departure, claim a right to rise above reality, and to look upon it with suspicion. . . . The idealist, like the ecclesiastic, carries all sorts of lofty concepts in his hand (—and not only in his hand!); he launches them with benevolent contempt against "understanding," "the senses," "honor," "good living," "science"; he sees such things as *beneath* him, as pernicious and seductive forces, on which "the soul" soars as a pure thing-in-itself—as if humility, chastity, poverty, in a word, *holiness,* had not already done much more damage to life than all imaginable horrors and vices. . . . The pure soul is a pure lie. . . . So long as the priest, that *professional* denier, calumniator and poisoner of life, is accepted as a *higher* variety of man, there can be no answer to the question, What *is* truth? Truth has already been stood on its head when the obvious attorney of mere emptiness is mistaken for its representative. . . .

The Christian concept of a god—the god as the patron of the sick, the god as a spinner of cobwebs, the god as a spirit—is one of the most corrupt concepts that has ever been set up in the world: it probably touches low-water mark in the ebbing evolution of the god-type. God degenerated into the *contradiction of life*. Instead of being its transfiguration and eternal Yea! In him war is declared on life, on nature, on the will to live! God becomes the formula for every slander upon the "here and now," and for every lie about the "beyond"! In him nothingness is deified, and the will to nothingness is made holy! . . .

When the centre of gravity of life is placed, *not* in life itself, but in "the beyond"—in *nothingness*—then one has taken away its centre of gravity altogether. The vast lie of personal immortality destroys all reason, all natural instinct—henceforth, everything in the instincts that is beneficial, that fosters life and that safeguards the future, is a cause of suspicion. So to live that life no longer has any meaning: *this* is now the "meaning" of life.

Christianity also stands in opposition to all *intellectual* well-being,— sick reasoning is the only sort that it *can* use as Christian reasoning; it takes the side of everything that is idiotic; it pronounces a curse upon "intellect," upon the *superbia* of the healthy intellect. Since sickness is inherent in Christianity, it follows that the typically Christian state of "faith" *must* be a form of sickness too, and that all straight, straightforward and scientific paths to knowledge *must* be banned by the church as *forbidden* ways. Doubt is thus a sin from the start. . . . "Faith" means the will to avoid knowing what is true. The pietist, the priest of either sex, is a fraud *because* he is sick: his instinct *demands* that the truth shall never be allowed its rights on any point. "Whatever makes for illness is *good; whatever issues from abundance, from superabundance, from power, is evil*": so argues the believer.

The whole labor of the ancient world gone for naught. To what end the Greeks? to what end the Romans?—All the prerequisites to a learned culture, all the *methods* of science, were already there; man had already perfected the great and incomparable art of reading profitably—that first necessity to the tradition of culture, the unity of the sciences; the natural sciences, in alliance with mathematics and mechanics, were on the right road—*the sense of fact*, the last and more valuable of all the senses, had its schools, and it traditions were already centuries old! Every *essential* to the beginning of the work was ready—and the *most* essential, it cannot be said too often, are methods, and also the most difficult to develop, and the longest opposed by habit and laziness. What we have today reconquered, with unspeakable self-discipline, for ourselves—for certain bad instincts, certain Christian instincts, still lurk in our bodies—that is to say, the keen eye for reality, the cautious hand, patience and seriousness in the smallest things, the whole *integrity* of knowledge—all these were already there, and had been there for 2,000 years! *All gone for naught!* Overnight it became merely a memory!

Here it becomes necessary to call up a memory that must be a hundred times more painful to Germans. The Germans have destroyed for Europe the last great harvest of civilization that Europe was ever to reap—the *Renaissance.* Is it understood at last, *will* it ever be understood, *what* the Renaissance was? *The transvaluation of Christian values,*—an attempt with all available means, all instincts and all the resources of genius to bring about a triumph of the *opposite* values, the more noble values. . . . This has been the one great war of the past; there has never been a more critical question than that of the Renaissance; there has never been a form of *attack* more fundamental, more direct, or more violently delivered by a whole front upon the center of the enemy! To attack at the critical place, at the very seat of Christianity, and there enthrone the more noble values—that is to say, to *insinuate* them into the instincts, into the most fundamental needs and appetites of those sitting there. . . . I see before me the *possibility* of a perfectly heavenly enchantment and spectacle:—it seems to me to scintillate with all the vibrations of a fine and delicate beauty, and within it there is an art so divine, so infernally divine, that one might search in vain for thousands of years for another such possibility; I see a spectacle so rich in significance and at the same time so wonderfully full of paradox that it should arouse all the gods on Olympus to immortal laughter—*Caesar Borgia as pope!* . . . Am I understood? . . . Well then, *that* would have been the sort of triumph that *I* alone am longing for today—: by it Christianity would have been *swept away!*

What happened? A German monk, Luther, came to Rome. This monk, with all the vengeful instincts of an unsuccessful priest in him, raised a rebellion *against* the Renaissance in Rome. . . . Instead of grasping, with profound thanksgiving, the miracle that had taken place: the conquest of Christianity at its *capital*—instead of this, his hatred was stimulated by the spectacle. A religious man thinks only of himself.— Luther saw only the *depravity* of the papacy at the very moment when the opposite was becoming apparent: the old corruption, the *peccatum orginale*, Christianity itself, no longer occupied the papal chair! Instead there was life! Instead there was the triumph of life! Instead there was a great yea to all lofty, beautiful and daring things! . . . And Luther *restored the church:* he attacked it. . . . The Renaissance—an event without meaning, a great futility!

—With this I come to a conclusion and pronounce my judgment. I *condemn* Christianity; I bring against the Christian church the most terrible of all the accusations that an accuser has ever had in his mouth. It is, to me, the greatest of all imaginable corruptions; it seeks to work the ultimate corruption, the worst possible corruption. The Christian church has left nothing untouched by its depravity; it has turned every value into worthlessness, and every truth into a lie, and every integrity into baseness of soul. Let anyone dare to speak to me of its "humanitarian" blessings! Its deepest necessities range it against any effort to abolish distress; it lives by distress, it *creates* distress to make *itself* immortal. . . . For example, the worm of sin; it was the church that first enriched mankind with this misery!—The "equality of souls before God"—this fraud, this *pretext* for the *rancunes* of all the base-minded—this explosive concept, ending in revolution, the modern idea, and the notion of overthrowing the whole social order—this is *Christian* dynamite. . . . The "humanitarian" blessings of Christianity forsooth! To breed out of *humanitas* a self-contradiction, an art of self-pollution, a will to lie at any price, an aversion and contempt for all good and honest instincts! All this, to me, is the "humanitarianism" of Christianity! Parasitism as the *only* practise of the church; with its anaemic and "holy" ideals, sucking all the blood, all the love, all the hope out of life; the beyond as the will to deny all reality; the cross as the distinguishing mark of the most subterranean conspiracy ever heard of—against health, beauty, well-being, intellect, *kindness* of soul—*against life itself.* . . .

This eternal accusation against Christianity I shall write upon all walls, wherever walls are to be found—I have letters that even the blind will be able to see. . . . I call Christianity the one great curse, the one great intrinsic depravity, the one great instinct of revenge, for which no means are venomous enough, or secret, subterranean and *small* enough,—I call it the one immortal blemish upon the human race.

CHAPTER THREE

In Defense of
Dismissing Mother and Father

*E*ven parents who do not believe in God might reasonably think their children owe them something. After all, many parents spend an enormous amount of time and a considerable percentage of their wealth on raising their children.

Traditional Christian and Muslim attitudes toward parents stem from Jewish law. According to *The Oxford Dictionary of the Jewish Religion,* "Rabbinic law permits only two exceptions to the duty of unquestioning obedience: parents must be disobeyed when they order their children to transgress the Torah, and a son may ignore his parents' wishes in choosing a wife. Otherwise the duty of honoring and revering parents knows no bounds." Indeed respect for parents extends after their death, respect Jews express ritually in the recitation of Qaddish (a special prayer for the dead). Christians and Muslims, it is fair to say, generally endorse this idea of a moral obligation to parents.

Jane English probes the idea that grown children owe their parents something. Can parents justify asking favors of their grown children, apart from appeals to the fifth commandment (to honor one's mother and father)? She concludes that we reasonably care for our parents because we love them or value them as friends, not because they once made sacrifices for us. This essay, from 1979, suggests the usefulness of the fifth commandment to needy parents whose children do not consider them friends.

∾

JANE ENGLISH was a faculty member in the Department of Philosophy at the University of North Carolina at Chapel Hill when she died climbing the Matterhorn in 1978. Prior to the fatal accident, she published several well-received articles and edited both *Sex Equality* (1977) and *Feminism and Philosophy* (1977).

WHAT DO GROWN CHILDREN OWE THEIR PARENTS?

Jane English

What do grown children owe their parents? I will contend that the answer is "nothing." Although I agree that there are many things that children *ought* to do for their parents, I will argue that it is inappropriate and misleading to describe them as things "owed." I will maintain that parents' voluntary sacrifices, rather than creating "debts" to be "repaid," tend to create love or "friendship." The duties of grown children are those of friends and result from love between them and their parents, rather than being things owed in repayment for the parents' earlier sacrifices. Thus, I will oppose those philosophers who use the word "owe" whenever a duty or obligation exists. Although the "debt" metaphor is appropriate in some moral circumstances, my argument is that a love relationship is not such a case.

Misunderstandings about the proper relationship between parents and their grown children have resulted from reliance on the "owing" terminology. For instance, we hear parents complain, "You owe it to us to write home (keep up your piano playing, not adopt a hippie lifestyle), because of all we sacrificed for you (paying for piano lessons, sending you to college)." The child is sometimes even heard to reply, "I didn't ask to be born (to be given piano lessons, to be sent to college)." This inappropriate idiom of ordinary language tends to obscure, or even to undermine, the love that is the correct ground of filial obligation.

FAVORS CREATE DEBTS

There are some cases, other than literal debts, in which talk of "owing," though metaphorical, is apt. New to the neighborhood, Max barely knows his neighbor, Nina, but he asks her if she will take in his mail while he is gone for a month's vacation. She agrees. If, subsequently, Nina asks Max to do the same for her, it seems that Max has a moral obligation to agree (greater than the one he would have had if Nina had not done the same for him), unless for some reason it would be a burden far out of proportion to the one Nina bore for him. I will call this a *favor:* when A, at B's request, bears some burden for B, then B incurs an obligation to reciprocate. Here the metaphor of Max's "owing" Nina is appropriate. It is not literally a debt, of course, nor can Nina pass this IOU on to heirs, demand payment in the form of Max's taking out her garbage, or sue Max. Nonetheless, since Max ought to perform one act of similar nature and amount of sacrifice in return, the term is suggestive. Once he reciprocates, the debt is "discharged"—that is, their obligations revert to the condition they were in before Max's initial request.

Contrast a situation in which Max simply goes on vacation and, to his surprise, finds upon his return that his neighbor has mowed his grass twice weekly in his absence. This is a voluntary sacrifice rather than a favor, and Max has no duty to reciprocate. It would be nice for him to volunteer to do so, but this would be supererogatory on his part. Rather than a favor, Nina's action is a friendly gesture. As a result, she might expect Max to chat over the back fence, help her catch her straying dog, or something similar—

she might expect the development of a friendship. But Max would be chatting (or whatever) out of friendship, rather than in repayment for mown grass. If he did not return her gesture, she might feel rebuffed or miffed, but not unjustly treated or indignant, since Max has not failed to perform a duty. Talk of "owing" would be out of place in this case.

It is sometimes difficult to distinguish between favors and non-favors, because friends tend to do favors for each other, and those who exchange favors tend to become friends. But one test is to ask how Max is motivated. Is it "to be nice to Nina" or "because she did x for me"? Favors are frequently performed by total strangers without any friendship developing. Nevertheless, a temporary obligation is created, even if the chance for repayment never arises. For instance, suppose that Oscar and Matilda, total strangers, are waiting in a long checkout line at the supermarket. Oscar, having forgotten the oregano, asks Matilda to watch his cart for a second. She does. If Matilda now asks Oscar to return the favor while she picks up some tomato sauce, he is obliged to agree. Even if she had not watched his cart, it would be inconsiderate of him to refuse, claiming that he was too busy reading the magazines. He may have a duty to help others, but he would not "owe" it to her. But if she has done the same for him, he incurs an additional obligation to help, and talk of "owing" is apt. It suggests an agreement to perform equal, reciprocal, canceling sacrifices.

THE DUTIES OF FRIENDSHIP

The terms "owe" and "repay" are helpful in the case of favors, because the sameness of the amount of sacrifice on the two sides is important; the monetary metaphor suggests equal quantities of sacrifice. But friendship ought to be characterized by mutuality rather than reciprocity: friends offer what they can give and accept what they need, without regard for the total amounts of benefits exchanged. And friends are motivated by love rather than by the prospect of repayment. Hence, talk of "owing" is singularly out of place in friendship.

For example, suppose Alfred takes Beatrice out for an expensive dinner and a movie. Beatrice incurs no obligation to "repay" him with a goodnight kiss or a return engagement. If Alfred complains that she "owes" him something, he is operating under the assumption that she should repay a favor, but on the contrary his was a generous gesture done in the hopes of developing a friendship. We hope that he would not want her repayment in the form of sex or attention if this was done to discharge a debt rather than from friendship. Since, if Alfred is prone to reasoning in this way, Beatrice may well decline the invitation or request to pay for her own dinner, his attitude of expecting a "return" on his "investment" could hinder the development of a friendship. Beatrice should return the gesture only if she is motivated by friendship.

Another common misuse of the "owing" idiom occurs when the Smiths have dined at the Joneses' four times, but the Joneses at the Smiths' only once. People often say, "We owe them three dinners." This line of thinking may be appropriate between business acquaintances, but not between friends. After all, the Joneses invited the Smiths not in order to feed them or to be fed in turn, but because of the friendly contact presumably enjoyed by all on such occasions. If the Smiths do not feel friendship toward the Joneses, they can decline future invitations and not invite the Joneses; they owe them nothing. Of course, between friends of equal resources and needs, roughly equal sacrifices (though not necessarily roughly equal dinners) will typically occur. If the sacrifices are highly out of proportion to the resources, the relationship is closer to servility than to friendship.[1]

Another difference between favors and friendship is that after a friendship ends, the duties of friendship end. The party that has sacrificed less owes the other nothing. For instance, suppose Elmer donated a pint of blood that his wife Doris needed during an operation. Years after their divorce, Elmer is in an accident and needs one pint of blood. His new wife, Cora, is also of the same blood type. It seems that Doris not only does not "owe" Elmer blood, but that she should actually refrain from coming forward if Cora has volunteered to donate. To insist on donating not only interferes with the newlyweds' friendship, but it belittles Doris and Elmer's former relationship by suggesting that Elmer gave blood in hopes of favors returned instead of simply out of love for Doris. It is one of the heart-rending features of divorce that it attends to quantity in a relationship previously characterized by mutuality. If Cora could not donate, Doris's obligation is the same as that for any former spouse in need of blood; it is not increased by the fact that Elmer similarly aided her. It *is* affected by the degree to which they are still friends, which in turn may (or may not) have been influenced by Elmer's donation.

In short, unlike the debts created by favors, the duties of friendship do not require equal quantities of sacrifice. Performing equal sacrifices does not cancel the duties of friendship, as it does the debts of favors. Unrequested sacrifices do not themselves create debts, but friends have duties regardless of whether they requested or initiated the friendship. Those who perform favors may be motivated by mutual gain, whereas friends should be motivated by affection. These characteristics of the friendship relation are distorted by talk of "owing."

PARENTS AND CHILDREN

The relationship between children and their parents should be one of friendship characterized by mutuality rather than one of reciprocal favors. The quantity of parental sacrifice is not relevant in determining what duties the grown child has. The medical assistance grown children ought to offer their ill mothers in old age depends upon the mothers' need, not upon whether they endured a difficult pregnancy, for example. Nor do one's duties to one's parents cease once an equal quantity of sacrifice has been performed, as the phrase "discharging a debt" may lead us to think.

Rather, what children ought to do for their parents (and parents for children) depends upon (1) their respective needs, abilities, and resources and (2) the extent to which there is an ongoing friendship between them. Thus, regardless of the quantity of childhood sacrifices, an able, wealthy child has an obligation to help his needy parents more than does a needy child. To illustrate, suppose sisters Cecile and Dana are equally loved by their parents, even though Cecile was an easy child to care for, seldom ill, while Dana was often sick and caused some trouble as a juvenile delinquent. As adults, Dana is a struggling artist living far away, while Cecile is a wealthy lawyer living nearby. When the parents need visits and financial aid, Cecile has an obligation to bear a higher proportion of these burdens than her sister. This results from her abilities, rather than from the quantities of sacrifice made by the parents earlier.

Sacrifices have an important causal role in creating an ongoing friendship, which may lead us to assume incorrectly that it is the sacrifices that are the source of the obligation. That the source is the friendship instead can be seen by examining cases in which the sacrifices occurred but the friendship, for some reason, did not develop or persist. For example, if a woman gives up her newborn child for adoption, and if no feelings of love ever develop on either side, it seems that the grown child does not have an obligation to "repay" her for her sacrifices in pregnancy. For that matter, if the adopted child has an unimpaired love relationship with the adoptive parents, he or she has the same obligations to help them as a natural child would have.

The filial obligations of grown children are a result of friendship, rather than owed for services rendered. Suppose that Vance married Lola despite his parents' strong wish that he marry within their religion, and that as a result, the parents refuse to speak to him again. As the years pass, the parents are unaware of Vance's problems, his accomplishments, the birth of his children. The love that once existed between them, let us suppose, has been completely destroyed by this event and thirty years of desuetude. At this point, it seems, Vance is under no obligation to pay his parents' medical bills in their old age, beyond his general duty to help those in need. An additional, filial obligation would only arise from whatever love he may still feel for them. It would be irrelevant for his parents to argue, "But look how much we sacrificed for you when you were young," for that sacrifice was not a favor but occurred as part of a friendship which existed at that time but is now, we have supposed, defunct. A more appropriate message would be, "We still love you, and we would like to renew our friendship."

I hope this helps to set the question of what children ought to do for their parents in a new light. The parental argument, "You ought to do *x* because we did *y* for you," should be replaced by, "We love you and you will be happier if you do *x*," or "We believe you love us, and anyone who loved us would do *x*." If the parents' sacrifice had been a favor, the child's reply, "I never asked you to do *y* for me," would have been relevant; to the revised parental remarks, this reply is clearly irrelevant. The child can either do *x* or dispute one of the parents' claims: by showing that a love relationship does not exist, or that love for someone does not motivate doing *x*, or that he or she will not be happier doing *x*.

Seen in this light, parental requests for children to write home, visit, and offer them a reasonable amount of emotional and financial support in life's crises are well founded, so long as a friendship still exists. Love for others does call for caring about and caring for them. Some other parental requests, such as for more sweeping changes in the child's lifestyle or life goals, can be seen to be insupportable, once we shift the justification from debts owed to love. The terminology of favors suggests that reasoning, "Since we paid for your college education, you owe it to us to make a career of engineering, rather than becoming a rock musician." This tends to alienate affection even further, since the tuition payments are depicted as investments for a return rather than done from love, as though the child's life goals could be "bought." Basing the argument on love leads to different reasoning patterns. The suppressed premise, "If A loves B, then A follows B's wishes as to A's lifelong career," is simply false. Love does not even dictate that the child adopt the parents' values as to the desirability of alternative life goals. So the parents' strongest available argument here is, "We love you, we are deeply concerned about your happiness, and in the long run you will be happier as an engineer." This makes it clear that an empirical claim is really the subject of the debate.

The function of these examples is to draw out our considered judgments as to the proper relation between parents and their grown children, and to show how poorly they fit the model of favors. What is relevant is the ongoing friendship that exists between parents and children. Although that relationship developed partly as a result of parental sacrifices for the child, the duties that grown children have to their parents result from the friendship rather than from the sacrifices. The idiom of owing favors to one's parents can actually be destructive if it undermines the role of mutuality and leads us to think in terms of quantitative reciprocal favors.

NOTES

1. Cf. Thomas E. Hill, Jr., "Servility and Self-Respect," *Monist* 57 (1973). Thus, during childhood, most of the sacrifices will come from the parents, since they have most of the resources and the child has most of the needs. When children are grown, the situation is usually reversed.

CHAPTER FOUR

In Defense of
Murder

𝔐urder happens regularly. We ourselves sometimes murder, as for example when we put murderers to death. Some argue that capital punishment, war, and even abortion all qualify as murder. Murder, it seems, is all around us.

Long before we started arguing about trimesters and the viability of a fetus, Jonathan Swift devised a solution to the raging problem of poverty in Ireland. Killing one-year-old children in order to cook them would lessen the number of hungry mouths in society while providing food for those who desperately needed it.

Gruesome as the idea may sound, plenty of people took Swift's satire seriously in 1729. They agreed that small children would not miss a world they never really knew. And waiting a year to do the deed would fatten the children nicely. Poverty, a problem that defied ready solution, had met its match in Swift's proposal.

Swift likely knew about the age-old Christian practice of exposing children, detailed by Yale Historian John Boswell in 1988 in the book *The Kindness of Strangers*. Families which could not accommodate another hungry mouth anonymously left infants in fields, forests, and town squares. Parents gradually began depositing infants on the doorsteps of monasteries and convents, where the children were educated and brought up to perform important labor that strengthened satellites of Roman Catholic power.

This essay, still provocative today, raises the question of how best to defend sin—any sin. By writing a send-up and pretending only to be joking, an author can effectively evade charges of immorality (Swift was an ordained Anglican priest) while planting in the heads of others the seeds of a defense.

Today, when we know how to transplant vital tissue and organs from one person to another, Swift's story takes on an eerie new significance. Selling organs is illegal in part, no doubt, because of the likelihood some poor families might consider such a proposal. In order to send a child through college or to finance an expensive medical procedure, a parent might well choose to auction off a kidney. In more extreme cases, someone might even sell his heart. Selling body parts remains prohibited throughout most of the world, just as murder does.

∾

JONATHAN SWIFT (1667–1745) is widely considered one of the greatest writers of the eighteenth century and one of the most gifted satirists of all times. An Irishman, he was ordained a priest in the Anglican Church. His masterpiece, *Gulliver's Travels,* was published anonymously in 1726.

A MODEST PROPOSAL FOR PREVENTING THE CHILDREN OF POOR PEOPLE

*from Being a Burden to Their Parents
Or the Country, and for Making
Them Beneficial to
the Public*

Jonathan Swift

It is a melancholy object to those who walk through this great town, or travel in the country, when they see the *streets,* the *roads,* and *cabin-doors* crowded with *beggars* of the female sex, followed by three, four, or six children, *all in rags,* and importuning every passenger for an alms. These *mothers* instead of being able to work for their honest livelihood, are forced to employ all their time in strolling to beg sustenance for their *helpless infants* who, as they grow up, either turn *thieves* for want of work, or leave their *dear Native Country to fight for the Pretender* in Spain, or sell themselves to the Barbadoes.

I think it is agreed by all parties that this prodigious number of children, in the arms, or on the backs, or at the *heels* of their *mothers,* and frequently of their fathers, is *in the present deplorable state of the kingdom,* a very great additional grievance; and therefore whoever could find out a fair, cheap and easy method of making these children sound useful members of the commonwealth would deserve so well of the public, as to have his statue set up for a preserver of the nation.

But my intention is very far from being confined to provide only for the children of *professed beggars,* it is of a much greater extent, and shall take in the whole number of infants at a certain age, who are born of parents in effect as little able to support them as those who demand our charity in the streets.

As to my own part, having turned my thoughts for many years upon this important subject, and maturely weighed the several *schemes of other projectors,* I have always found them grossly mistaken in their computation. It is true a child *just dropped from its dam* may be supported by her milk for a solar year with little other nourishment, at most not above the value of two shillings, which the mother may certainly get, or the value in scraps, by her lawful occupation of *begging.* And it is exactly at one year old that I propose to provide for them in such a manner as, instead of being a charge upon their *parents,* or the *parish,* or *wanting food and raiment* for the rest of their lives, they shall, on the contrary, contribute to the feeding and partly to the clothing of many thousands.

There is likewise another great advantage in my scheme, that it will prevent those *voluntary abortions,* and that horrid practice of *women murdering their bastard children,* alas! too frequent among us, sacrificing the *poor innocent babes,* I doubt, more to avoid the expense than the shame, which would move tears and pity in the most savage and inhuman breast.

The number of souls in this kingdom being usually reckoned one million and a half, of these I calculate there may be about two hundred thousand couple[s] whose wives are breeders, from which number I subtract thirty thousand couples who are able to maintain their own children, although I apprehend there cannot be so many under *the present distresses of the kingdom,* but this being granted, there will remain an hundred and seventy thousand breeders. I again subtract fifty thousand for those women who miscarry, or whose children die by accident, or disease within the year. There only remain an hundred and twenty thousand children of poor parents annually born. The question therefore is, how this number shall be reared and provided for, which, as I have already said, under the present situation of affairs is utterly impossible by all the methods hitherto proposed, for we can *neither employ them in handicraft,* or *agriculture;* we neither build houses (I mean in the county) nor cultivate land: they can very seldom pick up a livelihood *by stealing* till they arrive at six years old, except where they are of towardly parts, although I confess they learn the rudiments much earlier, during which time they can however be properly looked upon only as *probationers,* as I have been informed by a principal gentleman in the County of Cavan, who protested to me that he never knew above one or two instances under the age of six, even in a part of the kingdom *so renowned for the quickest proficiency in that art.*

I am assured by our merchants that a boy or a girl, before twelve years old, is no saleable commodity, and even when they come to this age, they will not yield above three pounds, or three pounds and half-a-crown at most on the Exchange, which cannot turn to account either to the parents or the kingdom, the charge of nutriment and rags having been at least four times that value.

I shall now therefore humbly propose my own thoughts, which I hope will not be liable to the least objection.

I have been assured by a very knowing American of my acquaintance in London, that a young healthy child, well nursed, is at a year old a most delicious, nourishing, and wholesome food, whether *stewed, roasted, baked,* or *boiled,* and I make no doubt that it will equally serve in a *fricassee,* or a *ragout.*

I do therefore humbly offer it to *public consideration,* that of the hundred and twenty thousand children, already computed, twenty thousand may be reserved for breed, whereof only one fourth part to be males, which is more than we allow to *sheep, black-cattle,* or *swine;* and my reason is that these children are seldom the fruits of marriage, *a circumstance not much regarded by our savages;* therefore *one male* will be sufficient to serve *four females.* That the remaining hundred thousand may at a year old be offered in sale to the *persons of quality* and *fortune,* through the kingdom, always advising the mother to let them suck plentifully of the last month, so as to render them plump and fat for a good table. A child will make two dishes at an entertainment for friends, and when the family dines alone the fore or hind quarter will make a reasonable dish, and seasoned with a little pepper or salt will be very good boiled on the fourth day, especially in *winter.*

I have reckoned upon a medium, that a child just born will weigh 12 pounds, and in a solar year if tolerably nursed increaseth to 28 pounds.

I grant this food will be somewhat dear, and therefore very *proper for landlords,* who, as they have already devoured most of the parents, seem to have the best title to the children.

Infants' flesh will be in season throughout the year, but more plentiful in *March,* and a little before and after, for we are told by a grave author, an eminent French physician, that *fish being a prolific diet,* there are more children born in *Roman Catholic countries* about nine months after *Lent,* than at any other season; therefore reckoning a year after *Lent,* the markets will be more glutted than usual, because the number of *Popish infants* is at least three to one in this kingdom, and therefore it will have one other collateral advantage by lessening the number of *Papists* among us.

I have already computed the charge of nursing a beggar's child (in which list I reckon all *cottagers, labourers,* and four firths of the *farmers*) to be about two shillings *per annum,* rags included, and I believe no gentleman would repine to give ten shillings for the *carcass of a good fat child,* which, as I have said, will make four dishes of excellent nutritive meat, when he hath only some particular friend, or his own family to dine with him. Thus the Squire will learn to be a good landlord, and grow popular among his tenants, the mother will have eight shillings net profit, and be fit for work till she produces another child.

Those who are more thrifty *(as I must confess the times require)* may flay the carcass; the skin of which, artificially dressed, will make admirable *gloves for ladies,* and *summer boots for fine gentlemen.*

As to our City of Dublin, shambles may be appointed for this purpose in the most convenient parts of it, and butchers we may be assured will not be wanting, although I rather recommend buying the children alive, and dressing them hot from the knife, as we do *roasting pigs.*

A very worthy person, *a true lover of his country,* and whose virtues I highly esteem, was lately pleased in discoursing on this matter, to offer a refinement upon my scheme. He said that many gentlemen of this kingdom, having of late destroyed their deer, he conceived that the want of venison might be well supplied by the bodies of young lads and maidens not exceeding fourteen years of age, nor under twelve, so great a number of both sexes in every country being now ready to starve for want of work and service: and these to be disposed of by their parents if alive, or otherwise by their nearest relations. But with due deference to so excellent a friend and so deserving a patriot, I cannot be altogether in his sentiments; for as to the males, my American acquaintance assured me from frequent experience that their flesh was generally tough and lean, like that of our schoolboys, by continual exercise, and their taste disagreeable, and to fatten them would not answer the charge. Then as to the females, it would I think with humble submission, *be a loss to the public,* because they soon would become breeders themselves. And besides, it is not improbable that some scrupulous people might be apt to censure such a practice (although indeed very unjustly) as a little bordering upon cruelty, which, I confess, hath always been with me the strongest objection against any project, however so well intended.

But in order to justify my friend, he confessed that this expedient was put into his head by the famous *Psalmanazar,* a native of the island Formosa, who came from thence to London above twenty years ago, and in conversation told my friend that in his county when any young person happened to be put to death, the executioner sold the carcass to *persons of quality,* as a prime dainty, and that in his time, the body of a plump girl of fifteen, who was crucified for an attempt to poison the emperor, was sold to his Imperial *Majesty's Prime Minister of State,* and other great *Mandarins* of the Court, *in joints from the gibbet,* at four hundred crowns. Neither indeed can I deny, that if the same use were made of several plump young girls in this town, who, without one single groat to their fortunes, cannot stir abroad without a chair, and appear at the *playhouse* and *assemblies* in foreign fineries which they never will pay for, the kingdom would not be the worse.

Some persons of a desponding spirit are in great concern about that vast number of poor people who are aged, diseased, or maimed, and I have been desired to employ my thoughts what course may be taken to ease the nation of so grievous an encumbrance. But I am not in the least pain upon that matter, because it is very well known that they are every day *dying,* and *rotting,* by *cold* and *famine,* and *filth,* and *vermin,* as fast as can be reasonably expected. And as to the younger labourers they are now in almost as hopeful a condition. They cannot get work, and consequently pine away for want of nourishment, to a degree that if at any time they are accidentally hired to common labour, they have not strength to perform it; and thus the country and themselves are happily delivered from the evils to come.

I have too long digressed, and therefore shall return to my subject. I think the advantages by the proposal which I have made are obvious and many, as well as of the highest importance.

For *first,* as I have already observed, it would greatly lessen the *number of Papists,* with whom we are yearly over-run, being the principal breeders of the nation as well as of our most dangerous enemies, and who stay at home on purpose with a design to *deliver the kingdom to the Pretender;* hoping to take their advantage by the absence of *so many good Protestants,* who have chosen rather to leave their country than stay at home and pay tithes against their conscience to an *Episcopal curate.*

Secondly, the poorer tenants will have something valuable of their own, which by law may be made liable to distress, and help to pay their landlord's rent, their corn and cattle being already seized, and *money a thing unknown.*

Thirdly, whereas the maintenance of an hundred thousand children, from two years old and upwards, cannot be computed at less than ten shillings a piece *per annum,* the nation's stock will be thereby increased fifty thousand pounds *per annum,* besides the profit of a new dish introduced to the tables of all *gentlemen of fortune* in the kingdom who have any refinement in taste; and the money will circulate among ourselves, the goods being entirely of our own growth and manufacture.

Fourthly, the constant breeders, besides the gain of eight shillings *sterling per annum* by the sale of their children, will be rid of the charge of maintaining them after the first year.

Fifthly, this food would likewise bring great *custom to taverns,* where the vintners will certainly be so prudent as to procure the best receipts for dressing it to perfection, and consequently have their houses frequented by all the *fine gentlemen,* who justly value themselves upon their knowledge in good eating; and a skilful cook, who understands how to oblige his guests, will contrive to make it as expensive as they please.

Sixthly, this would be a great inducement to marriage, which all wise nations have either encouraged by rewards, or enforced by laws and penalties. It would increase the care and tenderness of mothers toward their children, when they were sure of a settlement for life to the poor babes, provided in some sort by the public to their annual profit instead of expense. We should see an honest emulation among the married women, *which of them could bring the fattest child to the market.* Men would become as *fond* of their wives, during the time of their pregnancy, as they are now of the *mares* in foal, their *cows* in calf, or *sows* when they are ready to farrow; nor offer to beat or kick them (as it is too *frequent* a practice) for fear of a miscarriage.

Many other advantages might be enumerated. For instance, the addition of some thousand carcasses in our exportation of barrelled beef; the propagation of *swine's flesh* and improvement in the art of making good *bacon,* so much wanted among us by the great destruction of *pigs,* too frequent at our tables, which are no way comparable in taste, or magnificence to a well-grown, fat yearling child, which roasted whole will make a considerable figure at a *Lord Mayor's feast,* or any other public entertainment. But this and many others I omit, being studious of brevity.

Supposing that one thousand families in this city, would be constant customers for infants' flesh, besides others who might have it at *merry-meetings,* particularly *weddings* and *christenings,* I compute that Dublin would take off annually about twenty thousand carcasses, and the rest of the kingdom (where probably they will be sold somewhat cheaper) the remaining eighty thousand.

I can think of no one objection that will possibly be raised against this proposal, unless it should be urged that the number of people will be thereby much lessened in the kingdom. This I freely own, and it was indeed one principal design in offering it to the world. I desire the reader will observe, that I calculate my remedy *for this one individual Kingdom of IRELAND, and for no other that ever was, is, or, I think, ever can be upon earth.* Therefore let no man talk to me of other expedients: *Of taxing our absentees at five shillings a pound: Of using neither clothes, nor household furniture, except what is of our own growth and manufacture: Of utterly rejecting the materials and instruments that promote foreign luxury: Of curing the expensiveness of pride vanity, idleness, and gaming in our women: Of introducing a vein of parsimony, prudence and temperance: Of learning to love our Country, wherein we differ even from LAPLANDERS, and the inhabitants of TOPINAMBOO: Of quitting our animosities and factions, nor act any longer like the Jews, who were murdering one another at the very moment their city was taken: Of being a little cautious not to sell our country and consciences for nothing: Of teaching landlords to have at least one degree of mercy toward their tenants. Lastly of putting a spirit of honesty, industry and skill into our shopkeepers, who, if a resolution could now be taken to buy only our native goods, would immediately unite to cheat and exact upon us in the price, the measure, and the goodness, nor could ever yet be brought to make one fair proposal of just dealing, though often and earnestly invited to it.*

Therefore I repeat, let no man talk to me of these and the like expedients, till he hath at least some glimpse of hope that there will ever be some hearty and sincere attempt to put them in practice.

But as to myself, having been wearied out for many years with offering vain, idle, visionary thoughts, and at length utterly despairing of success, I fortunately fell upon this proposal, which as it is wholly new, so it hath something solid and real, of no expense and little trouble, full in our own power, and whereby we can incur no danger in *disobliging England*. For this kind of commodity will not bear exportation, the flesh being of too tender a consistence to admit a long continuance in salt, *although perhaps I could name a country which would be glad to eat up our whole nation without it.*

After all, I am not so violently bent upon my own opinion as to reject any offer proposed by wise men, which shall be found equally innocent, cheap, easy and effectual. But before something of that kind shall be advanced in contradiction to my scheme, and offering a better, I desire the author, or authors, will be pleased maturely to consider two points. *First,* as things now stand, how they will be able to find food and raiment for an hundred thousand useless mouths and backs. And *secondly,* there being a round million of creatures in human figure throughout this kingdom, whose whole subsistence put into a common stock would leave them in debt two millions of pounds *sterling;* adding those who are beggars by profession, to the bulk of farmers, cottagers and labourers with their wives and children, who are beggars in effect; I desire those *politicians* who dislike my overture and may perhaps be so bold to attempt an answer, that they will first ask the parents of these mortals, whether they would not at this day think it a great happiness to have been sold for food at a year old, in the manner I prescribe; and thereby have avoided such a perpetual scene of misfortunes as they have since gone through, by the *oppression of landlords,* the impossibility of paying rent without money or trade, the want of common sustenance, with neither house nor clothes to cover them from the inclemencies of the weather, and the most inevitable prospect of entailing the like, or greater miseries upon their breed for ever.

I profess in the sincerity of my heart that I have not the least personal interest in endeavouring to promote this necessary work, having no other motive than the *public good of my country, by advancing our trade, providing for infants, relieving the poor, and giving some pleasure to the rich.* I have no children, by which I can propose to get a single penny; the youngest being nine years old, and my wife past child-bearing.

CHAPTER FIVE

In Defense of
ADULTERY

Die: die for adultery! No:
The wren goes to't, and the small gilded fly
Does lecher in my sight.
Let copulation thrive.
—*King Lear,* IV.6.1

*P*eople get married in virtually every culture. In the United States, for example, census reports for the past century document that over ninety percent of men and women marry. No one knows how many spouses commit adultery, although studies tend to put the rate at about fifty percent.

Adultery has always troubled us. In ancient Israel, adultery was punishable by death, just as it was in Puritan New England (how often the penalty was inflicted is hard to determine). In 1959, New York refused to issue a license for the film *Lady Chatterley's Lover* because it "portrays adultery as proper behavior."[1]

In this essay from 1975, Richard Wasserstrom asks whether adultery is always immoral. He allows that adulterous behavior is wrong to the extent that it involves breaking a promise, taking unfair advantage, or deceiving another, but he questions whether adultery would be unjust if we eliminated these three conditions. One might wonder how we could eliminate these conditions, but nonetheless, adultery need not automatically lead to the demise of a marriage and often does not. We can defend adultery, Wasserstrom contends, provided that it is done thoughtfully.

Wasserstrom mentions here the highly influential Wolfenden Report, published in England in 1957. Chaired by Sir John Wolfenden, a parliamentary committee debated what to make of an anti-sodomy law still on the books but irregularly enforced. This signal move to renew public debate over the morality of homosexuality (Oscar Wilde had been condemned to prison in 1895 for acts of "gross indecency") helped usher in the modern gay rights movement. Because various social conservatives have viewed adultery and gay relationships as effective gauges of a society's moral health, they have worried that the greater the frequency of either, the greater the danger to a society. Wasserstrom challenges us to articulate just what is so wrong about adultery.

∾

RICHARD WASSERSTROM is Professor Emeritus of Philosophy at the University of California, Santa Cruz. He has published a number of articles in philosophy that examine the moral issues and arguments involved in topics such as racism and sexism, affirmative action, punishment, privacy, and war.

IS ADULTERY IMMORAL?

Richard Wasserstrom

Many discussions of the enforcement of morality by the law take as illustrative of the problem under consideration the regulation of various types of sexual behavior by the criminal law. It was, for example, the Wolfenden Report's recommendations concerning homosexuality and prostitution that led Lord Devlin to compose his now famous lecture, "The Enforcement of Morals." And that lecture in turn provoked important philosophical responses from H. L. A. Hart, Ronald Dworkin, and others.

Much, if not all, of the recent philosophical literature on the enforcement of morals appears to take for granted the immorality of the sexual behavior in question. The focus of discussion, at least, is whether such things as homosexuality, prostitution, and adultery ought to be made illegal even if they are immoral, and not whether they are immoral.

I propose in this paper to think about the latter, more neglected topic, that of sexual morality, and to do so in the following fashion. I shall consider just one kind of behavior that is often taken to be a case of sexual immorality—adultery. I am interested in pursuing at least two questions. First, I want to explore the question of in what respects adulterous behavior falls within the domain of morality at all: For this surely is one of the puzzles one encounters when considering the topic of sexual morality. It is often hard to see on what grounds much of the behavior is deemed to be either moral or immoral, for example, private homosexual behavior between consenting adults. I have purposely selected adultery because it seems a more plausible candidate for moral assessment than many other kinds of sexual behavior.

The second question I want to examine is that of what is to be said about adultery, without being especially concerned to stay within the area of morality. I shall endeavor, in other words, to identify and to assess a number of the major arguments that might be advanced against adultery. I believe that they are the chief arguments that would be given in support of the view that adultery is immoral, but I think they are worth considering even if some of them turn out to be nonmoral arguments and considerations.

A number of the issues involved seem to me to be complicated and difficult. In a number of places I have at best indicated where further philosophical exploration is required without having successfully conducted the exploration myself. The paper may very well be more useful as an illustration of how one might begin to think about the subject of sexual morality than as an elucidation of important truths about the topic.

Before I turn to the arguments themselves there are two preliminary points that require some clarification. Throughout the paper I shall refer to the immorality of such things as breaking a promise, deceiving someone, etc. In a very rough way, I mean by this that there is something morally wrong that is done in doing the action in question. I mean that the action is, in a strong sense of *"prima facie,"* prima facie wrong or unjustified. I do not mean that it may never be right or justifiable to do the action; just that the fact that it is an action of this description always does count against the rightness of the action. I leave entirely open the question of what it is that makes actions of this kind immoral in this sense of "immoral."

The second preliminary point concerns what is meant or implied by the concept of adultery. I mean by "adultery" any case of extramarital sex, and I want to explore the arguments for and against extramarital sex, undertaken in a variety of morally relevant situations. Someone might claim that the concept of adultery is conceptually connected with the concept of immorality, and that to characterize behavior as adulterous is already to characterize it as immoral or unjustified in the sense described above. There may be something to this. Hence the importance of making it clear that I want to talk about extramarital sexual relations. If they are always immoral, this is something that must be shown by argument. If the concept of adultery does in some sense entail or imply immorality, I want to ask whether that connection is a rationally based one. If not all cases of extramarital sex are immoral (again, in the sense described above), then the concept of adultery should either be weakened accordingly or restricted to those classes of extramarital sex for which the predication of immorality is warranted.

One argument for the immorality of adultery might go something like this: what makes adultery immoral is that it involves the breaking of a promise, and what makes adultery seriously wrong is that it involves the breaking of an important promise. For, so the argument might continue, one of the things the two parties promise each other when they get married is that they will abstain from sexual relationships with third persons. Because of this promise both spouses quite reasonably entertain the expectation that the other will behave in conformity with it. Hence, when one of the parties has sexual intercourse with a third person he or she breaks that promise about sexual relationships which was made when the marriage was entered into, and defeats the reasonable expectations of exclusivity entertained by the spouse.

In many cases the immorality involved in breaching the promise relating to extramarital sex may be a good deal more serious than that involved in the breach of other promises. This is so because adherence to this promise may be of much greater importance to the parties than is adherence to many of the other promises given or received by them in their lifetime. The breaking of this promise may be much more hurtful and painful than is typically the case.

Why is this so? To begin with, it may have been difficult for the nonadulterous spouse to have kept the promise. Hence that spouse may feel the unfairness of having restrained himself or herself in the absence of reciprocal restraint having been exercised by the adulterous spouse. In addition, the spouse may perceive the breaking of the promise as an indication of a kind of indifference on the part of the adulterous spouse. If you really cared about me and my feelings—the spouse might say— you would not have done this to me. And third, and related to the above, the spouse may see the act of sexual intercourse with another as a sign of affection for the other person and as an additional rejection of the non-adulterous spouse as the one who is loved by the adulterous spouse. It is not just that the adulterous spouse does not take the feelings of the spouse sufficiently into account, the adulterous spouse also indicates through the act of adultery affection for someone other than the spouse. I will return to these points later. For the present, it is sufficient to note that a set of arguments can be developed in support of the proposition that certain kinds of adultery are wrong just because they involve the breach of a serious promise which, among other things, leads to the intentional infliction of substantial pain by one spouse upon the other.

Another argument for the immorality of adultery focuses not on the existence of a promise of sexual exclusivity but on the connection between adultery and deception. According to this argument, adultery involves deception. And because deception is wrong, so is adultery.

Although it is certainly not obviously so, I shall simply assume in this paper that deception is always immoral. Thus the crucial issue for my purposes is the asserted connection between extramarital sex and deception. Is it plausible to maintain, as this argument does, that adultery always does involve deception and is on that basis to be condemned?

The most obvious person on whom deceptions might be practiced is the nonparticipating spouse; and the most obvious thing about which the nonparticipating spouse can be deceived is the existence of the adulterous act. One clear case of deception is that of lying. Instead of saying that the afternoon was spent in bed with A, the adulterous spouse asserts that it was spent in the library with B, or on the golf course with C.

There can also be deception even when no lies are told. Suppose, for instance, that a person has sexual intercourse with someone other than his or her spouse and just does not tell the spouse about it. Is that deception? It may not be a case of lying if, for example, the spouse is never asked by the other about the situation. Still, we might say, it is surely deceptive because of the promises that were exchanged at marriage. As we saw earlier, these promises provide a foundation for the reasonable belief that neither spouse will engage in sexual relationships with any other persons. Hence the failure to bring the fact of extramarital sex to the attention of the other spouse deceives that spouse about the present state of the marital relationship.

Adultery, in other words, can involve both active and passive deception. An adulterous spouse may just keep silent or, as is often the fact, the spouse may engage in an increasingly complex way of life devoted to the concealment of the facts from the nonparticipating spouse. Lies, half-truths, clandestine meetings, and the like may become a central feature of the adulterous spouse's existence. These are things that can and do happen, and when they do they make the case against adultery an easy one. Still, neither active nor passive deception is inevitably a feature of an extramarital relationship.

It is possible, though, that a more subtle but pervasive kind of deceptiveness is a feature of adultery. It comes about because of the connection in our culture between sexual intimacy and certain feelings of love and affection. The point can be made indirectly at first by seeing that one way in which we can, in our culture, mark off our close friends from our mere acquaintances is through the kinds of intimacies that we are prepared to share with them. I may, for instance, be willing to reveal my very private thoughts and emotions to my closest friends or to my wife, but to no one else. My sharing of these intimate facts about myself is from one perspective a way of making a gift to those who mean the most to me. Revealing these things and sharing them with those who mean the most to me is one means by which I create, maintain, and confirm those interpersonal relationships that are of most importance to me.

Now in our culture, it might be claimed, sexual intimacy is one of the chief currencies through which gifts of this sort are exchanged. One way to tell someone—particularly someone of the opposite sex—that you have feelings of affection and love for them is by allowing to them or sharing with them sexual behaviors that one doesn't share with the rest of the world. This way of measuring affection was certainly very much a part of the culture in which I matured. It worked something like this. If you were a girl, you showed how much you liked someone by the degree of sexual intimacy you would allow. If you liked a boy only a little, you never did more than kiss—and even the kiss was not very passionate. If you liked the boy a lot and if your feeling was reciprocated, necking, and possibly petting, was permissible. If the attachment was still stronger and you thought it might even become a permanent relationship, the sexual activity was correspondingly more intense and more intimate, although whether it would ever lead to sexual intercourse depended on whether the parties (and particularly the girl) accepted fully the prohibition on non-marital sex. The situation for the boy was related, but not exactly the same. The assumption was that males did not naturally link sex with affection in the way in which females did. However, since women did, males had to take this into account. That is to say, because a woman would permit sexual intimacies only if she had feelings of affection for the male and only if those feelings were reciprocated, the male had to have and express those feelings, too, before sexual intimacies of any sort would occur.

The result was that the importance of a correlation between sexual intimacy and feelings of love and affection was taught by the culture and assimilated by those growing up in the culture. The scale of possible positive feedings toward persons of the other sex ran from casual liking at the one end to the love that was deemed essential to and characteristic of marriage at the other. The scale of possible sexual behavior ran from brief, passionless kissing or hand-holding at the one end to sexual intercourse at the other. And the correlation between the two scales was quite precise. As a result, any act of sexual intimacy carried substantial meaning with it, and no act of sexual intimacy was simply a pleasurable set of bodily sensations. Many such acts were, of course, more pleasurable to the participants because they were a way of saying what the participants' feelings were. And sometimes they were less pleasurable for the same reason. The point is, however, that in any event sexual activity was much more than mere bodily enjoyment. It was not like eating a good meal, listening to good music, lying in the sun, or getting a pleasant back rub. It was behavior that meant a great deal concerning one's feelings for persons of the opposite sex in whom one was most interested and with whom one was most involved. It was among the most authoritative ways in which one could communicate to another the nature and degree of one's affection.

If this sketch is even roughly right, then several things become somewhat clearer. To begin with, a possible rationale for many of the rules of conventional sexual morality can be developed. If, for example, sexual intercourse is associated with the kind of affection and commitment to another that is regarded as characteristic of the marriage relationship, then it is natural that sexual intercourse should be thought properly to take place between persons who are married to each other. And if it is thought that this kind of affection and commitment is only to be found within the marriage relationship, then it is not surprising that sexual intercourse should only be thought to be proper within marriage.

Related to what has just been said is the idea that sexual intercourse ought to be restricted to those who are married to each other as a means by which to confirm the very special feelings that the spouses have for each other. Because the culture teaches that sexual intercourse means that the strongest of all feelings for each other are shared by the lovers, it is natural that persons who are married to each other should be able to say this to each other in this way. Revealing and confirming verbally that these feelings are present is one thing that helps to sustain the relationship; engaging in sexual intercourse is another.

In addition, this account would help to provide a framework within which to make sense of the notion that some sex is better than other sex. As I indicated earlier, the fact that sexual intimacy can be meaningful in the sense described tends to make it also the case that sexual intercourse can sometimes be more enjoyable than at other times. On this view, sexual intercourse will typically be more enjoyable where the strong feelings of affection are present than it will be where it is merely "mechanical." This is so in part because people enjoy being loved, especially by those whom they love. Just as we like to hear words of affection, so we like to receive affectionate behavior. And the meaning enhances the independently pleasurable behavior.

More to the point, moreover, an additional rationale for the prohibition on extramarital sex can now be developed. For given this way of viewing the sexual world, extramarital sex will almost always involve deception of a deeper sort. If the adulterous spouse does not in fact have the appropriate feelings of affection for the extramarital partner, then the adulterous spouse is deceiving that person about the presence of such feelings. If, on the other hand, the adulterous spouse does have the corresponding feelings for the extramarital partner but not toward the nonparticipating spouse, the adulterous spouse is very probably deceiving the nonparticipating spouse about the presence of such feelings toward that spouse. Indeed, it might be argued, whenever there is no longer love between the two persons who are married to each other, there is deception just because being married implies both to the participants and to the world that such a bond exists. Deception is inevitable, the argument might conclude, because the feelings of affection that ought to accompany any act of sexual intercourse can only be held toward one other person at any given time in one's life. And if this is so, then the adulterous spouse always deceives either the partner in adultery or the nonparticipating spouse about the existence of such feelings. Thus extramarital sex involves deception of this sort and is for this reason immoral even if no deception vis-à-vis the occurrence of the act of adultery takes place.

What might be said in response to the foregoing arguments? The first thing that might be said is that the account of the connection between sexual intimacy and feelings of affection is inaccurate. Not inaccurate in the sense that no one thinks of things that way, but in the sense that there is substantially more divergence of opinion than that account suggests. For example, the view I have delineated may describe reasonably accurately the concepts of the sexual world in which I grew up, but it does not capture the sexual *weltanschauung* of today's youth at all. Thus, whether or not adultery implies deception in respect to feelings depends very much on the persons who are involved and the way they look at the "meaning" of sexual intimacy.

Second, the argument leaves to be answered the question of whether it is desirable for sexual intimacy to carry the sorts of messages described above. For those persons for whom sex does have these implications, there are special feelings and sensibilities that must be taken into account. But it is another question entirely whether any valuable end—moral or otherwise—is served by investing sexual behavior with such significance. That is something that must be shown and not just assumed. It might, for instance, be the case that substantially more good than harm would come from a kind of demystification of sexual behavior: one that would encourage the enjoyment of sex more for its own sake and one that would reject the centrality both of the association of sex with love and of love with only one other person.

I regard these as two of the more difficult, unresolved issues that our culture faces today in respect to thinking sensibly about the attitudes toward sex and love that we should try to develop in ourselves and in our children. Much of the contemporary literature that advocates sexual liberation of one sort or another embraces one or the other of two different views about the relationship between sex and love.

One view holds that sex should be separated from love and affection. To be sure sex is probably better when the partners genuinely like and enjoy each other. But sex is basically an intensive, exciting sensuous activity that can be enjoyed in a variety of suitable settings with a variety of suitable partners. The situation in respect to sexual pleasure is no different from that of the person who knows and appreciates fine food and who can have a very satisfying meal in any number of good restaurants with any number of congenial companions. One question that must be settled here is whether sex can be so demystified; another, more important question is whether it would be desirable to do so. What would we gain and what might we lose if we all lived in a world in which an act of sexual intercourse was no more or less significant or enjoyable than having a delicious meal in a nice setting with a good friend? The answer to this question lies beyond the scope of this paper.

The second view seeks to drive the wedge in a different place. It is not the link between sex and love that needs to be broken; rather, on this view, it is the connection between love and exclusivity that ought to be severed. For a number of the reasons already given, it is desirable, so this argument goes, that sexual intimacy continue to be reserved to and shared with only those for whom one has very great affection. The mistake lies in thinking that any "normal" adult will only have those feelings toward one other adult during his or her lifetime—or even at any time in his or her life. It is the concept of adult love, not ideas about sex, that, on this view, needs demystification. What are thought to be both unrealistic and unfortunate are the notions of exclusivity and possessiveness that attach to the dominant conception of love between adults in our and other cultures. Parents of four, five, six, or even ten children can certainly claim and sometimes claim correctly that they love all of their children, that they love them all equally, and that it is simply untrue to their feelings to insist that the numbers involved diminish either the quantity or the quality of their love. If this is an idea that is readily understandable in the case of parents and children, there is no necessary reason why it is an impossible or undesirable ideal in the case of adults. To be sure, there is probably a limit to the number of intimate, "primary" relationships that any person can maintain at any given time without the quality of the relationship being affected. But one adult ought surely be able to love two, three, or even six other adults at any one time without that love being different in kind or degree from that of the traditional, monogamous, lifetime marriage. And as between the individuals in these relationships, whether within a marriage or without, sexual intimacy is fitting and good.

The issues raised by a position such as this one are also surely worth exploring in detail and with care. Is there something to be called "sexual love" which is different from parental love or the nonsexual love of close friends? Is there something about love in general that links it naturally and appropriately with feelings of exclusivity and possession? Or is there something about sexual love, whatever that may be, that makes these feelings especially fitting here? Once again the issues are conceptual, empirical, and normative all at once: What is love? How could it be different? Would it be a good thing or a bad thing if it were different?

Suppose, though, that having delineated these problems we were now to pass them by. Suppose, moreover, we were to be persuaded of the possibility and the desirability of weakening substantially either the links between sex and love or the links between sexual love and exclusivity. Would it not then be the case that adultery could be free from all of the morally objectionable features described so far? To be more specific, let us imagine that a husband and wife have what is today sometimes characterized as an "open marriage." Suppose, that is, that they have agreed in advance that extramarital sex is—under certain circumstances—acceptable behavior for each to engage in. Suppose, that as a result there is no impulse to deceive each other about the occurrence or nature of any such relationships, and that no deception in fact occurs. Suppose, too, that there is no deception in respect to the feelings involved between the adulterous spouse and the extramarital partner. And suppose, finally, that one or the other or both of the spouses then has sexual intercourse in circumstances consistent with these understandings. Under this description, so the agreement might conclude, adultery is simply not immoral. At a minimum, adultery cannot very plausibly be condemned either on the ground that it involves deception or on the ground that it requires the breaking of a promise.

At least two responses are worth considering. One calls attention to the connection between marriage and adultery; the other looks to more instrumental arguments for the immorality of adultery. Both issues deserve further exploration.

One way to deal with the case of the "open marriage" is to question whether the two persons involved are still properly to be described as being married to each other. Part of the meaning of what it is for two persons to be married to each other, so this argument would go, is to have committed oneself to have sexual relationships only with one's spouse. Of course, it would be added, we know that that commitment is not always honored. We know that persons who are married to each other often do commit adultery. But there is a difference between being willing to make a commitment to marital fidelity, even though one may fail to honor that commitment, and not making the commitment at all. Whatever the relationship may be between the two individuals in the case described above, the absence of any commitment to sexual exclusivity requires the conclusion that their relationship is not a marital one. For a commitment to sexual exclusivity is a necessary although not a sufficient condition for the existence of a marriage.

Although there may be something to this suggestion, as it is stated it is too strong to be acceptable. To begin with, I think it is very doubtful that there are many, if any, *necessary* conditions for marriage; but even if there are, a commitment to sexual exclusivity is not such a condition.

To see that this is so, consider what might be taken to be some of the essential characteristics of a marriage. We might be tempted to propose that the concept of marriage requires the following: a formal ceremony of some sort in which mutual obligations are undertaken between two persons of the opposite sex; the capacity on the part of the persons involved to have sexual intercourse with each other; the willingness to have sexual intercourse only with each other; and feelings of love and affection between the two persons. The problem is that we can imagine relationships that are clearly marital and yet lack one or more of these features. For example, in our own society, it is possible for two persons to be married without going through a formal ceremony, as in the common-law marriages recognized in some jurisdictions. It is also possible for two persons to get married even though one or both lacks the capacity to engage in sexual intercourse. Thus, two very elderly persons who have neither the desire nor the ability to have intercourse can, nonetheless, get married, as can persons whose sexual organs have been injured so that intercourse is not possible. And we certainly know of marriages in which love was not present at the time of the marriage, as, for instance, in marriages of state and marriages of convenience.

Counterexamples not satisfying the condition relating to the abstention from extramarital sex are even more easily produced. We certainly know of societies and cultures in which polygamy and polyandry are practiced, and we have no difficulty in recognizing these relationships as cases of marriages. It might be objected, though, that these are not counterexamples because they are plural marriages rather than marriages in which sex is permitted with someone other than with one of the persons to whom one is married. But we also know of societies in which it is permissible for married persons to have sexual relationships with persons to whom they were not married, for example, temple prostitutes, concubines, and homosexual lovers. And even if we knew of no such societies, the conceptual claim would still, I submit, not be well taken. For suppose all of the other indicia of marriage were present: suppose the two persons were of the opposite sex, suppose they had the capacity and desire to have intercourse with each other, suppose they participated in a formal ceremony in which they understood themselves voluntarily to be entering into a relationship with each other in which substantial mutual commitments were assumed. If all these conditions were satisfied, we would not be in any doubt about whether or not the two persons were married even though they had not taken on a commitment of sexual exclusivity and even though they had expressly agreed that extramarital sexual intercourse was a permissible behavior for each to engage in.

A commitment to sexual exclusivity is neither a necessary nor a sufficient condition for the existence of a marriage. It does, nonetheless, have this much to do with the nature of marriage: like the other indicia enumerated above, its presence tends to establish the existence of a marriage. Thus, in the absence of a formal ceremony of any sort, an explicit commitment to sexual exclusivity would count in favor of regarding the two persons as married. The conceptual role of the commitment to sexual exclusivity can, perhaps, be brought out through the following example. Suppose we found a tribe which had a practice in which all the other indicia of marriage were present but in which the two parties were *prohibited* ever from having sexual intercourse with each other. Moreover, suppose that sexual intercourse with others was clearly permitted. In such a case we would, I think, reject the idea that the two were married to each other and we would describe their relationship in other terms, for example, as some kind of formalized, special friendship relation—a kind of heterosexual "blood-brother" bond.

Compare that case with the following. Suppose again that the tribe had a practice in which all of the other indicia of marriage were present, but instead of a prohibition on sexual intercourse between the persons in the relationship there was no rule at all. Sexual intercourse was permissible with the person with whom one had this ceremonial relationship, but it was no more or less permissible than with a number of other persons to whom one was not so related (for instance, all consenting adults of the opposite sex). Although we might be in doubt as to whether we ought to describe the persons as married to each other, we would probably conclude that they were married and that they simply were members of a tribe whose views about sex were quite different from our own.

What all of this shows is that *a prohibition* on sexual intercourse between the two persons involved in a relationship is conceptually incompatible with the claim that the two of them are married. The *permissibility* of intramarital sex is a necessary part of the idea of marriage. But no such incompatibility follows simply from the added permissibility of extramarital sex.

These arguments do not, of course, exhaust the arguments for the prohibition on extramarital sexual relations. The remaining argument that I wish to consider—as I indicated earlier—is a more instrumental one. It seeks to justify the prohibition by virtue of the role that it plays in the development and maintenance of nuclear families. The argument, or set of arguments, might, I believe, go something like this.

Consider first a farfetched nonsexual example. Suppose a society were organized so that after some suitable age—say, 18, 19, or 20—

persons were forbidden to eat anything but bread and water with anyone but their spouse. Persons might still choose in such a society not to get married. Good food just might not be very important to them because they have underdeveloped taste buds. Or good food might be bad for them because there is something wrong with their digestive system. Or good food might be important to them, but they might decide that the enjoyment of good food would get in the way of the attainment of other things that were more important. But most persons would, I think, be led to favor marriage in part because they preferred a richer, more varied, diet to one of bread and water. And they might remain married because the family was the only legitimate setting within which good food was obtainable. If it is important to have society organized so that persons will both get married and stay married, such an arrangement would be well suited to the preservation of the family, and the prohibitions relating to food consumption could be understood as fulfilling that function.

It is obvious that one of the more powerful human desires is the desire for sexual gratification. The desire is a natural one, like hunger and thirst, in the sense that it need not be learned in order to be present within us and operative upon us. But there is in addition much that we do learn about what the act of sexual intercourse is like. Once we experience sexual intercourse ourselves—and in particular once we experience orgasm—we discover that it is among the most intensive, short-term pleasures of the body.

Because this is so, it is easy to see how the prohibition upon extramarital sex helps to hold marriage together. At least during that period of life when the enjoyment of sexual intercourse is one of the desirable bodily pleasures, persons will wish to enjoy those pleasures. If one consequence of being married is that one is prohibited from having sexual intercourse with anyone but one's spouse, then the spouses in a marriage are in a position to provide an important source of pleasure for each other that is unavailable to them elsewhere in the society.

The point emerges still more clearly if this rule of sexual morality is seen as of a piece with the other rules of sexual morality. When this prohibition is coupled, for example, with the prohibition on nonmarital sexual intercourse, we are presented with the inducement both to get married and to stay married. For if sexual intercourse is only legitimate within marriage, then persons seeking that gratification which is a feature of sexual intercourse are furnished explicit social directions for its attainment; namely marriage.

Nor, to continue the argument, is it necessary to focus exclusively on the bodily enjoyment that is involved. Orgasm may be a significant part of what there is to sexual intercourse, but it is not the whole of it. We need only recall the earlier discussion of the meaning that sexual intimacy has in our own culture to begin to see some of the more intricate ways in which sexual exclusivity may be connected with the establishment and maintenance of marriage as the primary heterosexual love relationship. Adultery is wrong, in other words, because a prohibition on extramarital sex is a way to help maintain the institutions of marriage and the nuclear family.

Now I am frankly not sure what we are to say about an argument such as this one. What I am convinced of is that, like the arguments discussed earlier, this one also reveals something of the difficulty and complexity of the issues that are involved. So, what I want now to do— in the brief and final portion of this paper—is to try to delineate with reasonable precision what I take several of the fundamental, unresolved issues to be.

The first is whether this last argument is an argument for the *immorality* of extramarital sexual intercourse. What does seem clear is that there are differences between this argument and the ones considered earlier. The earlier arguments condemned adulterous behavior because it was behavior that involved breaking a promise, taking unfair advantage, or deceiving another. To the degree to which the prohibition on extramarital sex can be supported by arguments which invoke considerations such as these, there is little question but that violations of the prohibition are properly regarded as immoral. And such a claim could be defended on one or both of two distinct grounds. The first is that things like promise-breaking and deception are just wrong. The second is that adultery involving promise-breaking or deception is wrong because it involves the straightforward infliction of harm on another human being—typically the nonadulterous spouse—who has a strong claim not to have that harm so inflicted.

The argument that connects the prohibition on extramarital sex with the maintenance and preservation of the institution of marriage is an argument for the instrumental value of the prohibition. To some degree this counts, I think, against regarding all violations of the prohibition as obvious cases of immorality. This is so partly because hypothetical imperatives are less clearly within the domain of morality than are categorical ones, and even more because instrumental prohibitions are within the domain of morality only if the end they serve or the way they serve it is itself within the domain of morality.

What this should help us see, I think, is the fact that the argument that connects the prohibition on adultery with the preservation of marriage is at best seriously incomplete. Before we ought to be convinced by it, we ought to have reasons for believing that marriage is a morally desirable and just social institution. And this is not quite as easy or obvious a task as it may seem to be. For the concept of marriage is, as we have seen, both a loosely structured and a complicated one. There may be all sorts of intimate, interpersonal relationships which will resemble but not be identical with the typical marriage relationship presupposed by the traditional sexual morality. There may be a number of distinguishable sexual and loving arrangements which can all legitimately claim to be called *marriages.* The prohibitions of the traditional sexual morality may be effective ways to maintain some marriages and ineffective ways to promote and preserve others. The prohibitions of the traditional sexual morality may make good psychological sense if certain psychological theories are true, and they may be purveyors of immense psychological mischief if other psychological theories are true. The prohibitions of the traditional sexual morality may seem obviously correct if sexual intimacy carries the meaning that the dominant culture has often ascribed to it, and they may seem equally bizarre when sex is viewed through the perspective of the counterculture. Irrespective of whether instrumental arguments of this sort are properly deemed moral arguments, they ought not to fully convince anyone until questions like these are answered.

NOTES

1. *Kingsley International Pictures Corp. v. Regents,* 360 U.S. 684.

CHAPTER SIX

In Defense of
DECEIT

𝒯he truth can hurt, we all know. Why hurt others unnecessarily? Should we really speak frankly when undistinguished friends confide that they dream of becoming a movie star, or winning the Nobel prize? And what about atheists? Isn't it somehow cruel of them to deride those who believe in God, when believers claim to find great solace in their religion?

In the following work from 1888, Oscar Wilde portrays lying as an art form. Socially skilled people can use deceit to their own advantage, certainly, but they can also lie to protect, even inspire, others. Think of what painters and poets do: They craft images that uplift and refine us, all the while deceiving us. So little in life is perfect that we find welcome solace in depictions of life as we would like it to be. Through the character of Vivian in the following dialogue, Wilde suggests that we reserve the compliments "gracious" and "sophisticated" for those among us who lie easily and artfully.

Wilde reminds us that brutal honesty deprives us of something valuable. Hardly a saint himself, Wilde nonetheless suffered terribly in real life as a result of honesty. He landed in jail not because of his sexual affairs with men but because of his reluctance to abide by a Victorian code of duplicity about his private life.

References to this clever defense of lying found their way into numerous news articles during the Monica Lewinsky scandal that plagued the Clinton White House.

∾

OSCAR WILDE (1854–1900), an Irishman, was educated at Magdalene College, Oxford and served two years in prison for acts of "gross indecency." Among his celebrated works figure *The Importance of Being Earnest* (1895); *Lady Windemere's Fan* (1892); *A Woman of No Importance* (1893); and *De Profundis* (1905). He died in poverty and disgrace in a Paris hotel after having hopelessly pursued an English aristocrat, Lord Alfred Douglas, who refused to resume their romance and later converted to Roman Catholicism. Wilde himself converted to Catholicism on his deathbed.

THE DECAY OF LYING

Oscar Wilde

AN OBSERVATION, A DIALOGUE.

Persons: *Cyril and Vivian*
Scene: *The library of a country house in Nottinghamshire.*

CYRIL (*coming in through the open window from the terrace*). My dear *Vivian,* don't coop yourself up all day in the library. It is a perfectly lovely afternoon. The air is exquisite. There is a mist upon the woods, like the purple bloom upon a plum. Let us go and lie on the grass, and smoke cigarettes, and enjoy Nature.

VIVIAN. Enjoy Nature! I am glad to say that I have entirely lost that faculty. People tell us that Art makes us love Nature more than we loved her before; that it reveals her secrets to us; and that after a careful study of Corot and Constable we see things in her that had escaped our observation. My own experience is that the more we study Art, the less we care for Nature. What Art really reveals to us is Nature's lack of design, her curious crudities, her extraordinary monotony, her absolutely unfinished condition. Nature has good intentions, of course, but, as Aristotle once said, she cannot carry them out. When I look at a landscape I cannot help seeing all its defects. It is fortunate for us, however, that Nature is so imperfect, as otherwise we should have had no art at all. Art is our spirited protest, our gallant attempt to teach Nature her proper place. As for the infinite variety of Nature, that is a pure myth. It is not to be found in Nature herself. It resides in the imagination, or fancy, or cultivated blindness of the man who looks at her.

CYRIL. Well, you need not look at the landscape. You can lie on the grass and smoke and talk.

VIVIAN. But Nature is so uncomfortable. Grass is hard and lumpy and damp, and full of dreadful black insects. Why, even Morris' poorest workman could make you a more comfortable seat than the whole of Nature can. Nature pales before the furniture of "the street which came from Oxford has borrowed its name," as the poet you love so much once vilely phrased it. I don't complain. If Nature had been comfortable, mankind would never have invented architecture, and I prefer houses to the open air. In a house we all feel of the proper proportions. Everything is subordinated to us, fashioned for our use and our pleasure. Egotism itself, which is so necessary to a proper sense of human dignity, is entirely the result of indoor life. Out of doors one becomes abstract and impersonal. One's individuality absolutely leaves one. And then Nature is so indifferent, so unappreciative. Whenever I am walking in the park here I always feel that I am no more to her than the cattle that browse on the slope, or the burdock that blooms in the ditch. Nothing is more evident than that Nature hates Mind. Thinking is the most unhealthy thing in the world, and people die of it just as they die of any other disease. Fortunately, in England, at any rate, thought is not catching. Our splendid physique as a people is entirely due to our national stupidity. I only hope we shall be able to keep this great historic bulwark of our happiness for many years to come; but I am afraid that we are beginning to be overeducated; at least, everybody who is incapable of learning has taken to teaching—that is really what our enthusiasm for education has come to. In the meantime, you had better go back to your wearisome uncomfortable Nature, and leave me to correct my proofs.

CYRIL. Writing an article! That is not very consistent after what you have just said.

VIVIAN. Who wants to be consistent? The dullard and the doctrinaire, the tedious people who carry out their principles to the bitter end of action, to the *reductio ad absurdum* of practice. Not I. Like Emerson, I write over the door of my library the word "Whim." Besides my article is really a most salutary and valuable warning. If it is attended to, there may be a new Renaissance of Art.

CYRIL. What is the subject?

VIVIAN. I intend to call it "The Decay of Lying: A Protest."

CYRIL. Lying! I should have thought that our politicians kept up that habit.

VIVIAN. I assure you that they do not. They never rise beyond the level of misrepresentation, and actually condescend to prove, to discuss, to argue. How different from the temper of the true liar, with his frank, fearless statements, his superb irresponsibility, his healthy, natural disdain of proof of any kind! After all, what is a fine lie? Simply that which is its own evidence. If a man is sufficiently unimaginative to produce evidence in support of a lie, he might just as well speak the truth at once. No, the politicians won't do. Something may, perhaps, be urged on behalf of the Bar. The mantle of the Sophist has fallen on its members. Their feigned ardours and unreal rhetoric are delightful. They can make the worse appear the better cause, as though they were fresh from Leontine schools, and have been known to wrest from reluctant juries triumphant verdicts of acquittal for their clients, even when those clients, as often happens, were clearly and unmistakably innocent. But they are briefed by the prosaic, and are not ashamed to appeal to precedent. In spite of their endeavours, the truth will out. Newspapers, even, have degenerated. They may now be absolutely relied upon. One feels it as one wades through their columns. It is always the unreadable that occurs. I am afraid that there is not much to be said in favour of either the lawyer or the journalist. Besides, what I am pleading for is Lying in art. Shall I read you what I have written? It might do you a great deal of good.

CYRIL. Certainly, if you give me a cigarette. Thanks. By the way, what magazine do you intend it for?

VIVIAN. For the *Retrospective Review*. I think I told you that the elect had revived it.

CYRIL. Whom do you mean by "the elect"?

VIVIAN. Oh, the Tired Hedonists, of course. It is a club to which I belong. We are supposed to wear faded roses in our button-holes when we meet, and to have a sort of cult for Domitian. I am afraid you are not eligible. You are too fond of simple pleasures.

CYRIL. I should be black-balled on the ground of animal spirits, I suppose?

VIVIAN. Probably. Besides, you are a little too old. We don't admit anybody who is of the usual age.

CYRIL. Well, I should fancy you are all a good deal bored with each other.

VIVIAN. We are. That is one of the objects of the club. Now, if you promise not to interrupt too often, I will read you my article.

CYRIL. You will find me all attention.

VIVIAN (*reading in a very clear, musical voice*). "THE DECAY OF LYING: A PROTEST.—One of the chief causes that can be assigned for the curiously commonplace character of most of the literature of our age is undoubtedly the decay of Lying as an art, a science, and a social pleasure. The ancient historians gave us delightful fiction in the form of fact; the modern novelist presents us with dull facts under the guise of fiction. The Blue-Book is rapidly becoming his ideal both for method and manner. He has his tedious *'document humain,'* his miserable little *'coin de la création,'* into which he peers with his microscope. He is to be found at the Librairie Nationale, or at the British Museum, shamelessly reading up his subject. He has not even the courage of other people's ideas, but insists on going directly to life for everything, and ultimately, between encyclopaedias and personal experience, he comes to the ground, having drawn his types from the family circle or from the weekly washerwoman, and having acquired an amount of useful information from which never, even in his most meditative moments, can he thoroughly free himself.

"The loss that results to literature in general from this false ideal of our time can hardly be over-estimated. People have a careless way of talking about a 'born liar,' just as they talk about a 'born poet.' But in both cases they are wrong. Lying and poetry are arts—arts, as Plato saw, not unconnected with each other—and they require the most careful study, the most disinterested devotion. Indeed, they have their technique, just as the more material arts of painting and sculpture have, their subtle secrets of form and colour, their craft-mysteries, their deliberate artistic methods. As one knows the poet by his fine music, so one can recognise the liar by his rich rhythmic utterance, and in neither case will the casual inspiration of the moment suffice. Here, as elsewhere, practice must precede perfection. But in modern days while the fashion of writing poetry has become far too common, and should, if possible, be discouraged, the fashion of lying has almost fallen into disrepute. Many a young man starts in life with a natural gift for exaggeration which, if nurtured in congenial and sympathetic surroundings, or by the imitation of the best models, might grow into something really great and wonderful. But, as a rule, he comes to nothing. He either falls into careless habits of accuracy——"

CYRIL. My dear fellow!

VIVIAN. Please don't interrupt in the middle of a sentence. "He either falls into careless habits of accuracy, or takes to frequenting the society of the aged and the well-informed. Both things are equally fatal to his imagination, as indeed they would be fatal to the imagination of anybody, and in a short time he develops a morbid and unhealthy faculty of truth-telling, begins to verify all statements made in his presence, has no hesitation in contradicting people who are much younger than himself, and often ends by writing novels which are so like life that no one can possibly believe in their probability. This is no isolated instance that we are giving. It is simply one example out of many; and if something cannot be done to check, or at least to modify, our monstrous worship of facts, Art will become sterile, and Beauty will pass away from the land.

"Even Mr. Robert Louis Stevenson, that delightful master of delicate and fanciful prose, is tainted with this modern vice, for we know positively no other name for it. There is such a thing as robbing a story of its reality by trying to make it too true, and *The Black Arrow* is so inartistic as not to contain a single anachronism to boast of, while the transformation of Dr. Jekyll reads dangerously like an experiment out of the *Lancet*. As for Mr. Rider Haggard, who really has, or had once, the makings of a perfectly magnificent liar, he is now so afraid of being suspected of genius that when he does tell us anything marvellous, he feels bound to invent a personal reminiscence, and to put it into a footnote as a kind of cowardly corroboration. Nor are our other novelists much better. Mr. Henry James writes fiction as if it were a painful duty, and wastes upon mean motives and imperceptible 'points of view' his neat literary style, his felicitous phrases, his swift and caustic satire. Mr. Hall Caine, it is true, aims at the grandiose, but then he writes at the top of his voice. He is so loud that one cannot hear what he says. Mr. James

Payn is an adept in the art of concealing what is not worth finding. He hunts down the obvious with the enthusiasm of a short-sighted detective. As one turns over the pages, the suspense of the offer becomes almost unbearable. The horses of Mr. William Black's phaeton do not soar towards the sun. They merely frighten the sky at evening into violent chromolithographic effects. On seeing them approach, the peasants take refuge in dialect. Mrs. Oliphant prattles pleasantly about curates, lawn-tennis parties, domesticity, and other wearisome things. Mr. Marion Crawford h[a]s immolated himself upon the altar of local colour. He is like the lady in the French comedy who talks about 'le beau ciel d'Italie.' Besides, he has fallen into a bad habit of uttering moral platitudes. He is always telling us that to be good is to be good, and that to be bad is to be wicked. At times he is almost edifying. *Robert Elsmere* is, of course, a masterpiece—a masterpiece of the 'genre ennuyeux,' the one form of literature that the English people seem to thoroughly enjoy. A thoughtful young friend of ours once told us that it reminded him of the sort of conversation that goes on at a meat tea in the house of a serious Noncomformist family, and we can quite believe it. Indeed it is only in England that such a book could be produced. England is the home of lost ideas. As for that great and daily increasing school of novelist for whom the sun always rises in the East-End, the only thing that can be said about them is that they find life crude, and leave it raw.

"In France, though nothing so deliberately tedious as *Robert Elsmere* has been produced, things are not much better. M. Guy de Maupassant, with his keen mordant irony and his hard vivid style, strips life of the few poor rags that still cover her, and shows us foul sore and festering wound. He writes lurid little tragedies in which everybody is ridiculous; bitter comedies at which one cannot laugh for very tears. M. Zola, true to the lofty principle that he lays down in one of his pronunciamientos on literature, 'L' homme de génie n'a jamais d'esprit,' is determined to show that, if he has not got genius, he can at least be dull. And how well he succeeds! He is not without power. Indeed at times, as in *Germinal,* there is something almost epic in his work. But his work is entirely wrong from beginning to end, and wrong not on the ground of morals, but on the ground of art. From any ethical standpoint it is just what it should be. The author is perfectly truthful and describes things exactly as they happen. What more can any moralist desire? We have no sympathy at all with the moral indignation of our time against M. Zola. It is simply the indignation of Tartuffe on being exposed. But from the standpoint of art, what can be said in favour of the author of *L'Assommoir, Nana,* and *Pot-Bouille?* Nothing. Mr. Ruskin once described the characters in George Eliot's novels as being like the sweepings of a Pentonville omnibus, but M. Zola's characters are much worse. They have their dreary vices, and their drearier virtues. The record of their lives is absolutely without interest. Who cares what happens to them? In literature we require distinction, charm, beauty, and imaginative power. We don't want to be harrowed and disgusted with an account of the doings of the lower orders. M. Daudet is better. He has wit, a light touch, and an amusing style. But he has lately committed literary suicide. Nobody can possibly care for Delobelle with his 'Il faut lutter pour l'art,' or for Valmajour with his eternal refrain about the nightingale, or for the poet in *Jack* with his 'mots cruels,' now that we have learned from *Vingt Ans de ma Vie littéraire* that these characters were taken directly from life. To us they seem to have suddenly lost all their vitality, all the few qualities they ever possessed. The only real people are the people who never existed, and if a novelist is base enough to go to life for his personages he should at least pretend that they are creations, and not boast of them as copies. The justification of a character in a novel is not that other persons are what they are, but that the author is what he is. Otherwise the novel is not a work of art. As for M. Paul Bourget, the master of the *roman psychologique,* he commits the error of imagining that the men and women of modern life are capable of being infinitely analysed for an innumerable series of chapters. In point of fact, what is interesting about people in good society—and M. Bourget rarely moves out to the Faubourg St. Germain, except to come to London—is the mask that each one of them wears, not the reality that lies behind the mask. It is a humiliating confession, but we are all of us made out of the same stuff. In Falstaff there is something of Hamlet, in Hamlet there is not a little of Falstaff. The fat knight has his moods of melancholy, and the young prince his moments of coarse humour. Where we differ from each other is purely in accidentals: in personal appearance, tricks of habit, and the like. The more one analyses people, the more all reasons for analysis disappear. Sooner or later one comes to that dreadful universal thing called human nature. Indeed, as any one who has ever worked among the poor knows only too well, the brotherhood of man is no mere poet's dream, it is a most depressing and humiliating reality; and if a writer insists upon analysing the upper classes, he might just as well write of match-girls and costermongers at once." However, my dear Cyril, I will not detain you any further just here. I quite admit that modern novels have many good points. All I insist on is that, as a class, they are quite unreadable.

CYRIL. That is certainly a very grave qualification, but I must say that I think you are rather unfair in some of your strictures. I like *The Deemster,* and *The Daughter of Heth,* and *Le Disciple,* and *Mr. Isaacs,* and for *Robert Elsmere,* I am quite devoted to it. Not that I can look upon it as a serious work. As a statement of the problems that confront the earnest Christian it is ridiculous and antiquated. It is simply Arnold's *Literature and Dogma* with the literature left out. It is as much behind the age as Paley's *Evidences,* or Colenso's method of Biblical exegesis. Nor could anything be less impressive than the unfortunate hero gravely heralding a dawn that rose long ago, and so completely missing its true significance that he proposes to carry on the business of the old firm under the new name. On the other hand, it contains several clever caricatures, and a heap of delightful quotations, and Green's philosophy very plentifully sugars the somewhat bitter pill of the author's fiction. I also cannot help expressing my surprise that you have said nothing about the two novelists whom you are always reading, Balzac and George Meredith. Surely they are realists, both of them?

VIVIAN. Ah! Meredith! Who can define him? His style is chaos illumined by flashes of lightning. As a writer he has mastered everything except language: as a novelist he can do everything, except tell a story: as an artist he is everything, except articulate. Somebody in Shakespeare—Touchstone, I think—talks about a man who is always breaking his shins over his own wit, and it seems to me that this might serve as a basis for a criticism of Meredith's method. But whatever he is, he is not a realist. Or, rather, I would say that he is a child of realism who is not on speaking terms with his father. By deliberate choice he has made himself a romanticist. He has refused to bow the knee to Baal, and after all, even if the man's fine spirit did not revolt against the noisy assertions of realism, his style would be quite sufficient of itself to keep life at a respectful distance. By its means he has planted round his garden a hedge full of thorns, and red with wonderful roses. As for Balzac, he was a most remarkable combination of the artistic temperament with the scientific spirit. The latter he bequeathed to his disciples: the former was entirely his own. The difference between such a book as M. Zola's *L'Assommoir* and Balzac's *Illusions Perdues* is the difference between unimaginative realism and imaginative reality. "All Balzac's characters," said Baudelaire, "are gifted with the same ardour of life that animated himself. All his fictions are as deeply coloured as dreams. Each mind is a weapon loaded to the muzzle with will. The very scullions have genius." A steady course of Balzac reduces our living friends to shadows, and our acquaintances to the shadows of shades. His characters have a kind of fervent fiery-coloured existence. They dominate us, and defy scepticism. One of the greatest tragedies of my life is the death of Lucien de Rubempré. It is a grief from which I have never been able to completely rid myself. It haunts me in my moments of pleasure. I remember it when I laugh. But Balzac is no more a realist than Holbein was. He created life, he did not copy it. I admit, however, that he set far too high a value on modernity of form, and that, consequently, there is no book of his that, as an artistic masterpiece, can rank with *Salammbô* or *Esmmond,* or *The Cloister and the Hearth,* or the *Vicomte de Bragelonne.*

CYRIL. Do you object to modernity of form, then?

VIVIAN. Yes. It is a huge price to pay for a very poor result. Pure modernity of form is always somewhat vulgarising. It cannot help being so. The public imagine that, because they are interested in their immediate surroundings, Art should be interested in them also, and should take them as her subject-matter. But the mere fact that they are interested in these things makes them unsuitable subjects for Art. The only beautiful things, as somebody once said, are the things that do not concern us. As long as a thing is useful or necessary to us, or affects us in any way, either for pain or for pleasure, or appeals strongly to our sympathies, or is a vital part of the environment in which we live, it is outside the proper sphere of art. To art's subject-matter we should be more or less indifferent. We should, at any rate, have no preferences, no prejudices, no partisan feelings of any kind. It is exactly because Hecuba is nothing to us that her sorrows are such an admirable motive for tragedy. I do not know anything in the whole history of literature sadder than the artistic career of Charles Reade. He wrote one beautiful book, *The Cloister and the Hearth,* a book as much above *Romola* as *Romola* is above *Daniel Deronda,* and wasted the rest of his life in a foolish attempt to be modern, to draw public attention to the state of our convict prisons, and the management of our private lunatic asylums. Charles Dickens was depressing enough in all conscience when he tried to arouse our sympathy for the victims of the poor-law administration; but Charles Reade, an artist, a scholar, a man with a true sense of beauty, raging and roaring over the abuses of contemporary life like a common pamphleteer or a sensational journalist, is really a sight for the angels to weep over. Believe me, my dear Cyril, modernity of form and modernity of subject-matter are entirely and absolutely wrong. We have mistaken the common livery of the age for the vesture of the Muses, and spend our days in the sordid streets and hideous suburbs of our vile cities when we should be out on the hillside with Apollo. Certainly we are a degraded race, and have sold our birthright for a mess of facts.

CYRIL. There is something in what you say, and there is no doubt that whatever amusement we may find in reading a purely modern novel, we have rarely any artistic pleasure in re-reading it. And this is perhaps the best rough test of what is literature and what is not. If one cannot enjoy reading a book over and over again, there is no use reading it at all. But what do you say about the return to Life and Nature? This is the panacea that is always being recommended to us.

VIVIAN. I will read you what I say on that subject. The passage comes later on in the article, but I may as well give it to you now:—
"The popular cry of our time is 'Let us return to Life and Nature; they will recreate Art for us, and send the red blood coursing through her veins; they will shoe her feet with swiftness and make her hand strong.' But, alas! we are mistaken in our amiable and well-meaning efforts. Nature is always behind the age. And as for Life, she is the solvent that breaks up Art, the enemy that lays waste her house."

CYRIL. What do you mean by saying that Nature is always behind the age?

VIVIAN. Well, perhaps that is rather cryptic. What I mean is this. If we take Nature to mean natural simple instinct as opposed to self-conscious culture, the work produced under this influence is always old-fashioned, antiquated, and out of date. One touch of Nature may make the whole world kin, but two touches of Nature will destroy any work of Art. If, on the other hand, we regard Nature as the collection of phenomena external to man, people only discover in her what they bring to her. She has no suggestions of her own. Wordsworth went to the lakes, but he was never a lake poet. He found in stones the sermons he had already hidden there. He went moralising about the district, but his good work was produced when he returned, not to Nature but to poetry. Poetry gave him "Laodamia," and the fine sonnets, and the great Ode, such as it is. Nature gave him "Martha Ray" and "Peter Bell," and the address to Mr. Wilkinson's spade.

CYRIL. I think that view might be questioned. I am rather inclined to believe in the "impulse from a vernal wood," though, of course, the artistic value of such an impulse depends entirely on the kind of temperament that receives it, so that the return to Nature would come to mean simply the advance to a great personality. You would agree with that, I fancy. However, proceed with your article.

VIVIAN (*reading*). "Art begins with abstract decoration, with purely imaginative and pleasurable work dealing with what is unreal and nonexistent. This is the first stage. Then Life becomes fascinated with this new wonder, and asks to be admitted into the charmed circle. Art takes life as part of her rough material, recreates it, and refashions it in fresh forms, is absolutely indifferent to fact, invents, imagines, dreams, and keeps between herself and reality the impenetrable barrier of beautiful style, of decorative or ideal treatment. The third stage is when Life gets the upper hand, and drives Art out into the wilderness. This is the true decadence, and it is from this that we are now suffering.

"Take the case of the English drama. At first in the hands of the monks Dramatic Art was abstract, decorative, and mythological. Then she enlisted Life in her service, and using some of life's external forms, she created an entirely new race of beings, whose sorrows were more terrible than any sorrow man has ever felt, whose joys were keener than lover's joys, who had the rage of the Titans and the calm of the gods, who had monstrous and marvellous sins, monstrous and marvellous virtues. To them she gave a language different from that of actual use, a language full of resonant music and sweet rhythm, made stately by solemn cadence, or made delicate by fanciful rhyme, jewelled with wonderful words, and enriched with lofty diction. She clothed her children in strange raiment and gave them masks, and at her bidding the antique world rose from its marble tomb. A new Caesar stalked through the streets of risen Rome, and with purple sail and flute-led oars another Cleopatra passed up the river to Antioch. Old myth and legend and dream took shape and substance. History was entirely re-written, and there was hardly one of the dramatists who did not recognise that the object of Art is not simple truth but complex beauty. In this they were perfectly right. Art itself is really a form exaggeration; and selection, which is the very spirit of art, is nothing more than an intensified mode of over-emphasis.

"But Life soon shattered the perfection of the form. Even in Shakespeare we can see the beginning of the end. It shows itself by the gradual breaking up of the blank-verse in the later plays, by the predominance given to prose, and by the over-importance assigned to characterisation. The passages in Shakespeare—and they are many—where the language is uncouth, vulgar, exaggerated, fantastic, obscene even, are entirely due to Life calling for an echo of her own voice, and rejecting the intervention of beautiful style, through which alone should Life be suffered to find expression. Shakespeare is not by any means a flawless artist. He is too fond of going directly to life, and borrowing life's natural utterance. He forgets that when Art surrenders her imaginative medium she surrenders everything. Goethe says, somewhere—'It is in working within limits that the master reveals himself,' and the limitation, the very condition of any art is style. However, we need not linger any longer over Shakespeare's realism. *The Tempest* is the most perfect of palinodes. All that we desired to point out was, that the magnificent work of the Elizabethan and Jacobean artists contained within itself the seeds of its own dissolution, and that, if it drew some of its strength from using life as a rough material, it drew all its weakness from using life as an artistic method. As the inevitable result of this substitution of an imitative for a creative medium, this surrender of an imaginative form, we have the modern English melodrama. The characters in these plays talk on the stage exactly as they would talk off it; they have neither aspirations nor aspirates; they are taken directly from life and reproduce its vulgarity down to the smallest detail; they present the gait, manner, costume, and accent of real people; they would pass unnoticed in a third-class railway carriage. And yet how wearisome the plays are! They do not succeed in producing even that impression of reality at which they aim, and which is their only reason for existing. As a method, realism is a complete failure.

"What is true about the drama and the novel is no less true about those arts that we call the decorative arts. The whole history of these arts in Europe is the record of the struggle between Orientalism, with its frank rejection of imitation, its love of artistic convention, its dislike to the actual representation of any object in Nature, and our own imitative spirit. Wherever the former has been paramount, as in Byzantium, Sicily, and Spain, by actual contact, or in the rest of Europe by the influence of the Crusades, we have had beautiful and imaginative work in which the visible things of life are transmuted into artistic conventions, and the things that Life has not are invented and fashioned for her delight. But wherever we have returned to Life and Nature, our work has always become vulgar, common, and uninteresting. Modern tapestry, with its aërial effects, its elaborate perspective, its broad expanses of waste sky, its faithful and laborious realism, has no beauty whatsoever. The pictorial glass of Germany is absolutely detestable. We are beginning to weave passable carpets in England, but only because we have returned to the method and spirit of the East. Our rugs and carpets of twenty years ago, with their solemn depressing truths, their inane worship of Nature, their sordid reproductions of visible objects, have become, even to the Philistine, a source of laughter. A cultured Mahomedan once remarked to us, 'You Christians are so occupied in misinterpreting the fourth commandment that you have never thought of making an artistic application of the second.' He was perfectly right, and the whole truth of the matter is this: The proper school to learn art in is not Life but Art."

And now let me read you a passage which seems to me to settle the question very completely:

"It was not always thus. We need not say anything about the poets, for they, with the unfortunate exception of Mr. Wordsworth, have been really faithful to their high mission, and are universally recognised as being absolutely unreliable. But in the works of Herodotus, who, in spite of the shallow and ungenerous attempts of modern sciolists to verify his history, may justly be called the 'Father of Lies'; in the published speeches of Cicero and the biographies of Suetonius; in Tacitus at his best; in Pliny's *Natural History;* in Hanno's *Periplus;* in all the early chronicles; in the Lives of the Saints; in Froissart and Sir Thomas Mallory; in the travels of Marco Polo; in Olaus Magnus, and Aldrovandus, and Conrad

Lycosthenes, with his magnificent *Prodigiorum et Ostentorum Chronicon;* in the autobiography of Benvenuto Cellini; in the memoirs of Casanuova; in Defoe's *History of the Plague;* in Boswell's *Life of Johnson;* in Napoleon's despatches, and in the works of our own Carlyle, whose *French Revolution* is one of the most fascinating historical novels ever written, facts are either kept in their proper subordinate position, or else entirely excluded on the general ground of dulness. Now, everything is changed. Facts are not merely finding a footing-place in history, but they are usurping the domain of Fancy, and have invaded the kingdom of Romance. Their chilling touch is over everything. They are vulgarising mankind. The crude commercialism of America, its materialising spirit, its indifference to the poetical side of things, and its lack of imagination and of high unattainable ideals, are entirely due to that country having adopted for its national hero a man, who, according to his own confession, was incapable of telling a lie, and it is not too much to say that the story of George Washington and the cherry-tree has done more harm, and in a shorter space of time, than any other moral tale in the whole of literature."

CYRIL. My dear boy!

VIVIAN. I assure you it is the case, and the amusing part of the whole thing is that the story of the cherry-tree is an absolute myth. However, you must not think that I am too despondent about the artistic future either of America or of our own country. Listen to this:—

"That some change will take place before this century has drawn to its close we have no doubt whatsoever. Bored by the tedious and improving conversation of those who have neither the wit to exaggerate nor the genius to romance, tired of the intelligent person whose reminiscences are always based upon memory, whose statements are invariably limited by probability, and who is at any time liable to be corroborated by the merest Philistine who happens to be present, Society sooner or later must return to its lost leader, the cultured and fascinating liar. Who he was who first, without ever having gone out to the rude chase, told the wondering cavemen at sunset how he had dragged the Megatherium from the purple darkness of its jasper cave, or slain the Mammoth in single combat and brought back its giant tusks, we cannot tell, and not one of our modern anthropologists, for all their much-boasted science, has had the ordinary courage to tell us. Whatever was his name or race, he certainly was the true founder of social intercourse. For the aim of the liar is simply to charm, to delight, to give pleasure. He is the very basis of civilised society, and without him a dinner party, even at the mansions of the great, is as dull as a lecture at the Royal Society, or a debate at the Incorporated Authors, or one of Mr. Burnand's farcical comedies.

"Nor will he be welcomed by society alone. Art, breaking from the prison-house of realism, will run to greet him, and will kiss his false, beautiful lips, knowing that he alone is in possession of the great secret of all her manifestations, the secret that Truth is entirely and absolutely a matter of style; while Life—poor, probable, uninteresting human life— tired of repeating herself for the benefit of Mr. Herbert Spencer, scientific historians, and the compilers of statistics in general, will follow meekly after him, and try to reproduce, in her own simple and untutored way, some of the marvels of which he talks.

"No doubt there will always be critics who, like a certain writer in the *Saturday Review,* will gravely censure the teller of fairy tales for his defective knowledge of natural history, who will measure imaginative work by their own lack of any imaginative faculty, and will hold up their inkstained hands in horror if some honest gentleman, who has never been farther than the yew-trees of his own garden, pens a fascinating book of travels like Sir John Mandeville, or, like great Raleigh, writes a whole history of the world, without knowing anything whatsoever about the past. To excuse themselves they will try and shelter under the shield of him who made Prospero the magician, and gave him Caliban and Ariel as his servants, who heard the Tritons blowing their horns round the coral reefs of the Enchanted Isle, and the fairies singing to each other in a wood near Athens, who led the phantom kings in dim procession across the misty Scottish heath, and hid Hecate in a cave with the weird sisters. They will call upon Shakespeare—they always do—and will quote that hackneyed passage about Art holding the mirror up to Nature, forgetting that this unfortunate aphorism is deliberately said by Hamlet in order to convince the bystanders of his absolute insanity in all art-matters."

CYRIL. Ahem! Another cigarette, please.

VIVIAN. My dear fellow, whatever you may say, it is merely a dramatic utterance, and no more represents Shakespeare's real views upon art than the speeches of Iago represent his real views upon morals. But let me get to the end of the passage:

"Art finds her own perfection within, and not outside of, herself. She is not to be judged by any external standard of resemblance. She is a veil, rather than a mirror. She has flowers that no forests know of, birds that no woodland possesses. She makes and unmakes many worlds, and can draw the moon from heaven with a scarlet thread. Hers are the 'forms more real than living man,' and hers the great archetypes of which things that have existence are but unfinished copies. Nature has, in her eyes, no laws, no uniformity. She can work miracles at her will, and when she calls monsters from the deep they come. She can bid the almond tree blossom in winter, and send the snow upon the ripe cornfield. At her word the frost lays its silver finger on the burning mouth of June, and the winged lions creep out from the hollows of the Lydian hills. The dryads peer from the thicket as she passes by, and the brown fauns smile strangely at her when she comes near them. She has hawk-faced gods that worship her, and the centaurs gallop at her side."

CYRIL. I like that. I can see it. Is that the end?

VIVIAN. No. There is one more passage, but it is perfectly practical. It simply suggests some methods by which we could revive this lost art of Lying.

CYRIL. Well, before you read it to me, I should like to ask you a question. What do you mean by saying that life, "poor, probable, uninteresting human life," will try to reproduce the marvels of art? I can quite understand your objection to art being treated as a mirror. You think it would reduce genius to the position of a cracked looking-glass. But you don't mean to say that you seriously believe that Life imitates Art, that Life in fact is the mirror, and Art the reality?

VIVIAN. Certainly I do. Paradox though it may seem—and paradoxes are always dangerous things—it is none the less true that Life imitates art far more than Art imitates life. We have all seen in our own day in England how a certain curious and fascinating type of beauty, invented and emphasised by two imaginative painters, has so influenced Life that whenever one goes to a private view or to an artistic salon one sees, here the mystic eyes of Rossetti's dream, the long ivory throat, the strange square-cut jaw, the loosened shadowy hair that he so ardently loved, there the sweet maidenhood of "The Golden Stair," the blossom-like mouth and weary loveliness of the "Laus Amoris," the passion-pale face of Andromeda, the thin hands and lithe beauty of the Vivien in "Merlin's Dream." And it has always been so. A great artist invents a type, and Life tries to copy it, to reproduce it in a popular form, like an enterprising publisher. Neither Holbein nor Vandyck found in England what they have given us. They brought their types with them, and Life with her keen imitative faculty set herself to supply the master with models. The Greeks, with their quick artistic instinct, understood this, and set in the bride's chamber the statue of Hermes or of Apollo, that she might bear children as lovely as the works of art that she looked at in her rapture or her pain. They knew that Life gains from Art not merely spirituality, depth of thought and feeling, soul-turmoil or soul-peace, but that she can form herself on the very lines and colours of art, and can reproduce the dignity of Phidias as well as the grace of Praxiteles. Hence came their objection to realism. They disliked it on purely social grounds. They felt that it inevitably makes people ugly, and they were perfectly right. We try to improve the conditions of the race by means of good air, free sunlight, wholesome water, and hideous bare buildings for the better housing of the lower orders. But these things merely produce health, they do not produce beauty. For this, Art is required, and the true disciples of the great artist are not his studio-imitators, but those who become like his works of art, be they plastic as in Greek days, or pictorial as in modern times; in a word, Life is Art's best, Art's only pupil.

As it is with the visible arts, so it is with literature. The most obvious and the vulgarest form in which this is shown is in the case of the silly boys who, after reading the adventures of Jack Sheppard or Dick Turpin, pillage the stalls of unfortunate apple-women, break into sweet-shops at night, and alarm old gentlemen who are returning home from the city by leaping out on them in suburban lanes, with black masks and unloaded revolvers. This interesting phenomenon, which always occurs after the appearance of a new edition of either of the books I have alluded to, is usually attributed to the influence of literature on the imagination. But this is a mistake. The imagination is essentially creative and always seeks for a new form. The boy-burglar is simply the inevitable result of life's imitative instinct. He is Fact, occupied as Fact usually is, with trying to reproduce Fiction, and what we see in him is repeated on an extended scale throughout the whole of life. Schopenhauer has analysed the pessimism that characterises modern thought, but Hamlet invented it. The world has become sad because a puppet was once melancholy. The Nihilist, that strange martyr who has no faith, who goes to the stake without enthusiasm, and dies for what he does not believe in, is a purely literary product. He was invented by Tourgénieff, and completed by Dostoieffski. Robespierre came out of the pages of Rousseau as surely as the People's Palace rose out of the *débris* of a novel. Literature always anticipates life. It does not copy it, but moulds it to its purpose. The nineteenth century, as we know it, is largely an invention of Balzac. Our Luciens de Rubempré, our Rastignacs, and De Marsays made their first appearance on the stage of the *Comédie Humaine.* We are merely carrying out, with footnotes and unnecessary additions, the whim or fancy or creative vision of a great novelist. I once asked a lady, who knew Thackeray intimately, whether he had had any model for Becky Sharp. She told me that Becky was an invention, but that the idea of the character had been partly suggested by a governess who lived in the neighbourhood of Kensington Square, and was the companion of a very selfish and rich old woman. I inquired what became of the governess, and she replied that, oddly enough, some years after the appearance of *Vanity Fair,* she ran away with the nephew of the lady with whom she was living, and for a short time made a great splash in society, quite in Mrs. Rawdon Crawley's style, and entirely by Mrs. Rawdon Crawley's methods. Ultimately she came to grief, disappeared to the Continent, and used to be occasionally seen at Monte Carlo and other gambling places. The noble gentleman from whom the same great sentimentalist drew Colonel Newcome died, a few months after *The Newcomes* had reached a fourth edition, with the word "Adsum" on his lips. Shortly after Mr. Stevenson published his curious psychological story of transformation, a friend of mine, called Mr. Hyde, was in the north of London, and being anxious to get to a railway station, took what he thought would be a short cut, lost his way, and found himself in a network of mean, evil-looking streets. Feeling rather nervous, he began to walk extremely fast, when suddenly out of an archway ran a child right between his legs. It fell on the pavement, he tripped over it, and trampled upon it. Being of course very much frightened and a little hurt, it began to scream and in a few seconds the whole street was full of rough people who came pouring out of the houses like ants. They surrounded him and asked him his name. He was just about to give it when he suddenly remembered the opening incident in Mr. Stevenson's story. He was so filled with horror at having realised in his own person that terrible and well-written scene, and at having done accidentally, though in fact, what the Mr. Hyde of fiction had done with deliberate intent, that he ran away as hard as he could go. He was, however, very closely followed, and finally he took refuge in a surgery, the door of which happened to be open, where he explained to a young assistant, who happened to be there, exactly what had occurred. The humanitarian crowd were induced to go away on his giving them a small sum of money, and as soon as the coast was clear he left. As he passed out, the name on the brass door-plate of the surgery caught his eye. It was "Jekyll." At least it should have been.

Here the imitation, as far as it went, was of course accidental. In the following case the imitation was self-conscious: In the year 1879, just after I had left Oxford, I met at a reception at the house of one of the Foreign Ministers a woman of very curious exotic beauty. We became great friends, and were constantly together. And yet what interested me most in her was not her beauty, but her character, her entire vagueness of character. She seemed to have no personality at all, but simply the possibility of many types. Sometimes she would give herself up entirely to art, turn her drawing-room into a studio, and spend two or three days a week at picture-galleries or museums. Then she would take to attending race-meetings, wear the most horsey clothes, and talk about nothing but betting. She abandoned religion for mesmerism, mesmerism for politics, and politics for the melodramatic excitements of philanthropy. In fact, she was a kind of Proteus, and as much a failure in all her transformations as was that wondrous sea-god when Odysseus laid hold of him. One day a serial began in one of the French magazines. At the time I used to read serial stories, and I will remember the shock of surprise I felt when I came to the description of the heroine. She was so like my friend that I brought her the magazine, and she recognised herself in it immediately, and seemed fascinated by the resemblance. I should tell you, by the way, that the story was translated from some dead Russian writer, so that the author had not taken his type from my friend. Well, to put the matter briefly, some months afterwards I was in Venice, and finding the magazine in the reading-room of the hotel, I took it up casually to see what had become of the heroine. It was a most piteous tale, as the girl had ended by running away with a man absolutely inferior to her, not merely in social station, but in character and intellect also. I wrote to my friend that evening about my views on John Bellini, and the admirable ices at Florio's, and the artistic value of gondolas, but added a postscript to the effect that her double in the story had behaved in a very silly manner. I don't know why I added that, but I remember I had a sort of dread over me that she might do the same thing. Before my letter had reached her, she had run away with a man who deserted her in six months. I saw her in 1884 in Paris, where she was living with her mother, and I asked her whether the story had had anything to do with her action. She told me that she had felt an absolutely irresistible impulse to follow the heroine step by step in her strange and fatal progress, and that it was with a feeling of real terror that she had looked forward to the last few chapters of the story. When they appeared, it seemed to her that she was compelled to reproduce them in life, and she did so. It was a most clear example of this imitative instinct of which I was speaking, and an extremely tragic one.

However, I do not wish to dwell any further upon individual instances. Personal experience is a most vicious and limited circle. All that I desire to point out is the general principle that Life imitates Art far more than Art imitates Life, and I feel sure that if you think seriously about it you will find that it is true. Life holds the mirror up to Art, and either reproduces some strange type imagined by painter or sculptor, or realises in fact what has been dreamed in fiction. Scientifically speaking, the basis of life—the energy of life, as Aristotle would call it—is simply the desire for expression, and Art is always presenting various forms through which this expression can be attained. Life seizes on them and uses them, even if they be to her own hurt. Young men have committed suicide because Rolla did so, have died by their own hand because by his own hand Werther died. Think of what we owe to the imitation of Christ, of what we owe to the imitation of Caesar.

CYRIL. The theory is certainly a very curious one, but to make it complete you must show that Nature, no less than Life, is an imitation of Art. Are you prepared to prove that?

VIVIAN. My dear fellow, I am prepared to prove anything.

CYRIL. Nature follows the landscape painter then, and takes her effects from him?

VIVIAN. Certainly. Where, if not from the Impressionists, do we get those wonderful brown fogs that come creeping down our streets, blurring the gas-lamps and changing the houses into monstrous shadows? To whom, if not to them and their master, do we owe the lovely silver mists that brood over our river, and turn to faint forms of fading grace, curved bridge and swaying barge? The extraordinary change that has taken place in the climate of London during the last ten years is entirely due to this particular school of Art. You smile. Consider the matter from a scientific or a metaphysical point of view, and you will find that I am right. For what is Nature? Nature is no great mother who has borne us. She is our creation. It is in our brain that she quickens to life. Things are because we see them, and what we see, and how we see it, depends on the Arts that have influenced us. To look at a thing is very different from seeing a thing. One does not see anything until one sees its beauty. Then, and then only, does it come into existence. At present, people see fogs, not because there are fogs, but because poets and painters have taught them the mysterious loveliness of such effects. There may have been fogs for centuries in London. I dare say there were. But no one saw them, and so we do not know anything about them. They did not exist until Art had invented them. Now, it must be admitted, fogs are carried to excess. They have become the mere mannerisms of a clique, and the exaggerated realism of their method gives dull people bronchitis. Where the cultured catch an effect, the uncultured catch cold. And so, let us be humane, and invite Art to turn her wonderful eyes elsewhere. She has done so already, indeed. That white quivering sunlight that one sees now in France, with its strange blotches of mauve, and its restless violet shadows, is her latest fancy, and, on the whole, Nature reproduces it quite admirably. Where she used to give us Corots and Daubignys, she gives us now exquisite Monets and entrancing Pissarros. Indeed, there are moments, rare, it is true, but still to be observed from time to time, when Nature becomes absolutely modern. Of course she is not always to be relied upon. The fact is that she is in this unfortunate position: Art creates an incomparable and unique effect, and, having done so, passes on to other things. Nature, upon the other hand, forgetting that imitation can be made the sincerest form of insult, keeps on repeating this effect until we all become absolutely wearied of it. Nobody of any real culture, for instance, ever talks nowadays about the beauty of a sunset. Sunsets are quite old-fashioned. They belong to the time when Turner was the last note in art. To admire them is a distinct sign of provincialism of temperament. Upon the other hand they go on. Yesterday evening Mrs. Arundel insisted on my going to the window, and looking at the glorious sky, as she called it. Of course I had to look at it. She is one of those absurdly pretty Philistines, to whom one can deny nothing. And what was it? It was simply a very second-rate Turner, a Turner of a bad period, with all the painter's worst faults exaggerated and overemphasised. Of course, I am quite ready to admit that Life very often commits the same error. She produces her false Renés and her sham Vautrins, just as Nature gives us, on one day a doubtful Cuyp, and on another a more than questionable Rousseau. Still, Nature irritates one more when she does things of that kind. It seems so stupid, so obvious, so unnecessary. A false Vautrin might be delightful. A doubtful Cuyp is unbearable. However, I don't want to be too hard on Nature. I wish the Channel, especially at Hastings, did not look quite so often like a Henry Moore, grey pearl with yellow lights, but then, when Art is more varied, Nature will, no doubt, be more varied also. That she imitates Art, I don't think even her worst enemy would deny now. It is the one thing that keeps her in touch with civilised man. But have I proved my theory to your satisfaction?

CYRIL. You have proved it to my dissatisfaction, which is better. But even admitting this strange imitative instinct in Life and Nature, surely you would acknowledge that Art expresses the temper of its age, the spirit of its time, the moral and social conditions that surround it, and under whose influence it is produced.

VIVIAN. Certainly not! Art never expresses anything but itself. This is the principle of my new aesthetics; and it is this, more than that vital connection between form and substance, on which Mr. Pater dwells, that makes music the type of all the arts. Of course, nations and individuals, with that healthy natural vanity which is the secret of existence, are always under the impression that it is of them that the Muses are talking, always trying to find in the calm dignity of imaginative art some mirror of their own turbid passions, always forgetting that the singer of life is not Apollo, but Marsyas. Remote from reality, and with her eyes turned away from the shadows of the cave, Art reveals her own perfection, and the wondering crowd that watches the opening of the marvellous, many-petalled rose fancies that it is its own history that is being told to it, its own spirit that is finding expression in a new form. But it is not so. The highest art rejects the burden of the human spirit, and gains more from a new medium or a fresh material than she does from any enthusiasm for art, or from any great awakening of the human consciousness. She develops purely on her own lines. She is not symbolic of any age. It is the ages that are her symbols.

Even those who hold that Art is representative of time and place and people, cannot help admitting that the more imitative an art is, the less it represents to us the spirit of its age. The evil face of the Roman emperors look out at us from the foul porphyry and spotted jasper in which the realistic artists of the day delighted to work, and we fancy that in those cruel lips and sensual jaws we can find the secret of the ruin of the Empire. But it was not so. The vices of Tiberius could not destroy that supreme civilisation, any more than the virtues of the Antonines could save it. It fell for other, for less interesting reasons. The sibyls and prophets of the Sistine may indeed serve to interpret for some that new birth of the emancipated spirit that we call the Renaissance; but what do the drunken boors and brawling peasants of Dutch art tell us about the great soul of Holland? The more abstract, the more ideal an art is, the more it reveals to us the temper of its age. If we wish to understand a nation by means of its art, let us look at its architecture or its music.

CYRIL. I quite agree with you there. The spirit of an age may be best expressed in the abstract ideal arts, for the spirit itself is abstract and ideal. Upon the other hand, for the visible aspect of an age, for its look, as the phrase goes, we must, of course, go to the arts of imitation.

VIVIAN. I don't think so. After all, what the imitative arts really give us are merely the various styles of particular artists, or of certain schools of artists. Surely you don't imagine that the people of the Middle Ages bore any resemblance at all to the figures on mediaeval stained glass, or in the mediaeval stone and wood carving, or on mediaeval metal-work, or tapestries, or illuminated MSS. They were probably very ordinary-looking people, with nothing grotesque, or remarkable, or fantastic in their appearance. The Middle Ages, as we know them in art, are simply a definite form of style, and there is no reason at all why an artist with this style should not be produced in the nineteenth century. No great artist ever sees things as they really are. If he did, he would cease to be an artist. Take an example from our own day. I know that you are fond of Japanese things. Now, do you really imagine that the Japanese people, as they are presented to us in art, have any existence? If you do, you have never understood Japanese art at all. The Japanese people are the deliberate self-conscious creation of certain individual artists. If you set a picture by Hokusai, or Hokkei, or any of the great native painters, beside a real Japanese gentleman or lady, you will see that there is not the slightest resemblance between them. The actual people who live in Japan are not unlike the general run of English people; that is to say, they are extremely commonplace, and have nothing curious or extraordinary about them. In fact the whole of Japan is a pure invention. There is no such country, there are no such people. One of our most charming painters went recently to the Land of the Chrysanthemum in the foolish hope of seeing the Japanese. All he saw, all he had the chance of painting, were a few lanterns and some fans. He was quite unable to discover the inhabitants, as his delightful exhibition at Messrs. Dowdeswell's Gallery showed only too well. He did not know that the Japanese people are, as I have said, simply a mode of style, an exquisite fancy of art. And so, if you desire to see a Japanese effect, you will not behave like a tourist and go to Tokio. On the contrary, you will stay at home, and steep yourself in the work of certain Japanese artists, and then, when you have absorbed the spirit of their style, and caught their imaginative manner of vision, you will go some afternoon and sit in the Park or stroll down Piccadilly, and if you cannot see an absolutely Japanese effect there, you will not see it anywhere. Or, to return again to the past, take as another instance the ancient Greeks. Do you think that Greek art ever tells us what the Greek people were like? Do you believe that the Athenian women were like the stately dignified figures of the Parthenon frieze, or like those marvellous goddesses who sat in the triangular pediments of the same building? If you judge from the art, they certainly were so. But read an authority, like Aristophanes, for instance. You will find that the Athenian ladies laced tightly, wore high-heeled shoes, dyed their hair yellow, painted and rouged their faces, and were exactly like any silly fashionable or fallen creature of our own day. The fact is that we look back on the ages entirely through the medium of Art, and Art, very fortunately, has never once told us the truth.

CYRIL. But modern portraits by English painters, what of them? Surely they are like the people they pretend to represent?

VIVIAN. Quite so. They are so like them that a hundred years from now no one will believe in them. The only portraits in which one believes are portraits where there is very little of the sitter and a very great deal of the artist. Holbein's drawings of the men and women of his time impress us with a sense of their absolute reality. But this is simply because Holbein compelled life to accept his conditions, to restrain itself within his limitations, to reproduce his type, and to appear as he wished it to appear. It is style that makes us believe in a thing—nothing but style. Most of our modern portrait painters are doomed to absolute oblivion. They never paint what they see. They paint what the public sees, and the public never sees anything.

CYRIL. Well, after that, I think I should like to hear the end of you article.

VIVIAN. With pleasure. Whether it will do any good, I really cannot say. Ours is certainly the dullest and most prosaic century possible. Why, even Sleep has played us false, and has closed up the gates of ivory, and opened the gates of horn. The dreams of the great middle classes of the country, as recorded in Mr. Myers's two bulky volumes on the subject, and in the transactions of the Psychical Society, are the most depressing things that I have ever read. There is not even a fine nightmare among them. They are commonplace, sordid, and tedious. As for the Church, I cannot conceive anything better for the culture of a country than the presence in it of a body of men whose duty it is to believe in the supernatural, to perform daily miracles, and to keep alive that mythopoeic faculty which is so essential for the imagination. But in the English Church a man succeeds, not through his capacity for belief, but through his capacity for disbelief. Ours is the only Church where the sceptic stands at the altar, and where St. Thomas is regarded as the ideal apostle. Many a worthy clergyman, who passes his life in admirable works of kindly charity, lives and dies unnoticed and unknown; but it is sufficient for some shallow, uneducated passman out of either University to get up in his pulpit and express his doubts about Noah's Ark, or Balaam's ass, or Jonah and the whale, for half of London to flock to hear him, and to sit open-mouthed in rapt admiration at his superb intellect. The growth of common sense in the English Church is a thing very much to be regretted. It is really a degrading concession to a low form of realism. It is silly, too. It springs from an entire ignorance of psychology. Man can believe the impossible, but man can never believe the improbable. However, I must read the end of my article:

"What we have to do, what at any rate it is out duty to do, is to revive this old art of Lying. Much, of course, may be done, in the way of educating the public, by amateurs in the domestic circle, at literary lunches, and at afternoon teas. But this is merely the light and graceful side of lying, such as was probably heard at Cretan dinner parties. There are many other forms. Lying for the sake of gaining some immediate personal advantage, for instance—lying with a moral purpose, as it is usually called—though of late it has been rather looked down upon, was extremely popular with the antique world. Athena laughs when Odysseus tells her 'his words of sly devising,' as Mr. William Morris phrases it, and the glory of mendacity illumines the pale brow of the stainless hero of Euripedean tragedy, and sets among the noble women of the past the young bride of one of Horace's most exquisite odes. Later on, what at first had been merely a natural instinct was elevated into a self-conscious science. Elaborate rules were laid down for the guidance of mankind, and an important school of literature grew up round the subject. Indeed, when one remembers the excellent philosophical treatise of Sanchez on the whole question, one cannot help regretting that no one has ever thought of publishing a cheap and condensed edition of the works of that great casuist. A short primer, 'When to Lie and How,' if brought out in an attractive and not too expensive a form, would, no doubt, command a large sale, and would prove of real practical service to many earnest and deep-thinking people. Lying for the sake of the improvement of the young, which is the basis of home education, still lingers amongst us, and its advantages are so admirably set forth in the early books of Plato's *Republic* that it is unnecessary to dwell upon them here. It is a mode of lying for which all good mothers have peculiar capabilities, but it is capable of still further development, and has been sadly overlooked by the School Board. Lying for the sake of a monthly salary is, of course, well known in Fleet Street, and the profession of a political leader-writer is not without its advantages. But it is said to be a somewhat dull occupation, and it certainly does not lead to much beyond a kind of ostentatious obscurity. The only form of lying that it is absolutely beyond reproach is Lying for its own sake, and the highest development of this is, as we have already pointed out, Lying in Art. Just as those who do not love Plato more than Truth cannot pass beyond the threshold of the Academe, so those who do not love Beauty more than Truth never know the inmost shrine of Art. The solid, stolid British intellect lies in the desert sands like the Sphinx in Flaubert's marvellous tale, and fantasy, *La Chimère*, dances round it, and calls to it with her false, flute-toned voice. It may not hear her now, but surely some day, when we are all bored to death with the commonplace character of modern fiction, it will hearken to her and try to borrow her wings.

"And when that day dawns, or sunset reddens, how joyous we shall all be! Facts will be regarded as discreditable, Truth will be found mourning over her fetters, and Romance, with her temper of wonder, will return to the land. The very aspect of the world will change to our startled eyes. Out of the sea will rise Behemoth and Leviathan, and sail round the high-pooped galleys, as they do on the delightful maps of those ages when books on geography were actually readable. Dragons will wander about the waste places, and the phoenix will soar from her nest of fire into the air. We shall lay our hands upon the basilisk, and see the jewel in the toad's head. Champing his gilded oats, the Hippogriff will stand in our stalls, and over our heads will float the Blue Bird, singing of beautiful and impossible things, of things that are lovely and that never happen, of things that are not and that should be. But before this comes to pass, we must cultivate the lost art of Lying."

CYRIL. Then we must certainly cultivate it at once. But in order to avoid making any error, I want you to tell me briefly the doctrines of the new aesthetics.

VIVIAN. Briefly, then, they are these. Art never expresses anything but itself. It has an independent life, just as Thought has, and develops purely on its own lines. It is not necessarily realistic in an age of realism, nor spiritual in an age of faith. So far from being the creation of its time, it is usually in direct opposition to it, and the only history that it preserves for us is the history of its own progress. Sometimes it returns upon its footsteps, and revives some antique form, as happened in the archaistic movement of late Greek Art, and in the pre-Raphaelite movement of our own day. At other times it entirely anticipates its age, and produces in one century work that it takes another century to understand, to appreciate, and to enjoy. In no case does it reproduce its age. To pass from the art of a time to the time itself is the great mistake that all historians commit.

The second doctrine is this. All bad art comes from returning to Life and Nature, and elevating them into ideals. Life and Nature may sometimes be used as a part of Art's rough material, but before they are of any real service to art they must be translated into artistic conventions. The moment Art surrenders its imaginative medium it surrenders everything. As a method, Realism is a complete failure, and the two things that every artist should avoid are modernity of form and modernity of subject-matter. To us, who live in the nineteenth century, any century is a suitable subject for art except our own. The only beautiful things are the things that do not concern us. It is, to have the pleasure of quoting myself, exactly because Hecuba is nothing to us that her sorrows are so suitable a motive for a tragedy. Besides, it is only the modern that ever becomes old-fashioned. M. Zola sits down to give us a picture of the Second Empire. Who cares for the Second Empire now? It is out of date. Life goes faster than Realism, but Romanticism is always in front of Life.

The third doctrine is that Life imitates Art far more than Art imitates Life. This results not merely from Life's imitative instinct, but from the fact that the self-conscious aim of Life is to find expression, and that Art offers it certain beautiful forms through which it may realise that energy. It is a theory that has never been put forward before, but it is extremely fruitful, and throws an entirely new light upon the history of Art.

It follows, as a corollary from this, that external Nature also imitates Art. The only effects that she can show us are effects that we have already seen through poetry, or in paintings. This is the secret of Nature's charm, as well as the explanation of Nature's weakness.

The final revelation is that Lying, the telling of beautiful untrue things, is the proper aim of Art. But of this I think I have spoken at sufficient length. And now let us go out on the terrace, where "droops the milk-white peacock like a ghost," while the evening star "washes the duck with silver." At twilight nature becomes a wonderfully suggestive effect, and is not without loveliness, though perhaps its chief use is to illustrate quotations from the poets. Come! We have talked long enough.

CHAPTER SEVEN

In Defense of
GREED

$\mathcal{P}$arents often struggle with children who resist sharing toys and candy. Those children grow into adults who regularly worry about being accused of greediness. Greed comes naturally, it seems, but finds only public condemnation.

Some say that capitalism is greed institutionalized. The Vatican, for example, has denounced capitalism as largely immoral for well over a century. Is it true that an economic system founded on self-interest will inevitably lead to neglect of the poor, the disabled, and the unintelligent? Perhaps.

One can contest this position, though. There may be no more compelling a refutation than Bernard Mandeville's work *The Fable of the Bees,* first published in 1714, which argues cogently that we should make a virtue of necessity. Since people everywhere seem more motivated by greed than by altruism, why not capitalize on greed? The truth is, Mandeville reasons in this provocative piece, the happier each individual is, the stronger the nation of which he is a part.

Selfishness qualifies as greed. We think of selfishness as something bad, yet it is hard to imagine how anyone could become an Olympic champion, a corporate executive, or a medical doctor without having spent years focused on herself. What if the truth were that the hardest-working people turned out to be the greedy?

Mandeville likens human society to a beehive. Bees don't really understand why or what they're doing, but by following their instincts, they improve life for other bees. All the while, they make themselves happy as well. By analogy, people who stop working hard will diminish the gross national product. As the economy falters, life will become harder not so much for the rich as for the poor.

How should we make sense of the prevalence of greed? Is it simply an unfortunate effect of human nature? Or, is it the key to human advancement?

The French philosopher Voltaire ridiculed the Christian belief that we live in "the best of all possible worlds." (His play from 1759, *Candide,* raised blasphemy to new heights.) Christians explained evil in the world by saying that God has a reason for everything, which is invariably to make this life as good as it can possibly be. In *The Fable of the Bees,* which the German philosopher Kant admired, Mandeville harnesses optimism about possible worlds: Given how many greedy souls there are in the world, could it not be that God wants, even needs, people to be greedy?

I have taken the liberty of modernizing some of the spelling in the following verse. This is not an exact reproduction of Mandeville's original from 1714, nor of his subsequent revisions.

BERNARD MANDEVILLE (1670–1733) enjoyed a spectacular rise to fame on the strength of his verse *The Fable of the Bees,* published in England. A physician interested in ethical matters, he grew up and wrote in a country wracked by controversy over modern commerce and its moral consequences. His work anticipated the philosophical doctrine of utilitarianism, the idea that acts should be evaluated on the basis of how happy they make people.

THE GRUMBLING HIVE:

or,

KNAVES TURNED HONEST [1]

from The Fable of the Bees

Bernard Mandeville

A Spacious Hive well-stocked with Bees,
That lived in Luxury and Ease;
And yet as famed for Laws and Arms,
As yielding large and early Swarms;
Was counted the great Nursery
Of Sciences and Industry.
No Bees had better Government,
More Fickleness, or less Content:
They were not Slaves to Tyranny,
Nor ruled by wild *Democracy;*
But Kings, that could not wrong, because
Their Power was circumscribed by Laws.

THESE Insects lived like Men, and all
Our Actions they performed in small:

They did whatever's done in Town,
And what belongs to Sword or Gown:
Though the Artful Works, by nimble Slight
Of minute Limbs, escaped Human Sight;
Yet we've no Engines, Laborers,
Ships, Castles, Arms, Artificers,
Craft, Science, Shop, or Instrument,
But they had an Equivalent:
Which, since their Language is unknown,
Must be called, as we do our own.
As grant, that among other Things,
They wanted Dice, yet they had Kings;
And those had Guards; from whence we may
Justly conclude, they had some Play;
Unless a Regiment be shown
Of Soldiers, that make use of none.

    VAST Numbers thronged the fruitful Hive;
Yet those vast Numbers made them thrive;
Millions endeavouring to supply
Each other's Lust and Vanity;
While other Millions were employed,
To see their Handy-works destroyed;
They furnished half the Universe;
Yet had more Work than Labourers.
Some with vast Stocks, and little Pains,
Jumped into Business of great Gains;
And some were damned to Scythes and Spades,
And all those hard laborious Trades;
Where willing Wretches daily sweat,
And wear out Strength and Limbs to eat:
While others followed Mysteries,
To which few Folks bind 'Prentices;
That want no Stock, but that of Brass,

And may set up without a Cross;
As Sharpers, Parasites, Pimps, Players,
Pick-pockets, Coiners, Quacks, Sooth-sayers,
And all those, that in Enmity,
With downright Working, cunningly
Convert to their own Use the Labor
Of their good-natured heedless Neighbor.
These were called Knaves, but bar the Name,
The grave Industrious were the same:
All Trades and Places knew some Cheat,
No Calling was without Deceit.

THE Lawyers, of whose Art the Basis
Was raising Feuds and splitting Cases,
Opposed all Registers, that Cheats
Might make more Work with dipt Estates;
As it wasn't unlawful, that one's own,
Without a Law-Suit, should be known.
They kept off Hearings willfully,
To finger the refreshing Fee;
And to defend a wicked Cause,
Examined and surveyed the Laws,
As Burglars Shops and Houses do,
To find out where they'd best break through.

PHYSICIANS valued Fame and Wealth
Above the drooping Patient's Health,
Or their own Skill: The greatest Part
Studied, instead of Rules of Art,
Grave pensive Looks and dull Behaviour,
To gain the Apothecary's Favour;
The Praise of Midwives, Priests, and all
That served at Birth or Funeral.
To bear with the ever-talking Tribe,

And hear my Lady's Aunt prescribe;
With formal Smile, and kind How do ye,
To fawn on all the Family;
And, which of all the greatest Curse is,
To endure the Impertinence of Nurses.

AMONG the many Priests of *Jove*,
Hired to draw Blessings from Above,
Some few were Learned and Eloquent,
But thousands Hot and Ignorant:
Yet all passed Muster that could hide
Their Sloth, Lust, Avarice and Pride;
For which they were as famed as Tailors
For Cabbage, or for Brandy Sailors:
Some, meager-looked, and meanly clad,
Would mystically pray for Bread,
Meaning by that an ample Store,
Yet literally received no more;
And, while these holy Drudges starved,
The lazy Ones, for which they served,
Indulged their Ease, with all the Graces
Of Health and Plenty in their Faces.

THE Soldiers, that were forced to fight,
If they survived, got Honour by it;
Though some, that shunned the bloody Fray,
Had Limbs shot off, that ran away:
Some valiant Generals fought the Foe;
Others took Bribes to let them go:
Some ventured always where 'twas warm,
Lost now a Leg, and then an Arm;
Till quite disabled, and put by,
They lived on half their Salary;
While others never came in Play,
And stayed at Home for double Pay.

THEIR Kings were served, but Knavishly,
Cheated by their own Ministry;
Many, that for their Welfare slaved,
Robbing the very Crown they saved:
Pensions were small, and they lived high,
Yet boasted of their Honesty.
Calling, whenever they strained their Right,
The slippery Trick a Perquisite;
And when Folks understood their Cant,
They changed that for Emolument;
Unwilling to be short or plain,
In any thing concerning Gain;
For there was not a Bee but would
Get more, I won't say, than he should;
But than he dared to let them know,
That paid for it; as your Gamesters do,
That, though at fair Play, never will own
Before the Losers what they've won.

BUT who can all their Frauds repeat?
The very Stuff, which in the Street
They sold for Dirt to enrich the Ground,
Was often by the Buyers found
Sophisticated with a quarter
Of good-for-nothing Stones and Mortar;
Though *Flail* had little Cause to mutter,
Who sold the other Salt for Butter.

JUSTICE herself, famed for fair Dealing,
By Blindness had not lost her Feeling;
Her Left Hand, which the Scales should hold,
Had often dropped them, bribed with Gold;
And, though she seemed Impartial,
Where Punishment was corporal,
Pretended to a regular Course,

In Murder, and all Crimes of Force;
Though some, first pilloried for Cheating,
Were hanged in Hemp of their own beating;
Yet, it was thought, the Sword she bore
Checked but the Desperate and the Poor;
That, urged by mere Necessity,
Were tied up to the wretched Tree
For Crimes, which not deserved that Fate,
But to secure the Rich and Great.

    THUS every Part was full of Vice,
Yet the whole Mass a Paradise;
Flattered in Peace, and feared in Wars,
They were the Esteem of Foreigners,
And lavish of their Wealth and Lives,
The Balance of all other Hives.
Such were the Blessings of that State;
Their Crimes conspired to make them Great:
And Virtue, who from Politicks
Had learned a Thousand Cunning Tricks,
Was, by their happy Influence,
Made Friends with Vice: And ever since,
The worst of all the Multitude
Did something for the Common Good.

    THIS was the State's Craft, that maintained
The Whole of which each Part complained:
This, as in Music Harmony,
Made Jarrings in the main agree;
Parties directly opposite,
Assist each other, as 'twere for Spite;
And Temperance with Sobriety,
Serve Drunkenness and Gluttony.

THE Root of Evil, Avarice,
That damned ill-natured baneful Vice,
Was Slave to Prodigality,
That noble Sin; whilst Luxury
Employed a Million of the Poor,
And odious Pride a Million more:
Envy itself, and Vanity,
Were Ministers of Industry;
Their darling Folly, Fickleness,
In Diet, Furniture and Dress,
That strange ridiculous Vice, was made
The very Wheel that turned the Trade.
Their Laws and Clothes were equally
Objects of Mutability;
For, what was well done for a time,
In half a Year became a Crime;
Yet while they altered thus their Laws,
Still finding and correcting Flaws,
They mended by Inconstancy
Faults, which no Prudence could foresee.

THUS Vice nursed Ingenuity,
Which joined with Time and Industry,
Had carried Life's Conveniences,
It's real Pleasures, Comforts, Ease,
To such a Height, the very Poor
Lived better than the Rich before,
And nothing could be added more.

HOW Vain is Mortal Happiness!
Had they but known the Bounds of Bliss;
And that Perfection here below
Is more than Gods can well bestow;

The Grumbling Brutes had been content
With Ministers and Government.
But they, at every ill Success,
Like Creatures lost without Redress,
Cursed Politicians, Armies, Fleets;
While every one cried, *Damn the Cheats*
And would, though conscious of his own,
In others barbarously bear none.

ONE, that had got a Princely Store,
By cheating Master, King and Poor,
Dared cry aloud, *The Land must sink*
For all its Fraud; And whom do you think
The Sermonizing Rascal chide?
A Glover that sold Lamb for Kid.

THE least thing was not done amiss,
Or crossed the Public Business;
But all the Rogues cried brazenly,
Good Gods, Had we but Honesty!
Mercy smiled at the Impudence,
And others called it want of Sense,
Always to rail at what they loved:
But *Jove* with Indignation moved,
At last in Anger swore, *He'd rid*
The bawling Hive of Fraud; and did.
The very Moment it departs,
And Honesty fills all their Hearts;
There shows them, like the Instructive Tree,
Those Crimes which they're ashamed to see;
Which now in Silence they confess,
By blushing at their Ugliness:
Like Children, that would hide their Faults,
And by their Colour own their Thoughts:

Imagining, when they're looked upon,
That others see what they have done.

BUT, Oh ye Gods! What Consternation,
How vast and sudden was the Alteration!
In half an Hour, the Nation round,
Meat fell a Penny in the Pound.
The Mask Hypocrisy's flung down,
From the great Statesman to the Clown:
And some in borrowed Looks well known,
Appeared like Strangers in their own.
The Bar was silent from that Day;
For now the willing Debtors pay,
Even what's by Creditors forgot;
Who quitted them that had it not.
Those, that were in the Wrong, stood mute,
And dropped the patched vexatious Suit:
On which since nothing less can thrive,
Than Lawyers in an honest Hive,
All, except those that got enough,
With Inkhorns by their sides trooped off.

JUSTICE hanged some, set others free;
And after Goal delivery,
Her Presence being no more required,
With all her Train and Pomp retired.
First marched some Smiths with Locks and Grates,
Fetters, and Doors with Iron Plates:
Next Goalers, Turnkeys and Assistants:
Before the Goddess, at some distance,
Her chief and faithful Minister,
'Squire CATCH, Law's great Finisher,
Bore not the imaginary Sword,
But his own Tools, an Ax and Cord:

Then on a Cloud the Hood-winked Fair,
JUSTICE her self was pushed by Air:
About her Chariot, and behind,
Were Serjeants, Bums of every kind,
Tip-staffs, and all those Officers,
That squeeze a Living out of Tears.

THOUGH Physic lived, while Folks were ill,
None would prescribe, but Bees of skill,
Which through the Hive dispersed so wide,
That none of them had need to ride;
Waved vain Disputes, and strove to free
The Patients of their Misery;
Left Drugs in cheating Countries grown,
And used the Product of their own;
Knowing the Gods sent no Disease
To Nations without Remedies.

THEIR Clergy roused from Laziness,
Laid not their Charge on Journey-Bees;
But served themselves, exempt from Vice,
The Gods with Prayer and Sacrifice;
All those, that were unfit, or knew
Their Service might be spared, withdrew:
Nor was there Business for so many,
(If the Honest stand in need of any,)
Few only with the High-Priest stayed,
To whom the rest Obedience paid:
Himself employed in Holy Cares,
Resigned to others State-Affairs.
He chased no Starv'ling from his Door,
Nor pinched the Wages of the Poor;
But at his House the Hungry's fed,
The Hireling finds unmeasured Bread,
The needy Traveler Board and Bed.

AMONG the King's great Ministers,
And all the inferior Officers
The Change was great; for frugally
They now lived on their Salary:
That a poor Bee should ten times come
To ask his Due, a trifling Sum,
And by some well-hired Clerk be made
To give a Crown, or never be paid,
Would now be called a downright Cheat,
Though formerly a Perquisite.
All Places managed first by Three,
Who watched each other's Knavery,
And often for a Fellow-feeling,
Promoted one another's stealing,
Are happily supplied by One,
By which some thousands more are gone.

NO Honour now could be content,
To live and owe for what was spent;
Liv'ries in Brokers Shops are hung,
They part with Coaches for a Song;
Sell stately Horses by whole Sets;
And Country-Houses, to pay Debts.

VAIN Cost is shunned as much as Fraud;
They have no Forces kept Abroad;
Laugh at the Esteem of Foreigners,
And empty Glory got by Wars;
They fight, but for their Country's sake,
When Right or Liberty's at Stake.

NOW mind the glorious Hive, and see
How Honesty and Trade agree.
The Show is gone, it thins apace;

And looks with quite another Face.
For 'twas not only that They went,
By whom vast Sums were Yearly spent;
But Multitudes that lived on them,
Were daily forced to do the same.
In vain to other Trades they'd fly;
All were over-stocked accordingly.

THE Price of Land and Houses falls;
Miraculous Palaces, whose Walls,
Like those of *Thebes,* were raised by Play,
Are to be let; while the once gay,
Well-seated Household Gods would be
More pleased to expire in Flames, than see
The mean Inscription on the Door
Smile at the lofty ones they bore.
The building Trade is quite destroyed,
Artificers are not employed;
No Limner for his Art is famed,
Stone-cutters, Carvers are not named.

THOSE, that remained, grown temperate, strive,
Not how to spend, but how to live,
And, when they paid their Tavern Score,
Resolved to enter it no more:
No Vintner's Jilt in all the Hive
Could wear now Cloth of Gold, and thrive;
Nor *Torcol* such vast Sums advance,
For *Burgundy* and *Ortelans;*
The Courtier's gone, that with his Miss
Supped at his House on *Christmas* Peas;
Spending as much in two Hours stay,
As keeps a Troop of Horse a Day.

THE haughty Chloe, to live Great,
Had made her Husband rob the State:
But now she sells her Furniture,
Which the *Indies* had been ransacked for;
Contracts the expensive Bill of Fare,
And wears her strong Suit a whole Year:
The slight and fickle Age is past;
And Clothes, as well as Fashions, last.
Weavers, that joined rich Silk with Plate,
And all the Trades subordinate,
Are gone. Still Peace and Plenty reign,
And every Thing is cheap, though plain:
Kind Nature, free from Gardeners Force,
Allows all Fruits in her own Course;
But Rarities cannot be had,
Where Pains to get them are not paid.

AS Pride and Luxury decrease,
So by degrees they leave the Seas.
Not Merchants now, but Companies
Remove whole Manufactories.
All Arts and Crafts neglected lie;
Content, the Bane of Industry,
Makes them admire their homely Store,
And neither seek nor covet more.

SO few in the vast Hive remain,
The hundredth Part they can't maintain
Against the Insults of numerous Foes;
Whom yet they valiantly oppose:
'Till some well-fenced Retreat is found,
And here they die or stand their Ground.
No Hireling in their Army's known;

But bravely fighting for their own,
Their Courage and Integrity
At last were crowned with Victory.
They triumphed not without their Cost,
For many Thousand Bees were lost.
Hardened with Toils and Exercise,
They counted Ease it self a Vice;
Which so improved their Temperance;
That, to avoid Extravagance,
They flew into a hollow Tree,
Blest with Content and Honesty.

THE MORAL

THEN leave Complaints: Fools only strive
To make a Great an Honest Hive
To enjoy the World's Conveniences,
Be famed in War, yet live in Ease,
Without great Vices, is a vain
UTOPIA seated in the Brain.
Fraud, Luxury and Pride must live,
While we the Benefits receive:
Hunger's a dreadful Plague, no doubt,
Yet who digests or thrives without?
Do we not owe the Growth of Wine
To the dry shabby crooked Vine?
Which, while its Shoots neglected stood,
Choked other Plants, and ran to Wood;
But blest us with its noble Fruit,
As soon as it was tied and cut:
So Vice is beneficial found,
When it's by Justice lopped and bound;
Nay, where the People would be great,

As necessary to the State,
As Hunger is to make 'em eat.
Bare Virtue can't make Nations live
In Splendor; they, that would revive
A Golden Age, must be as free,
For Acorns, as for Honesty.

FINIS.

CHAPTER EIGHT

In Defense of
BREAKING
THE GOLDEN
RULE

One of the most familiar lessons from the New Testament is to love your neighbor as yourself.

In the following excerpt from 1930, Freud questions whether it is psychologically possible to love your neighbor as yourself, given how inherently aggressive he conceives human beings to be. Beyond that, he strongly disapproves of the idea that we should make ourselves feel toward strangers the way we do toward people whom we care about deeply. Freud proposes reciprocity as a more logical and morally superior standard by which to judge human behavior: He gives us permission to dislike those who purposely offend or humiliate us.

Essentially, Freud rebuts Jesus. It is one thing to admire moral ideals and strive for them; Freud makes us wonder if there is really any point to reaching for the impossible, in this instance.

Ominously, Freud mentions human beings acting monstrously toward one another. Had he written this essay ten or fifteen years later, Freud, a Jew, would certainly have included as an example of cruelty the systematic hunting, torturing, and slaying of Jews in Europe before the end of World War II.

∿

SIGMUND FREUD (1856–1939) refined the techniques of psycho-analysis for the treatment of psychological and emotional disorders. On March 12, 1938, Nazi troops marched into Austria and assumed power. On June 4, following numerous international interventions, Freud was allowed to emigrate to London with his wife, his youngest daughter Anna, his housekeeper, and his medical caretaker. Freud's other children also managed to escape. Four elderly and infirm sisters were forced to remain in Vienna and eventually died in concentration camps in 1941.

from

CIVILIZATION
AND ITS DISCONTENTS

Sigmund Freud

translated by James Strachey

. . . Reality shows us that civilization is not content with the ties we have so far allowed it. It aims at binding the members of the community together in a libidinal way as well and employs every means to that end. It favours every path by which strong identifications can be established between the members of the community, and it summons up aim-inhibited libido on the largest scale so as to strengthen the communal bond by relations of friendship. In order for these aims to be fulfilled, a restriction upon sexual life is unavoidable. But we are unable to understand what the necessity is which forces civilization along this path and which causes its antagonism to sexuality. There must be some disturbing factor which we have not yet discovered.

The clue may be supplied by one of the ideal demands, as we have called them, of civilized society. It runs: "Thou shalt love they neighbour as thyself." It is known throughout the world and is undoubtedly older than Christianity, which puts it forward as its proudest claim. Yet it is certainly not very old; even in historical times it was still strange to mankind. Let us adopt a naïve attitude towards it, as though we were hearing it for the first time; we shall be unable then to suppress a feeling of surprise and bewilderment. Why should we do it? What good will it do us? But, above all, how shall we achieve it? How can it be possible? My love is something valuable to me which I ought not to throw away without reflection. It imposes duties on me for whose fulfilment I must be ready to make sacrifices. If I love someone, he must deserve it in some way. (I leave out of account the use he may be to me, and also his possible significance for me as a sexual object, for neither of these two kinds of relationship comes into question where the precept to love my neighbour is concerned.) He deserves it if he is so like me in important ways that I can love myself in him; and he deserves it if he is so much more perfect than myself that I can love my ideal of my own self in him. Again, I have to love him if he is my friend's son, since the pain my friend would feel if any harm came to him would be my pain too—I should have to share it. But if he is a stranger to me and if he cannot attract me by any worth of his own or any significance that he may already have acquired for my emotional life, it will be hard for me to love him. Indeed, I should be wrong to do so, for my love is valued by all my own people as a sign of my preferring them, and it is an injustice to them if I put a stranger on a par with them. But if I am to love him (with this universal love) merely because he, too, is an inhabitant of this earth, like an insect, an earthworm or a grass-snake, then I fear that only a small modicum of my love will fall to his share—not by any possibility as much as, by the judgement of my reason, I am entitled to retain for myself. What is the point of a precept enunciated with so much solemnity if its fulfilment cannot be recommended as reasonable?

On closer inspection, I find still further difficulties. Not merely is this stranger in general unworthy of my love; I must honestly confess that he has more claim to my hostility and even my hatred. He seems not to have the least trace of love for me and shows me not the slightest consideration. If it will do him any good he has no hesitation in injuring me, nor does he ask himself whether the amount of advantage he gains bears any proportion to the extent of the harm he does to me. Indeed, he need not even obtain an advantage; if he can satisfy any sort of desire by it, he thinks nothing of jeering at me, insulting me, slandering me and showing his superior power; and the more secure he feels and the more helpless I am, the more certainly I can expect him to behave like this to me. If he behaves differently, if he shows me consideration and forbearance as a stranger, I am ready to treat him in the same way, in any case and quite apart from any precept. Indeed, if this grandiose commandment had run "Love thy neighbour as thy neighbour loves thee," I should not take exception to it. And there is a second commandment, which seems to me even more incomprehensible and arouses still stronger opposition in me. It is "Love thine enemies." If I think it over, however, I see that I am wrong in treating it as a greater imposition. At bottom it is the same thing.[1]

I think I can now hear a dignified voice admonishing me: "It is precisely because your neighbour is not worthy of love, and is on the contrary your enemy, that you should love him as yourself." I then understand that the case is one like that of *Credo quia absurdum.*[2]

Now it is very probable that my neighbour, when he is enjoined to love me as himself, will answer exactly as I have done and will repel me for the same reasons. I hope he will not have the same objective grounds for doing so, but he will have the same idea as I have. Even so, the behaviour of human beings shows differences, which ethics, disregarding the fact that such differences are determined, classifies as "good" or "bad." So long as these undeniable differences have not been removed, obedience to high ethical demands entails damage to the aims of civilization, for it puts a positive premium on being bad. One is irresistibly reminded of an incident in the French Chamber when capital punishment was being debated. A member had been passionately supporting its abolition and his speech was being received with tumultuous applause, when a voice from the hall called out: "Que messieurs les assassins commencent!"[3]

The element of truth behind all this, which people are so ready to disavow, is that men are not gentle creatures who want to be loved, and who at the most can defend themselves if they are attacked; they are, on the contrary, creatures among whose instinctual endowments is to be reckoned a powerful share of aggressiveness. As a result, their neighbour is for them not only a potential helper or sexual object, but also someone who tempts them to satisfy their aggressiveness on him, to exploit his capacity for work without compensation, to use him sexually without his consent, to seize his possessions, to humiliate him, to cause him pain, to torture and to kill him. *Homo homini lupus.*[4] Who, in the face of all his experience of life and of history, will have the courage to dispute this assertion? As a rule this cruel aggressiveness waits for some provocation or puts itself at the service of some other purpose, whose goal might also have been reached by milder measures. In circumstances that are favourable to it, when the mental counter-forces which ordinarily inhibit it are out of action, it also manifests itself spontaneously and reveals man as a savage beast to whom consideration towards his own kind is something alien. Anyone who calls to mind the atrocities committed during the racial migrations or the invasions of the Huns, or by the people known as Mongrols under Jenghiz Khan and Tamerlane, or at the capture of Jerusalem by the pious Crusaders, or even, indeed, the horrors of the recent World War—anyone who calls these things to mind will have to bow humbly before the truth of this view.

The existence of this inclination to aggression, which we can detect in ourselves and justly assume to be present in others, is the factor which disturbs our relations with our neighbour and which forces civilization into such a high expenditure [of energy]. In consequence of this primary mutual hostility of human beings, civilized society is perpetually threatened with disintegration. The interest of work in common would not hold it together; instinctual passions are stronger than reasonable interests. Civilization has to use its utmost efforts in order to set limits to man's aggressive instincts and to hold the manifestations of them in check by psychical reaction-formations. Hence, therefore, the use of methods intended to incite people into identifications are aim-inhibited relationships of love, hence the restriction upon sexual life, and hence too the idea's commandment to love one's neighbour as oneself—a commandment which is really justified by the fact that nothing else runs so strongly counter to the original nature of man. In spite of every effort, these endeavours of civilization have not so far achieved very much. It hopes to prevent the crudest excesses of brutal violence by itself assuming the right to use violence against criminals, but the law is not able to lay hold of the more cautious and refined manifestations of human aggressiveness. The time comes when each one of us has to give up as illusions the expectations which, in his youth, he pinned upon his fellow-men, and when he may learn how much difficulty and pain has been added to his life by their ill-will. At the same time, it would be unfair to reproach civilization with trying to eliminate strife and competition from human activity. These things are undoubtedly indispensable. But opposition is not necessarily enmity; it is merely misused and made an *occasion* for enmity.

The communists believe that they have found the path to deliverance from our evils. According to them, man is wholly good and is well-disposed to his neighbour; but the institution of private property has corrupted his nature. The ownership of private wealth gives the individual power and with it the temptation to ill-treat his neighbour; while the man who is excluded from possession is bound to rebel in hostility against his oppressor. If private property were abolished, all wealth held in common, and everyone allowed to share in the enjoyment of it, ill-will and hostility would disappear among men. Since everyone's needs would be satisfied, no one would have any reason to regard another as his enemy; all would willingly undertake the work that was necessary. I have no concern with any economic criticisms of the communist system; I cannot enquire into whether the abolition of private property is expedient or advantageous.[5] But I am able to recognize that the psychological premises on which the system is based are an untenable illusion. In abolishing private property we deprive the human love of aggression of one of its instruments, certainly a strong one, though certainly not the strongest; but we have in no way altered the differences in power and influence which are misused by aggressiveness, nor have we altered anything in its nature. Aggressiveness was not created by property. It reigned almost without limit in primitive times, when property was still very scanty, and it already shows itself in the nursery almost before property has given up its primal, anal form; it forms the basis of every relation of affection and love among people. . . .

It is clearly not easy for men to give up the satisfaction of this inclination to aggression. They do not feel comfortable without it. The advantage which a comparatively small cultural group offers of allowing this instinct an outlet in the form of hostility against intruders is not to be despised. It is always possible to bind together a considerable number of people in love, so long as there are other people left over to receive the manifestations of their aggressiveness. I once discussed the phenomenon that it is precisely communities with adjoining territories, and related to each other in other ways as well, who are engaged in constant feuds and in ridiculing each other—like the Spaniards and Portuguese, for instance, the North Germans and South Germans, the English and Scotch, and so on.[6] I gave this phenomenon the name of "the narcissism of minor differences," a name which does not do much to explain it. We can now see that it is a convenient and relatively harmless satisfaction of the inclination to aggression, by means of which cohesion between the members of the community is made easier. In this respect the Jewish people, scattered everywhere, have rendered most useful services to the civilizations of the countries that have been their hosts; but unfortunately all the massacres of the Jews in the Middle Ages did not suffice to make that period more peaceful and secure for their Christian fellows. When once the Apostle Paul had posited universal love between men as the foundation of his Christian community, extreme intolerance on the part of Christendom towards those who remained outside it became the inevitable consequence. To the Romans, who had not founded their communal life as a State upon love, religious intolerance was something foreign, although with them religion was a concern of the State and the State was permeated by religion. Neither was it an unaccountable chance that the dream of a Germanic world-dominion called for antisemitism as its complement; and it is intelligible that the attempt to establish a new, communist civilization in Russia should find its psychological support in the persecution of the bourgeois. One only wonders, with this concern, what the Soviets will do after they have wiped out their bourgeois. . . .

NOTES

1. A great imaginative writer may permit himself to give expression—jokingly, at all events—to psychological truths that are severely proscribed. Thus Heine confesses: "Mine is a most peaceable disposition. My wishes are: a humble cottage with a thatched roof, but a good bed, good food, the freshest milk and butter, flowers before my window, and a few fine trees before my door; and if God wants to make my happiness complete, he will grant me the joy of seeing some six or seven of my enemies hanging from those trees. Before their death I shall, moved in my heart, forgive them all the wrong they did me in their lifetime. One must, it is true, forgive one's enemies—but not before they have been hanged." *(Gedanken und Einfälle* [Section I].)

2. [See Chapter V of *The Future of an Illusion* (1927c).]

3. ["It's the murderers who should make the first move."]

4. ["Man is a wolf to man." Derived from Plautus, Asinaria II, iv, 88.]

5. Anyone who has tasted the miseries of poverty in his own youth and has experienced the indifference and arrogance of the well-to-do, should be safe from the suspicion of having no understanding or good will towards endeavours to fight against the inequality of wealth among men and all that it leads to. To be sure, if an attempt is made to base this fight upon an abstract demand, in the name of justice, for equality for all men, there is a very obvious objection to be made— that nature, by endowing individuals with extremely unequal physical attributes and mental capacities, has introduced injustices against which there is no remedy.

6. [See Chapter VI of *Group Psychology* (1921c), *Standard Ed.,* 18, 101, and "The Taboo of Virginity" (1918a), ibid., 11, 199.]

CHAPTER NINE

In Defense of
REFUSING TO FORGIVE

$\mathcal{J}$ews are taught to imitate God, who is proclaimed as forgiving iniquity, transgression, and sin (Exodus 346-7). And Christians regularly recite the "Our Father" (or the "Lord's Prayer"), which concludes with the plea, "Forgive us our trespasses as we forgive those who trespass against us."

On Yom Kippur, the holiest day of the Jewish year, forgiveness abounds. The observant ask forgiveness from those they've wronged, who, in turn, are expected to grant it.

In the following essay from 1998, David Novitz probes the philosophical psychology of human forgiveness. He claims that, despite religious injunctions to do so, it is not possible to forgive someone through an act of will. We can't simply force ourselves to change our feelings in the way forgiveness requires.

To forgive too readily, Novitz argues, is just as wrong as a steadfast refusal to attempt to forgive. While we may reasonably consider the disposition to undertake the task of forgiving as a virtue, there are circumstances, Novitz argues, in which it would be wrong to keep trying—even when the Bible, our priests, and our rabbis tell us to do so.

For to be too willing to undertake the task of forgiveness, or to undertake it in inappropriate circumstances, is a vice borne of low self-respect.

We can hardly hope to find a group of people better known for evil, and consequently harder to forgive, than the Nazis. In the late 1960s, Holocaust survivor Elie Weisel, who won the Nobel Peace Prize in 1986, urged fellow Jews never to forgive: "Every Jew, somewhere in his being, should set apart a zone of hate—healthy, virile hate—for what the German personifies and for what persists in the German. To do otherwise would be a betrayal of the dead."

Novitz disagrees with Weisel's thinking, arguing instead: (1) that one can only coherently attempt to forgive someone who has wronged you; and (2) that in order to posses the virtue of forgiveness, one must be disposed to attempt to forgive. Novitz would fault Weisel in supposing that all Germans, especially ones who were not even alive at the time of the Third Reich, can plausibly be blamed for the genocide of the Jews. These Germans (and many besides) have done no wrong, and there is nothing to forgive. Although Novitz advocates what he calls the virtue of forgiveness, he also insists that to possess this virtue requires knowing when not to forgive.

Whether we *can* forgive others depends in part on our own intelligence and in part on social factors beyond our control. Whether we *should* persist in our attempts to forgive others when our self-esteem is at stake is answered by Novitz with a resounding and well-argued "No."

∾

DAVID NOVITZ studied at Rhodes University in South Africa before finishing his doctorate in philosophy at Oxford University. He is author of *Pictures and Their Use in Communication* (1977); *Knowledge, Fiction and Imagination* (1987), and *The Boundaries of Art* (1992) as well as numerous journal articles. He has also coedited two well-known collections of essays on New Zealand society (together with sociologist Bill Willmott).

FORGIVENESS AND SELF-RESPECT

David Novitz

Of all the virtues to which people commonly appeal, the Judaeo-Christian virtue of forgiveness is perhaps the most obscure. To possess it, we are told, is to be a forgiving person: someone who dutifully declines to harbour grudges and thoughts of revenge, who is ready and able to turn the other cheek, to trust when trust has been betrayed, to restore relationships with those who have violated them, and, above all, to abandon feelings of bitterness and resentment at will.

On the view that I shall defend, all of these claims are importantly misguided. People who forgive too readily, I argue, do not manifest the right degree of self-respect; they underestimate their own worth and fail to take their projects and entitlements seriously enough. If there is a virtue of forgiveness, it would seem to consist in being disposed to forgive in the appropriate circumstances. However, since one cannot abandon one's feelings of anger and resentment just by deciding to do so, I also argue that forgiveness cannot consist in any one act that a person can perform at will, and this poses obvious problems for the claim that forgiveness can properly be considered a virtue.[1] Even so, I contend in the concluding section that, although not a classical Greek virtue, forgiveness may be considered a virtue in the Aristotelian sense of this word.

My concern will be with human rather than divine forgiveness.[2] Among other things, I shall want to know how it is possible for one human being to forgive another, and in attempting to explain this, I attempt to make sense of, or reconstruct along rational lines, the Judaeo-Christian virtue of forgiveness. Put differently, my aim is to explain the virtue of forgiveness within the bounds of rationally defensible, so-called secular, ethical theory. For this reason, my argument makes no assumptions of a theological nature.[3]

1. PRELIMINARIES

The verb "to forgive" always takes an object. What one forgives, however, is not a wrongful action; rather, one forgives the person who is believed to be responsible and who is blamed and resented for that action. Still, not every action that we deem to be wrong calls for forgiveness. Usually one tries to forgive only in situations where one believes oneself to have been seriously wronged and harmed; hence in situations that have resulted in strong feelings of anger and resentment. People speak, for instance, of Nelson Mandela as a forgiving man because of his decision not to avenge himself on those who were responsible for the practice and the legacy of apartheid. Or they might speak of a betrayed spouse as forgiving or as unforgiving. Here talk about forgiveness seems entirely appropriate because these are the sorts of wrongs that we can normally count on to produce feelings of outrage and resentment.

It seems less appropriate to speak of forgiveness where minor wrongs are concerned. Your failure to return a book as promised, or your borrowing my eraser without my permission are wrongs of a sort, but not of the sort that normally warrant forgiveness. This is so, I think, because these are not the sorts of wrongs that usually cause serious harm and which can reasonably give rise to enduring resentment. People being what they are, however, trivial wrongs of this sort may nonetheless result in strong feelings of resentment, and when they do it certainly is appropriate to speak of, to urge, or to seek forgiveness. This, I think, explains why we sometimes request forgiveness for perfectly trivial misdemeanours, for we recognize, albeit tacitly, that it is always possible that others will see these wrongs differently, take umbrage, or feel resentful.

The trivial transgressions that we suffer can easily be condoned or pardoned without lingering feelings of resentment and mistrust. But the serious wrongs that require our forgiveness cannot morally be condoned, and their pardon, if secured, will only involve the renouncement of our claims against the wrongdoer but will not straightforwardly result in the abandonment of the bitter feelings that these wrongs have occasioned.[4] And it is this (as well as the renouncement of our claims against the persons who have wronged us) that the traditional Judaeo-Christian act of forgiving must secure if it is to take place at all.[5]

It is, of course, possible for a person who has been seriously wronged not to feel resentful or angry, and in such a case there would be no need to forgive. But the absence of resentment in such circumstances is odd, for if a person has been badly used and unfairly wronged, it is appropriate to feel a strong sense of injustice, resentment, and anger. Not to feel this, Jeffrie Murphy suggests, is to fail to take oneself, one's projects, and one's entitlements seriously enough. According to him, the "primary value defended by the passion of resentment is self-respect."[6] So while we can agree that resentment is a dangerous emotion—one that can easily subvert social stability—it is also useful, since it draws attention to the rights and the respect that are due to oneself.

Sometimes, it is true, I may appear to forgive just by saying "I forgive you"—where this performative utterance is thought to constitute and exhaust the act of forgiving. But it does not do so. All that it can do is renounce the claims that I have on you. What it cannot ensure is that I will somehow relinquish the hard feelings that your action occasioned. Since, as we have now seen, one mark of having forgiven a person (at least in the traditional Judaeo-Christian sense) is that one no longer harbours feelings of anger or bitterness,[7] and since the utterance "I forgive you" cannot ensure this, it is much more like an act of pardoning than it is like forgiving. So while it is true that ordinary language sometimes permits us to use the word "forgive" when we mean "pardon," this is a second sense of the verb "to forgive" and is not one that I shall consider here.

Suppose, though, that one has been seriously wronged but does not believe this to be the case. Since this is so, there can no feelings of anger and resentment consequent upon the wrong; hence no need to banish these feelings through forgiveness. This is why forgiveness is called for only when we believe ourselves to have been wronged. It is well known, though, that people occasionally exaggerate the wrongs done to them, or imagine that they have been severely harmed by others when nothing of the sort has occurred. The feelings of anger or the desire for revenge consequent upon these illusions are not themselves illusory, so that forgiveness may be called for even in situations where a wrong has not actually been done but is only believed to have been done. It is true that people will not welcome the fact that they have been forgiven, for this clearly (and unfairly) implies their responsibility for the putative injury. Nonetheless, if it is true that the discourse of forgiveness is meant, among other things, to preserve and partially restore the social fabric, then whenever major wrongs are sincerely but falsely attributed by an individual to some innocent party, it makes sense to urge forgiveness.

However, it is only the (supposed) victim of a (putative) wrong who can properly be said to forgive the wrongdoer. It is not up to me, for instance, to forgive those British policemen who were responsible for ensuring the wrongful imprisonment and conviction of the Guildford Four. Only the Guildford Four can do that. This, of course, is not to deny that people may be wronged by the grave and unwarranted harm that someone does not to them but to others who are close to them. Even so, the father who claims to forgive a drunken driver for crippling his child in a collision cannot plausibly claim to forgive the driver on behalf of his quadriplegic child. All that he can plausibly do is claim to forgive the driver for the wrong and the harm that he, the father, has suffered through the willfully negligent behaviour that maimed his child.[8]

If all of this is right, a number of conditions are plainly necessary for speaking of forgiveness in the traditional—the Judaeo-Christian—sense of this word. The first is that one cannot be said to forgive a person unless one believes oneself to have been wrongfully harmed by that person. Second, one must believe that the putative wrong was either deliberate or else the result of willful negligence. Third, one must experience certain negative feelings as a result of the putative wrong—including the anger and bitterness that normally accompany resentment, as well as a strong desire for justice or revenge. A person who, for whatever reason, does not experience at least some of these emotions when badly wronged has no need to forgive, and it would of course be false to maintain that that such a person has either forgiven or failed to forgive. And finally, forgiveness (by contrast with pardoning) must not just involve the renunciation of one's claims against the wrongdoer but must also result in the dissolution of one's negative feelings: of the resentment and the anger that one feels on account of the wrong one has suffered.

It is arguable, though, that not all of these conditions are necessary for forgiveness in the traditional sense. People, we are told, do not just forgive (or fail to forgive) others for the wrongful injuries that are believed to have been done to them; they sometimes forgive (or fail to forgive) others for qualities they possess or for relationships in which they stand: things that have not been *done* at all but which nonetheless affect them adversely. Thus, for instance, an older sister may be said never to have forgiven her brother for being the favourite of her parents, for being good-looking, graceful, or athletic—even though these are not actions that he has performed. Or, in a somewhat different vein, it might be argued that it makes sense to speak of forgiveness even when one has not been wronged or injured. I may fail, for instance, to forgive you for trouncing me at tennis, or for doing so maddeningly well in your career, even though I know that you have done me no wrong, and that you certainly have not harmed me.

In the light of examples such as these, it is tempting to conclude that I have not isolated necessary conditions for Judaeo-Christian forgiveness, for it seems appropriate to speak of forgiveness even when no action was performed and no wrongful injury done. But this inference is unwarranted. All that these examples establish is that we sometimes use the verb "to forgive" non-literally. This is apparent from the fact that while we occasionally say of a person that she never forgave him for being so handsome, or that he failed to forgive her for beating him at tennis or for being so much more intelligent than he is, the converse makes no proper sense. We never speak, except as a joke, of one person forgiving another for being handsome, or for winning at tennis, or for being intelligent. And this suggests that I cannot literally forgive someone for the qualities that they possess, for the relationships in which they stand, or for an action that has not wronged me.

It appears, then, that the conditions that I have isolated are necessary for the Judaeo-Christian notion of forgiveness. But they are not, of course, sufficient. In order to see what else is required, we need to consider some of the many different ways in which people experience a change of heart, not all of which count as forgiveness.

2. PUNISHMENT, PITY, AND FORGIVENESS

The passage of time and the development of new interests and a new lifestyle may gradually displace feelings of bitterness and the desire for revenge. But this, of course, is not to forgive; if anything, it is to forget: it is to have one's attention diverted, and is (in consequence) to develop new and different priorities, so that the wrong and the harm that one has suffered gradually loses its sting. The process is entirely passive and depends not so much on one's character as it does on what has lately happened in one's life.

Like the passage of time, punishment would also seem to have the obviously beneficial effect of assuaging feelings of bitterness and resentment. But the demand for punishment often amounts to nothing more than a demand for revenge, and when it does, it is straightforwardly incompatible with forgiveness. Nelson Mandela is regarded as forgiving precisely because he has not avenged himself on the perpetrators of apartheid; were he to do so, he would be regarded as retributive and unforgiving. If, however, one's aim in punishing is not primarily to exact revenge, but is either to reform and so benefit the wrongdoer, or else to treat the wrongdoer with the respect due to all persons, then the demand for punishment, far from being incompatible with forgiveness, actually requires the prior forgiveness of the wrongdoer whom one now wishes to benefit or else treat with respect.[9] But since this is so, punishment in the present case does not result in forgiveness; rather, it presupposes it. From which we can see that forgiveness is not conditional on punishment, for one can punish (in the sense of exacting revenge) yet not forgive; and one can forgive without ever punishing (in any sense of this word).[10]

It is true that we are less likely to feel badly towards those who have wronged us if they show themselves to be contrite and express sincere regret for what they have done. There are good reasons for this, since such people have genuinely dissociated themselves from their past actions, which they now find wholly unacceptable. So although one may continue to think their actions unjust and immoral, it no longer seems as appropriate to harbour hard feelings towards them.[11] Even so, the fact that it no longer seems as appropriate to have such emotions will not guarantee that one does not have them; it will not guarantee forgiveness. Hard feelings often linger and, for a range of complex reasons that have much to do with our personal histories, cannot simply be banished at will.[12]

Matters are further complicated by the fact that expressions of regret can take different forms, so that whether or not one continues to harbour hard feelings in the face of apparent contrition will depend in part on the content, in part on the context, of the apology. To say "I really am sorry about what happened," rather than "I really am sorry for what I did," is straight away to seek to absolve oneself from blame. Even when one apologizes for what one did, but at the same time maintains that the consequences of one's action could not have been foreseen, one effectively attempts to demonstrate that one was not responsible for what was done, and hence that one is not properly to be blamed. In such cases, if the expression of regret is believed, the person is taken to be blameless, but this is not at all the same as forgiving that person. One can forgive people, I have argued, only when they are believed to be responsible and so are blamed for the wrong that was done. Certainly, excuses of this sort do not always exonerate; sometimes they mitigate, and when they do, we may cease to feel quite so strongly about the people who harmed us.[13] But this, we should notice, does not amount to forgiveness. Forgiveness is called for in precisely those situations where the emotions that we have are appropriate to the wrong and the harm that we believe to have been done.

Suppose, then, that in apologizing to me for what was done, you accept full responsibility for your actions and express your profound regret. Would this secure my forgiveness? Again, the matter is far from straightforward. Since any sincere apology implies an undertaking on your part not to repeat the offending behaviour, I will usually require evidence to the effect that you are able and willing to stop behaving in the way that has so wronged me before I can believe the undertaking and so accept your apology. The trouble, of course, is that it is often difficult to believe this. There is something erratic about the weakness of resolve involved in a person deliberately wronging and harming others at a certain time, and expressing regret for these actions soon after. And this makes it inappropriate to accept the apology since one has no reason to believe that the offending behaviour will not be repeated. In the face of this, it is not just difficult to forgive but it would arguably be remiss of one to seek to do so, since forgiveness, in this case, seems to overlook and thereby condone the strong potential for further wrongful action.

Your apology and contrition are more acceptable in those cases where some time has elapsed between the commission of the wrong and the expression of regret, or where I have reason to believe that you have learned something about the suffering that you have inflicted, about human vulnerability, and the importance of respecting others. But if there is no reason to suppose that you have learned any of this, I would have no grounds at all for accepting the expression of even the most abject regret, and since I would still have every good reason to resent what you have done, your apology would do little to resolve my hard feelings.[14]

Of course, some people do accept the most perfunctory and insincere apologies, and certainly seem to forgive as a result of them. There are many reasons for this. A wronged wife, for instance, may be motivated by her emotional and economic dependence on her husband to accept his apology and resume her trusting behaviour towards him, even though there are very good reasons why she should not.[15] After all, there is no reason, on the basis of his truculent "I'm sorry," to think that he has abandoned the principles on which he earlier behaved, or that he would be unlikely to repeat the offending behaviour as soon as it suited him to do so.

Whether this counts as an instance of forgiveness, however, is doubtful. For in these circumstances, to accept the apology is either to condone or ignore the wrongful behaviour, and this can hardly count as a virtue. If forgiveness is to be a virtue, it will have to acknowledge and attend to the wrong that was done, *and* deliberately seek to banish the bitter feelings associated with it. Hence, if the wife's emotional dependence, or her commitment to the story of Christianity, or her view of self as a dedicated homemaker, prompts her to accept an apology that ought not on rational or moral grounds to be accepted, then she is not so much a forgiving person as she is weak-willed or self-deceived: either unable or unwilling to acknowledge the disrespect and abuse that her husband's behaviour evinces.

It may, of course, be possible for the wife to forgive despite the fact that she does not possess the virtue of forgiveness and is not (as yet) a genuinely forgiving person. For just as a dishonest person may occasionally be honest, so a retributive and unforgiving person may occasionally forgive. However, an act cannot count as one of forgiveness (or as honest) if it is incompatible with the corresponding virtue—if, that is, it is grounded on principles for action, which, were they to become part of the character of that person, would make them unforgiving (or dishonest). And this explains why, in this instance, the wife's all-too-ready acceptance of her husband's apology cannot qualify as an act of forgiveness.

But there is another and a kinder construal that may be placed on the wife's behaviour. For she may believe that by refusing to dwell on the wrong that her husband has done to her, and by behaving normally and decently towards him, she may eventually reform his behaviour, and that this, in its turn, will help rekindle her trust and dissolve her bitterness and resentment. This, in Joanna North's opinion, is what forgiveness amounts to.[16] But she cannot be correct, since kind or decent behaviour of this sort does not amount to forgiveness. For one thing, as Bishop Butler observes, goodwill—and certainly the sort of kindliness that the wronged wife manifests in this case towards her husband—is compatible with a large degree of resentment, so that to act in this way is not to forgive.[17] Then again, to construe forgiveness as North does is to require the wife to divert her attention from the wrong that was done, and to fixate instead on more acceptable behaviour. But this, if successful, is just a way of coming to forget, not forgive. Forgiving, I have said, requires that we attend to and acknowledge the wrong while at the same time divesting ourselves of the resentment it occasioned.

Suppose, then, that it is obvious that you deeply regret the wrong you have done to me. You can now see that your behaviour was both harmful and immoral, and you are not just contrite but mortified and pained by what you have done. Suppose, too, that I recognize your pain, see that you are suffering, and that I accept your apology. Would this amount to forgiving you? Again I do not think so, for by accepting your apology I do not automatically cease to feel hurt and angry; all that I do (if I am sincere) is undertake to control those feelings, and to relinquish the claims that I have on you.

Let us suppose, then, that because of your penitence, I do not just accept your apology but find, to my relief, that I am no longer resentful and angry. But even this does not entail that I have forgiven you. For the fact, if it is one, that I no longer harbour strong feelings against you may come about in a number of ways, not all of which are compatible with forgiveness. Thus, for instance, it could be the case that my earlier desire to see you suffer—my desire for revenge—has at last been satisfied, and that I feel relief and release as a result. But if this is the case then it is doubtful whether I have forgiven you, for I have let your conscience exact the revenge that I had earlier desired. Since (as I argued earlier) forgiveness is never conditional on the satisfaction of one's demand for revenge, this cannot be a case of forgiveness.

But what if, instead of relief, your penitence and suffering brings me to pity you—or feel sorry for you—and that as a result I find that I no longer wish you ill? Does this mean that I have forgiven you? This comes close to the Judaeo-Christian notion of forgiveness, but there are problems with it. Pity may have different sources and may take different forms, not all of which are appropriate to forgiveness. To pity someone does not always amount to genuine compassion, for by pitying one may deliberately diminish and belittle a person, and to do this is not to forgive that person. In some cases, too, the pity I feel may arise from a sense of guilt or shame—my guilt, say, at the pleasure I take in your discomfort. Here the way in which I prefer to think of myself helps transform my initial delight at your pain into guilt, which, in its turn, is alleviated only by persuading myself that I now feel sorry for you. But this, of course, has nothing to do with the traditional notion of forgiveness. For if forgiveness is a virtue, it should not be motivated by a desire to free oneself from guilt or shame. Forgiveness, at least as traditionally construed, is not self-interested but other-regarding; from which it follows that my pity will have to come from a very different source, and be of a very different kind, if it is to play any role at all in forgiveness. What such pity amounts to, and what its source is, is something that we will turn to presently.

Before doing so, however, we need to notice another difficulty that arises when we distinguish between the temporary disappearance of my hard feelings on the one hand, and their permanent removal on the other. It is true that my pitying you may result in the total and permanent loss of my negative feelings towards you. But such feelings may equally disappear only for so long as I feel some pity for you. Here my pity may be said to occlude rather than remove my anger and resentment. However, the temporary occlusion of negative feelings is never sufficient for forgiveness. My resentment could also be momentarily hidden by my joy at having won a game of tennis or at having made a new friend. When the joy (or the pity) wanes, the resentment and anger will return.

However, if my pity is appropriately derived and of a suitable form, and is so integrated into my emotional life that I cease altogether to harbour feelings of resentment, then, it does indeed seem appropriate to say that I have forgiven you. This, at least, is what I now propose to argue. The trouble, of course, is that whether or not my pity for someone endures depends on a range of factors, not all of which will be seen to be within my full control. This suggests that forgiveness does not consist in any one act that a person can perform at will and that directly results in the banishment of hard feelings. Rather, on the view that I shall defend, to have forgiven someone is to have achieved success in a complex task, and it is this task, I argue, that one can and sometimes ought to undertake at will.

3. THE TASK OF FORGIVING

Even if there is no act of forgiving that can directly terminate my resentment and my rage, there is nonetheless a good deal that I can do indirectly in order to ease my negative feelings. It is a disposition to engage in this complex activity or task under the appropriate conditions, I now want to suggest, that needs to be cultivated and ingrained if one is properly to be regarded as a forgiving person—as a person, that is, who possesses the virtue of forgiveness.

It is well known that people can fuel their resentment. One obvious way in which I may do so is by offering a history that fixates on my grievances and emphasizes only those events that reinforce my sense of injustice and bruised pride. In so doing, I marginalize your point of view and ignore those factors that might otherwise have helped explain the offending behaviour. Were I disposed to do so, however, I could seek out "the other side of the story," and try to place your wrongful action in the context of your life and your needs, and in this way seek to undermine my grievance. By trying to see events from your point of view, I grasp, sometimes "from the inside," what motivated you, what errors of judgement prevailed, and why they had such a grip on your imagination.

Any such attempt to identify imaginatively with your situation, and the resultant (perhaps imperfect) understanding of what it was like to be in that situation, may help destabilize my attitudes towards you. For my new understanding places your actions in a different perspective and may enable me to feel, for a moment at least, as you must have felt. I may feel the urgency of your needs and so see differently why you acted as you did.

The willingness and the ability to see things differently and to depart from our own settled perspective is, I think, a necessary part of the task of forgiving, and requires some degree of empathic thinking. However, it is not enough to say, as North does, that forgiveness requires that we try "to view the wrongdoer with compassion, benevolence and love. . . ."[18] For in order to view someone with compassion and love, one must at least try to understand that person, their reasons, feelings, and hopes, and this will invariably involve an attempt to identify imaginatively with them. Even when we attempt to forgive "for old time's sake," we do so because we already identify feelingly with the wrongdoer we once knew.[19]

However, empathy is not something that comes naturally to us. The many wars and tribal conflicts, the endless betrayals, rapes, and murders that help constitute our common history, suggest that our capacity to empathise has to be developed, and that it is, and has always been, more or less limited. The development of this capacity depends greatly on prevailing cultural values; on whether such imaginative projections and their accompanying emotions are not just countenanced but encouraged by the societies in which we live. A culture that elevates honour, pride, and self-respect will be short on empathy and compassion, and will tend to urge revenge and praise retribution. In such a culture, empathy is believed to undermine one's sense of self—and not without reason, for whenever we empathise we run the risk of losing ourselves in the other; of failing, that is, to attend sufficiently to our own needs and desires, and hence of failing to take our own claims on the world seriously enough. There is a straightforward tension, then, between retaining a full view of our own importance and the empathy that requires one to lose sight of oneself and to fixate on the claims and the emotions of the other.

Our ability to empathise with others depends as well on whether or not there are models of empathic thinking that are readily available to us. As it happens, there is, in our society at present, a range of artifacts and practices that, if properly attended to, unquestionably develops our capacity to think empathically. Some fiction—especially drama and the novel, television and cinema—has done an enormous amount to allow people to escape the narrow, sometimes sectarian points of view encouraged by an awareness of their own interests, or by religious and political ideologies.[20] For fiction brings readers, theatre-goers, and viewers to grasp the points of view of fictional characters in ways that particular interests, politics, or religions sometimes expressly forbid. In the process, movies, television, and novels arguably alter the understanding (and the values) of countless individuals—and they do so, for the most part, without the pain and upheaval that often accompany such changes in real life. Our identification with Emma Bovary, Stephen Dedalus, and Dorothea Brooke enlarges our sympathies, makes us susceptible to new ways of thinking and feeling. In bringing us, in this way, to identify imaginatively with fictional creatures, novels (like television and the cinema) have given us a way of thinking about actual people; a way, I have suggested, that helps us not just to understand their actions from their point of view but also, on occasions, to abandon some or all of the feelings of resentment and hostility that might previously have been occasioned by their actions.

If I am right, one cannot forgive unless one tries to understand the other side of the story; unless, that is, one attempts to construe events from the point of view of the person who has acted wrongly towards you. But while this is a necessary component of the task of forgiving, it cannot itself ensure forgiveness. For one thing, I may try but fail to see things from your point of view. Such a failure can take at least two forms: First, I may fail simply because I believe, mistakenly, that I have succeeded in understanding things from your point of view when I have not. In such a case, something like forgiveness may eventually be secured, but that the forgiveness is not genuine is clear from the fact that my resentment may very well be rekindled when once my misunderstanding becomes apparent to me. Second, no matter how hard I try, I may simply be unable to empathise; I may remain baffled about the motives and feelings, the dreams, desires, and values that led to such untoward behaviour. In some circumstances, this may incline me to doubt your sanity, but when once I assume that you are not sane, questions of forgiveness do not properly arise for I can no longer hold you responsible for your actions.

Even in those situations where my empathic thinking results in a relatively full understanding, and I do indeed come to see from your point of view and to share some of your feelings, this need not, and sometimes should not, result in forgiveness. For I may come, in the process, to understand just how selfish your behaviour was, how cruel, and the extent to which you delight in, and continue to gain from, your malevolence. And on grasping this, I am even more degraded by your past behaviour and your current lack of concern for what you have done to me. As a result, my feelings of resentment and anger may quite properly intensify.

However, even if by empathising I come to feel the sharp edge of your shame and remorse, I may still be unable to dispel my resentment and so forgive you. For if I am angry and hurt, I may take pleasure in your discomfort; I may experience a higher-order delight—a kind of *Schadenfreude*—at your guilt and contrition. In addition to empathic identification, therefore, I will need (if I am to forgive you) to sympathize with, or have compassion for, you—where this involves the higher-order emotional attitude of concern or sadness on account of my empathic grasp of your remorse and suffering.[21] Most importantly, my compassion or sympathy will have to endure. It is only when one's empathic understanding and the compassion it engenders become a secure part of one's emotional life that one will be able, permanently, to forego one's resentment. For if one has an empathic grasp of the motivations, temptations, and remorse of the wrongdoer, and if one also feels an enduring compassion on account of this, it is both conceptually and psychologically impossible to continue to feel resentment and anger because of the wrong and the harm that was done to you. Forgiveness will be assured.

This, of course, is a particularly tall order. According to Lawrence Blum, compassion involves, among other things, "the imaginative dwelling on the condition of the other person, an active regard for his good, [and] a view of him as a fellow human being."[22] But people have no direct control over whether or not they can sustain all of this, and hence over whether or not their compassion will endure. In part, this depends on the intensity of their resentment and anger; something which is influenced not just by the perceived seriousness of the wrong and how recently it occurred, but also, and most importantly, by their sense of self—their self-esteem (that is, their self-regard or self-respect) and hence their self-confidence.[23] An inability to pick up the pieces and so heal one's life is likely to fuel one's resentment, for no matter one's empathic endeavours, and no matter one's attempts at sympathy, one will constantly be forced to return to one's own deprivations and to one's inability to cope with them.

By the same token, those who have comparatively high self-esteem and who are well able to resume their lives will usually need less in the way of empathic understanding in order to forego their resentment than those who feel less secure and are in need of greater assurance of the pain and remorse felt by a wrongdoer. This is why one cannot state with precision the degree of empathic understanding that is required for forgiveness, for depending on their personal histories, different people will have different needs. Even so, the conceptual point remains: a person must understand enough not to turn out simply to have condoned the wrong or to have compromised the respect due to them as persons, for this, I have argued, is not to forgive, and may easily result in an impoverished view of self.

We can see from this that to be too ready to attempt the task of forgiveness, and too eager to abandon feelings of resentment, is itself a character-flaw—not just because it indicates a tendency to underestimate one's own worth, but also because low self-esteem works to prevent eventual forgiveness.[24] The problem always is to embark on this task without further compromising one's self-esteem, and with it one's self-confidence, for to do so is to undermine one's chances of ever forgiving the wrongdoer.

Matters are further complicated by the fact that the worth that people attach to themselves is not entirely of their own making but is very largely the product of their social environment. This is why it is so much more difficult even to attempt to forgive in those societies where nobility, honour, and self-respect are greatly valued than it is in a society that prizes empathy and the understanding and harmony that derive from it. In the latter society, moreover, forgiveness may actually add to rather than diminish one's self-esteem, since it earns one the approval of others. Hence it is wrong to think that forgiveness always tends to corrode one's self-respect. It need not, and whether or not it does depends very largely on prevailing social values and attitudes.[25]

Success in the task of forgiveness, we can now see, is only as durable as one's self-image. A different sense of self at some time in the future, that results either in higher or in lower self-esteem, may rekindle the feelings of anger and resentment that were previously believed to have been banished. One obvious consequence of this is that it is difficult to know that one has finally forgiven someone for their wrongs against you. But this should come as no surprise; time alone can tell whether the feelings which we have struggled to control are finally conquered, or whether what is vanquished today will return by the backdoor tomorrow. Whether or not such feelings do return, I have suggested, has much to do with our personal histories, and, as a result, with factors that fall beyond our rational control.

It is clear from all of this that there can be no duty to forgive; this simply because it is not directly within one's power to do so.[26] There may, of course, be a duty to undertake the task of forgiveness, but when people forgive it is only because they have succeeded in this task. Whether or not they do succeed clearly depends on a range of factors, many of which lie beyond their full control. Sympathy and empathic projection, we have seen, are both necessary components of this task, but neither (whether considered individually or jointly) can guarantee its success. Occasionally, it is true, people fail to forgive simply because they are callous, unimaginative, and unfeeling, and if they can be brought to recognize these shortcomings, they plainly have a duty to try to improve themselves. But such a duty falls far short of the duty to forgive.

4. THE VIRTUE OF FORGIVENESS

If I am right, we can forgive people only if we establish some degree of sustained emotional contact with them. We need to feel with and for them, share some of their hopes, grasp their fears, their regrets, and their uncertainties. And, as I have suggested, we cannot do this for so long as they remain wholly alien to us; locked out, as it were, by the barrier of our unrelenting feelings. To be a forgiving person, on this view, is to be disposed to try and establish that contact in the appropriate circumstances. It requires that one be inclined to rise above or ignore the intensity of one's feelings in order to project oneself imaginatively and compassionately into the situation of others.

To possess the virtue of forgiveness, then, is to possess this disposition; no more. It is to be a person who wishes to, and who tries to, restore damaged relationships to something like their former good health. Clearly, then, one can be a forgiving person even though one is unable, on a particular occasion, to forgive—for, as we have seen, it is not always emotionally possible or ethically desirable to abjure one's feelings of resentment. Nor, I have argued, ought one even to attempt to forgive a person, and so become reconciled, if there are no relevant reasons for doing so. If the person will clearly re-offend, does not regret what has been done, or continues to behave in similar ways, attempts to forgive are inappropriate and a violation of one's own sense of self—

of the importance that one should attach to one's own projects and aspirations.

Forgiveness—by which is meant the disposition to undertake what I have called the task of forgiving—is like any Aristotelian virtue. For one thing, it is acquired through habituation, example, and practice, since, as I have already intimated, it will be acquired only in the right social conditions.[27] In part, the acquisition of this disposition depends on good fortune, for people who have been badly hurt, who have been scorched by the actions of others, may not be willing or able to think empathically and feel compassion. Their view of others may be permanently skewed, and there is not much that can be done about this; they will remain embittered and unforgiving, sometimes through no fault of their own.

Like all Aristotelian virtues, the virtue of forgiveness is "concerned with feelings and actions, in which excess and deficiency are in error and incur blame, while the intermediate condition is correct and wins praise."[28] To be too eager to forgive is a vice since, as we have seen, the attempt to forgive may not be rationally warranted, may very well signal a willingness to condone what is immoral, and may not only underestimate one's own worth but, in the process, may perpetuate and aggravate the harm and the wrong that one has suffered, and may do so in ways that preclude eventual forgiveness. On the other hand, to be too unwilling to embark on the task of forgiving is also a vice—although (as we have just learned) not always one for which one is fully responsible. The task of the rational person, whose heart is neither too hard nor too soft, is to find the Aristotelian mean—and to be willing to undertake and persist in the task of forgiving only if it is rationally and morally warranted.[29] So although, on Aristotle's view, "the mild person is ready to pardon, not eager to exact a penalty," it is also the case that "those who are not angered by the right things, or in the right way, or at the right times, or towards the right people, all seem to be foolish . . . "[30]

Clearly, then, those who have acquired the virtue of forgiveness— those, that is, who are disposed to undertake the task of forgiving in the appropriate circumstances—are more likely to succeed in this task than those who have not acquired this virtue. They will be practised at empathy and compassion and will tend, more often than not, to forgive in situations where it is appropriate to do so.

Their task, then, is to attempt to restore those relationships that can reasonably be restored so that their lives can proceed unencumbered by unresolved anger, bitterness, and resentment. For a life that is encumbered in this way is hardly a good life; it is one that sees others through the distorted lens of its own anger and that sacrifices community with them at every turn. Sometimes, too, it is a life in which one can no longer relate freely and openly to those with whom one once had a great deal in common; a fragmented life, therefore, that is exiled from its own past, that loses touch with the person one once was, and that forces one, in the end, to become a stranger to much that was previously of value to oneself.[31]

NOTES

1. The view that people can choose to forgive, and can somehow forgive at will, is widespread in the literature. See, for example, Jeffrie G. Murphy, "Forgiveness and Resentment," in *Forgiveness and Mercy* by Jeffrie G. Murphy and Jean Hampton (Cambridge: Cambridge University Press, 1988), where Jeffrie Murphy argues that forgiveness is an act that we perform for certain reasons (p. 24), and "that sometimes it is not merely permissible that I forgive but that I *ought* to forgive and can be properly criticized if I do not" (p. 29). Cheshire Calhoun, in "Changing One's Heart," *Ethics* 103 (1992), pp. 76–96, esp. p. 81, claims that "forgiveness is an elective response to culpable wrongdoing." The same view is shared by R. S. Downie, "Forgiveness," *Philosophical Quarterly* 15 (1965), pp. 128–134, especially p. 132, where forgiveness is also described as an action that we perform. See, as well, Joanna North, "Wrongdoing and Forgiveness," *Philosophy* 62 (1987), pp. 499–508, esp. pp. 500 and 503, who agrees with this view. Aurel Kolnai, "Forgiveness," *Proceedings of the Aristotelian Society* 74 (1973–74), pp. 91–106, thinks of forgiveness as "reaccepting" a person (p. 104) and as a "venture of trust"—that is, as something that we *do* trustingly (pp. 105–106). See, as well, Norvin Richards, "Forgiveness," *Ethics* 99 (1988), pp. 77–97. Richards thinks of forgiveness as an action that is largely, if not entirely, within one's control. At one point, he says it "would always be wrong not to forgive . . ." (p.87). Later (p. 95) he speaks of "a refusal or an inability to forgive," where the implication is that forgiving is sometimes subject to a person's control.

2. For some of the problems associated with this, see Anne C. Minas, "God and Forgiveness," *Philosophical Quarterly* 25 (1975), pp. 139–150.

3. Cf. L. Gregory Jones, *Embodying Forgiveness: A Theological Analysis* (Grand Rapids, Michigan: William B. Eerdmans, 1995), pp. 150ff.; and Marilyn McCord Adams, "Forgiveness: A Christian Model," *Faith and Philosophy* 8 (1991), pp. 277–304, esp. p. 300, whose accounts of what is involved in human forgiveness assume at crucial points the adoption of specific Christian beliefs.

4. A similar observation is made by Downie, "Forgiveness," pp. 128–134; and by Kolnai, "Forgiveness," pp. 91–106.

5. See, for example, A. Cohen, *Everyman's Talmud* (London: J.M. Dent, 1932), pp. 229–230; and R. C. Mortimer, *Christian Ethics* (London: Hutchinson University Library, 1950), pp. 46–47. Cf. Downie, "Forgiveness," p.130, who thinks that a change in behaviour is the sole mark of successfully forgiving someone. My claim, however, is that there must also be a genuine change of heart. A change of behaviour is insufficient for forgiveness since it will frequently do no more than hide bitter feelings and the desire for revenge. It is fully compatible with deceit and hypocrisy.

6. Jeffrie Murphy, "Forgiveness and Resentment," in Murphy and Hampton, *Forgiveness and Mercy,* p. 16.

7. According to *Leviticus* xix, 18, "Thou shalt not take vengeance nor bear a grudge."

8. Cf. Downie, "Forgiveness," p. 128 for an interesting discussion of this same point.

9. Immanuel Kant, *The Metaphysical Problems of Virtue,* Part I, translated by James W. Ellington, in Immanuel Kant, *Ethical Philosophy* (Indianapolis: Hackett Publishing Co., 1983), pp. 97–98. Kant says, for instance, that "the humanity in one's person is the object of the respect which he can require of every other human being. . . ."

10. Cf. North, "Wrongdoing and Forgiveness," pp. 501, 503, who thinks that retribution may actually play a part in forgiveness.

11. This, at least, is what Murphy suggests, for "to the extent that the agent is separated from his evil act, forgiveness *of him* is possible without tacit approval of his evil act." See "Forgiveness and Resentment" in Murphy and Hampton, *Forgiveness and Mercy,* pp. 24–25.

12. For an account of the effect of personal history on emotion, see Martha C. Nussbaum, *Need and Recognition: A Theory of the Emotions,* The Gifford Lectures, Lecture Three: "Emotions and Infancy," The University of Edinburgh, April/May 1993. At this time, the lectures still await publication. I am grateful to Professor Nussbaum for allowing me access to her manuscript.

13. Cf. Joseph Butler, "Upon Forgiveness of Injuries," in *The Works of the Right Reverend Father in God, Joseph Butler, D.C.L., Late Bishop of Durham,* edited by Samuel Halifax (New York: Carter, 1846), p.111.

14. Cf. Norvin Richards, "Forgiveness," p. 87, who thinks that the fact that someone wronged you is good reason to resent them despite their repentance.

15. For more on this, see my "Love, Friendship and the Aesthetics of Character," *American Philosophical Quarterly* 28 (1991), pp. 207–216, esp. pp. 210–214.

16. North, "Wrongdoing and Forgiveness," pp. 504 and 506.

17. See Butler, "Upon Forgiveness of Injuries," pp. 106–107.

18. North, "Wrongdoing and Forgiveness," p. 502.

19. On this, see Murphy, "Forgiveness and Resentment," pp. 29–30.

20. On this, see Iris Murdoch, *The Sovereignty of the Good* (New York: Schocken, 1971), pp. 65, 84–87. See, as well, Murray Smith, "Film Spectatorship and the

Institution of Fiction," *The Journal of Aesthetics and Art Criticism,* 53 (1995), pp. 113–127.

21. Here I am indebted to Susan Feagin, "The Pleasures of Tragedy," *American Philosophical Quarterly* 20 (1983), pp. 95–104. Cf. Patricia S. Greenspan, *Emotions & Reasons: An Inquiry into Emotional Justification* (New York & London: Routledge, 1988), Ch. 3, who tends to the view that "identificatory" emotions are also compassionate ones (p. 37). However, if "identificatory emotions" are always empathic, then they need not always be compassionate. To think this is to overlook the fact, of which much is made by Feagin, that we can respond emotionally to our identification with the emotions of others.

22. Lawrence Blum, "Compassion" in *Explaining Emotions,* edited by Amélie Oksen-berg Rorty (Berkeley & Los Angeles: University of California Press, 1980), p. 509.

23. Although I use the terms "self-respect" and "self-esteem" interchangeably in this context, there are nonetheless contexts in which it is useful to distinguish them. On this, see Richard Keshen, *Reasonable Self-Esteem* (Montreal & Kingston: McGill Queen's University Press, 1996), pp. 91–95.

24. Cf. Murphy, "Forgiveness and Resentment" in *Forgiveness and Mercy,* p. 17; as well as Richards, "Forgiveness," p. 82.

25. Cf. Adrian S. Piper, "Impartiality, Compassion, and Modal Imagination," *Ethics* 101 (1991), pp. 726–757. Piper rightly contends that compassion may sometimes violate one's boundaries and one's self-esteem. On her view, compassion must preserve the integrity of the self. What she does not properly acknowledge is that what *counts* as the integrity of the self varies from one social situation to another.

26. Cf. Kolnai, "Forgiveness," p. 101. See, as well, Murphy, "Forgiveness and Resentment," p. 29, who takes the opposite point of view.

27. Here it useful to consult Aristotle, *Nicomachean Ethics,* translated by Terence Irwin (Indianapolis: Hackett, 1985), Book 2, Ch. 2.

28. *Ibid.,* 1106b 25.

29. *Ibid.,* 1107a 1.

30. *Ibid.,* 1126a 2–9.

31. This paper was read as the Presidential Address of the Australasian Association of Philosophy (NZ Division), August, 1995. It is dedicated to Professor R. H. Stoothoff in appreciation of his many years of service to New Zealand philosophy. I am indebted to Alex Baird, Philip Catton, Tim Dare, Stan Godlovitch, Paul Harrison, Carolyn Mason, Christine Swanton, and two anonymous referees of this journal for comments on earlier drafts of this paper.

CHAPTER TEN

In Defense of
PRIDE, THE WORST OF THE SEVEN DEADLY SINS

*C*hristian theology condemns pride as the worst sin of all, for in pride a person supposedly turns his back on God. In extreme cases, pride leads people to imagine that they are themselves God, rulers of their own fate. Humility is urged instead.

What is humility? St. Bernard of Clairvaux (1090–1153), a nobleman who abandoned material comforts to revive the failing monastery of Citeaux, maintains in his most famous work, *The Steps of Humility:* "Humility is that thorough self-examination which makes a man contemptible in his own sight. It is acquired by those who set a ladder in their hearts whereby to ascend from virtue to virtue, that is, from step to step, until they attain the summit of humility, from where, as from the Zion of speculation, they can see the truth." The modern world, the competitive "rat race" that consumes so much of our energy, seems to make humility a curious anachronism—even a very bad idea.

In the following essay, written in 1999, Jerome Neu shows us the cost of condemning pride. To its credit, pride enables us to compete against others. Moreover, pride can elevate, even ennoble, racial and sexual minorities. Particularly in the age of identity politics, pride seems an excellent way of ramping up the downtrodden. It may well be pride that prevents us from renouncing our sins and turning to God, but it is also pride that pulls us to independent, fulfilling lives.

∾

JEROME NEU holds a doctorate in philosophy from Oxford University. He is Professor of Philosophy at the University of California, Santa Cruz, where he has at various times been Chair of the programs in Philosophy, History of Consciousness, and Legal Studies. He is the author of *Emotion, Thought, and Therapy* (1977) and of *A Tear Is an Intellectual Thing: The Meanings of Emotion* (2000) and editor of *The Cambridge Companion to Freud* (1991).

PRIDE AND IDENTITY

Jerome Neu

How is it that pride has gone from being one of the traditional seven deadly sins to becoming, in recent decades, the banner under which social movements have declared their objectives (Black Pride, Gay Pride, and so on)? How are we to understand the shift from a theology of sin to a politics of self-assertion (and an accompanying psychology of self-esteem)? Is it simply that times have changed? That, God having died, attitudes have changed—so that what once was thought to precede a fall now seems a condition of rising? Or is it perhaps that the nature of pride is to be understood differently in the two contexts? There may be an inherent ambiguity in pride: associating it on the one hand with arrogance, conceit, egotism, and vanity, and on the other hand with self-respect, self-esteem, self-confidence, dignity. (On certain readings, these may *all* be seen as different kinds or degrees of self-love.) Thus at different times, different aspects of the nature of the emotion come to be given prominence. Or is the difference in the objects? One place to start is with the recognition that the object, and the subject, of the traditional sin was the individual. The social movements that argue for pride are concerned with groups. How do individual and group identity come together in pride?

"WE'RE NUMBER ONE!"

"We're number one! We're number one!" It is the ecstatic chant of fans around the world when their sports team wins. The shout has gone up quite often in San Francisco in recent years from fans of the 49ers football team. But who exactly is the "we" that is claiming exalted status? It is most often not the players themselves. Their claim to victory and so status would seem straightforward enough. But what have the fans done to deserve credit? They have often watched the game (but is that necessary?) and cheered their heroes on to victory. Perhaps the cheers of encouragement do help (there is said to be a "home team advantage"). But if the watching is done through television, as it most often is, the cheers can hardly reach and so encourage the players. So the causal contribution of the ecstatic fans to victory may be minimal. But even where it is great, some would doubt that cheering itself is enough. The "49er Faithful" is a group of long-term fans who resent the Johnny-come-latelies who jump on the winning bandwagon to claim the 49ers as their own. After all, the Faithful had done their cheering and buying of merchandise during the many fallow years before a string of victories made the team so immensely popular. So is length of commitment a condition of group membership, and so credit for (subgroup) achievement? Is the motive of commitment relevant? Does it matter whether a fan decides to attach his or her good wishes to only winning teams or sticks (more or less consistently) to the home or nearest local team? Is identification with a winning team simply a matter of individual choice at all?

Surely some aspects of our identity are fixed independently of what we think or would like to think. Thus we can be embarrassed *by* something our parents say, where we might just be embarrassed *for* a stranger (such as an actor who forgets his lines on stage when we are in the audience). Thus also we can be ashamed of something our country does, even if we are part of a vocal minority that actively opposes the policy. (This was the situation of many Americans during the Vietnam War. [See Walsh 1970.]) For certain purposes, who we are is fixed by who others think we are. Their criteria are the relevant ones—though our endorsing and incorporating their perspective may also be crucial. (If we reject their perspective, we perhaps ought to be free of the consequent emotions.) If those around us take family membership to be determined by blood, and citizenship to be determined by place of birth or other factors not directly chosen or readily disavowable, then insofar as family membership or citizenship provides grounds for pride or shame, those emotions too can become independent of our actions and preferences.

Surely, some aspects of our identity depend on choices we make and allegiances we adopt. Sports fans are notably self-selecting—but as we have noted, there may be complications even there. The complications are especially obvious where the organization is more formal: joining an organization may be voluntary, but acceptance may be uncertain, and so membership may itself become a special source of pride. This is true for colleges, clubs, gangs, fraternities, and many other groups, including military organizations ("The Few, The Proud, The Marines"). Even where a voluntary choice is essential to group membership, and so to pride based on group membership, the reactions and other conditions placed on our choice by others may be equally essential.

But the complications of choice in relation to group membership and so individual identity are only a part of the picture. That they *are* a part of the picture, we should be clear, is due to the internal structure of pride. David Hume treats pride (like all passions) as a "simple and uniform impression" (*Treatise* II: 277) that cannot be defined or analyzed into parts. Nonetheless, he manages to bring out some of what should be regarded as the conceptual conditions of pride (he himself mistakenly regarded them as simply causal conditions and consequences). His general scheme treats pride as a pleasure of self-approval, such "that all agreeable objects, related to ourselves, by an association of ideas and of impressions, produce pride, and disagreeable ones, humility" (*Treatise*

II: 290ff.; see Neu 1977, part I). He includes *closeness to self* among the modifications or "limitations" to that scheme. According to Hume, the agreeable object must be *closely* related to ourselves (otherwise only "joy" and not pride is produced) and only to ourselves or at most to ourselves and a few others (hence the comparative and competitive nature of pride). Again, while Hume mistook these conceptual constraints for merely causal ones, a proper pride (here meaning a conceptually coherent pride, not necessarily a morally justified one) must indeed depend on a suitably valuable object being suitably related to one. For Hume, value was simply a matter of approval and disapproval, ultimately traceable to reactions of pleasure and pain. We shall see that the contemporary politics of pride must depend on a different notion of value and of what is valuable. And while individual identity was notoriously a special problem within Hume's narrowly empiricist philosophy of mind, tracing chains of credit back to a self must be problematic on any philosophy, at least so far as credit is taken to depend on group membership. Relation to self is a conceptual condition of pride, and closeness to self is, inevitably, open to complication and challenge.

PRIDE THE SIN

Christian *pride* has some connections with Classical *hubris* (and even Jewish *chutzpah*), but the Christian notion is wider than just insolence or defiance against the gods. Nonetheless, such defiance was what gave the sin its medieval preeminence. Pride was given first place (one might say, "pride of place") back in the seventh century in Gregory the Great's now-conventional list of seven deadly sins (Bloomfield 1952, 72–74). The arrogance of pride was for him the root of all evil, "the beginning of all sin" (Lyman 1978, 136). There is biblical ground for giving pride such primacy (Ecclesiaticus 10:15 in the Vulgate), though 1 Timothy 6:10 gives avarice the prize. (St. Thomas made one of his usual efforts to reconcile the texts [Bloomfield, 88].) Pride isolates and alienates from both God and society; it is a form of self-satisfied and self-sufficient withdrawal (Fairlie 1978, 42). For a medieval world committed to discipline, hierarchy, and corporate order, this made it particularly heinous. As Bloomfield puts it, pride "is the sin of rebellion against God, the sin of exaggerated individualism" (75).

The negative view of pride that has carried over to our more individualistic times picks up on the arrogance and error associated with the earlier notion, though a modifier is sometimes added to spell out the problem: *false* pride is explicitly seen as based on false beliefs, just as *overweening* pride is by definition excessive. Must pride by its very nature fall into error and excess?

Pride is, in part, a sin of judgment, an intellectual deviation, involving bias in favor of one's self. The bias is of course motivated, so the defect is not purely intellectual. Spinoza's definition captures this aspect of pride quite precisely: "Pride is thinking more highly of oneself than is just, out of love of oneself" (*Ethics* III, Definitions of the Affects XXVIII). The source of pride in self-love makes clear its link to self-esteem (understood in a sense that allows for excess), as Spinoza puts it: "Pride is an effect or property of Self-love. Therefore, it can also be defined as Love of oneself, or Self-esteem, insofar as it so affects a man that he thinks more highly of himself than is just." Oddly to the modern mind, Spinoza argues, "There is no opposite of this affect. For no one, out of hate, thinks less highly of himself than is just." But today's many self-help psychologies that insist on self-love and self-esteem as a precondition for a happy and effective life assume that failures of self-love are pervasive. Spinoza's argument actually depends on a rather special point: that if you think you cannot do something, you *therefore* cannot do it, certainly you will not try, and (however self-defeating) you therefore cannot be underestimating your abilities, for your estimate and your abilities are conceptually (in this negative direction) linked. Spinoza goes on to acknowledge a number of ways in which a person can think less highly of himself than is just and describes the relevant affect as "despondency" ("as Pride is born of Self-esteem, so Despondency is born of Humility," which is a form of sadness [Definition XXIX, Exp.]). Whatever the relation of pride and humility (is humility a virtue or simply an opposing error of judgment?) and of pride and shame (there are grounds for regarding them as true emotional, if not moral, opposites), we should not too quickly follow Spinoza in building error into our definition of pride. As a matter of modern usage, while pride may sometimes indeed be *false* and *overweening,* that we speak of *wounded* pride in connection with various forms of humiliation shows pride can also be a matter of dignity and self-respect. Similarly, Adam Smith remarks in his *The Theory of Moral Sentiments:* "We frequently say of a man that he is too proud, or that he has too much noble pride, ever to suffer himself to do a mean thing" (1969 [1759]: 416). Spinoza himself tells us that "Self-esteem [sometimes the Latin is translated as "self-satisfaction," sometimes "self-approval," and is understood by many as what they mean by "pride"] is a Joy born of the fact that a man considers himself and his own power of acting" (Definition XXV). He opposes such self-esteem to humility and tells us it "is really the highest thing we can hope for," so far as it arises from reason (*Ethics* IV, P52 Schol.). But that is not the point I wish to pursue here. I think we can now begin to see how an error of judgment can start looking like a sin in a God-centered world—at least when the error involves taking undeserved credit.

Spinoza picks up on Gregory the Great's vision of pride as bias in one's own favor, a tyranny of bad judgment: "it comes about that all the good things of others become displeasing to him, and the things he has done himself, even when they are mistaken, alone please him . . . he favours himself in his thought; and when he thinks he surpasses others in all things, he walks with himself along the broad spaces of his thought and silently utters his own praises" (*Moralia,* XXIV, 48, quoted in Payne 1960, 72–73). One might go further and think whatever praises are in fact due are due elsewhere, that when credit is traced to its ultimate source, pride in oneself is always misplaced.

RESPONSIBILITY

One might think that responsibility should be a condition of pride—that, for example, pride should be for virtue and achievements rather than natural endowment and gifts. Responsibility in turn might be seen as conditioned on causal role or individual choice. (The relevant conditions depend on the various purposes one might have in allocating responsibility; and for certain purposes, e.g., legal ones, getting the conditions precisely right might be extremely important [Hart 1968].) But despite the many possible senses of "responsibility," responsibility is *not* a condition of pride. While there are conceptual constraints of other sorts on pride, there is no *conceptual* error in claiming to be proud where one cannot claim responsibility (whether one is proud of the 49ers, one's cultural heritage, one's parents, or one's height). If responsibility were a condition of pride, a politics of pride in group identity, where the characteristic defining group identity (whether skin color or sexual preference, ethnic or national origin) was not itself something deliberately chosen, would make no sense. The point of claiming such pride is different (and we shall return to it shortly), but it is worth lingering a moment longer on the temptation to condition pride on responsibility.

It might seem that, so far as group membership is dependent on factors outside of one's control, group membership cannot provide appropriate grounds for pride or, for that matter, for shame. One no more chooses one's family (or, more precisely, one's biological parents) than one chooses to be unattractive or unintelligent. Shame would seem as misplaced in the one case as in the others. But then, one typically does not become attractive or intelligent by one's choice and efforts; such advantages are typically gifts rather than achievements. So is pride appropriate in relation to such advantages? Certainly many are in fact proud of their looks or their intelligence. While such pride is not conceptually misplaced (responsibility is not, as a matter of language, a condition of pride), insofar as proper pride is thought to depend on achievements rather than gifts, it is perhaps morally misplaced. This may be part of the intuition of those who think of God as the author of our gifts, and so of individual pride in gifts as misappropriation of credit (if not sin). Leaving God aside, supposing one thinks proper pride must be limited to achievements rather than gifts (just as proper shame must be limited to faults rather than natural disadvantages or handicaps), the problem becomes most pointed when one asks whether perhaps *everything* is not a gift. After all, traced far enough, even apparent achievements depend on conditions outside one's control.

The notion of "moral" appropriateness here connects with Kant's emphasis on the distinction between moral characteristics and natural characteristics. One's moral identity, for Kant, depends on factors outside the natural order. Appeal to the noumenal realm may take one beyond what empirically makes sense, but Kant's point connects with the ordinary intuition that there are some aspects of our character for which we are responsible (whether we try to work hard or are simply lazy, what we try to do with our intelligence, etc.) and there are others that are not subject to our will, but are simply (say biologically) given, and so not appropriate grounds for moral judgment. But then, will there not always be some empirical explanation for why some are lazy, why some try to do good with their intelligence, and so on? If one traces the causal chains far enough, won't we always come to factors outside the sphere of the individual will? One comes to doubt the line that depends on appeal to the individual (nonempirical) will. Kant's desire to isolate the sphere of the moral, marking it off as a sphere of freedom and autonomy, where moral worth is a matter of virtue rather than natural endowment or talents viewed as gifts, may lead to a contracting self, a self with ultimately no content at all (Nagel 1979c). Certainly that is the result if everything ultimately is a gift. One writer, Arnold Isenberg (1980 [1949]), sees the difficulty but tries to differentiate shame and pride, regarding pride as widely appropriate and shame as widely inappropriate, because he thinks shame does no good—it just adds misery to misery, and the reflexive misery is avoidable. But the pleasantness of an experience does not itself make that experience well grounded, and even misery can sometimes do some good (the spurrings of painful conscience may redirect just as bitter medicine may cure). Whatever the savings in individual misery, a society of the shameless is not highly to be desired.

While responsibility is not a condition of pride, something like "closeness to self" is. Seen as "close enough to ourselves," however that notion is unpacked, we can be proud or, equally, ashamed of our family or our country: they are a part of who one is and, even if one has not chosen them, one cannot wholly dissociate from them. That shame arguably should not extend to certain things outside our control—some things that are not our fault, such as physical limitations, handicaps, or deformities—is more a matter of what we regard as our "essential" self and what counts as valuable than of responsibility or control or the will (though some, like Kant, would shrink the essential self to a transcendent will). What should be regarded as essential and what as valuable are obviously contestable. That the chain of credit, "closeness to self" in Hume's phrase, is open to question in cases of group pride, such as that of the 49ers fans, opens the way to the insight that the chain of credit is in fact *always* open to question, even in cases of individual pride. The world in which individual pride was inevitably a sin took certain views of essential identity and of value as obvious. The politics of group pride seeks to question such views.

VALUE

The political value of pride in identity politics partly derives from the internal place of values within pride. (When O. J. Simpson allowed as how he was "not proud" of his wife abuse, he was using "pride" to mark his choice of values, in this case to show his acceptance of community values.) On all accounts, the source of pride must be seen as an achievement or an advantage; pride involves positive valuation. Like "closeness to self," that is a conceptual condition.

The point of pride as a member of a group, the pride of belonging, depends on some distinctive virtue of the group, on its perceived value. Claiming group membership is a way of claiming the associated value for oneself. This reflects the conceptual dependence of pride on positive valuation. (On Hume's excessively mechanical account, lacking the belief in value, one would lack the double association needed to produce pride. Rather, I would say, lacking the needed belief, whatever was produced would not be considered pride [Foot 1978 (1958–59)].) That is, group pride, the pride of membership or belonging, like the pride of ownership, depends on value—the subject, like the owned object, is seen as valuable. The twist in recent identity politics is in the seeing of value.

Identity politics involves transvaluation, a reversal of received values. A previously despised property comes to be seen as valuable: "Black is Beautiful." Earlier majority values or norms are rejected as mistaken, biased, blind. A previous source of shame becomes a source of pride. The point is *not* that one should not be ashamed of one's skin color (for example) because one cannot help it, did not choose it, and so is not responsible. The point rather is that one should not be ashamed of one's skin color because there is nothing wrong with it in the first place.

One response is to see this as the politics of "sour grapes"—what "everyone knows" is valuable is rejected in self-defense against the shame of exclusion, of failure by the received standards. But if all that can be said in favor of a received standard is that "everyone knows" it is correct, that in itself provides grounds for suspicion. First there is the general bias in one's own favor that Spinoza warns of in connection with pride. The favored majority, the so-called "everyone," must beware of such self-reinforcing bias. Then there are more particular psychological tendencies to distortion, some especially prominent in recent local rivalries and nationalistic struggles. Issues of national identity are especially pressing in the many parts of the world where linguistic, religious, historical, and other divisions have taken on importance, sometimes leading to civil war. Such accentuation of small differences in the midst of overwhelming commonalities may be an inherent feature of human psychology, described by Freud under the heading of "the narcissism of minor differences." (The relation of such narcissism to identity formation and to aggression we will return to.) What differences are taken to matter and the value that is attached to the privileged position may very much depend on an individual's own situational circumstances and the accidents of history. Adjusting one's preferences to suit one's possibilities, making a virtue out of necessity (Elster 1983, 110), is as much a temptation for majorities as for minorities. Values are not to be reduced to uncriticized preferences. Better arguments, more grounded in human nature and human needs, must be provided if an accusation of "sour grapes" is to stick. And universal claims to dignity and justice weigh against it.

How is one to argue that one condition is better than another, that it ought to be preferred (even if it cannot be chosen, it is given or a "gift")? One should note first of all that such an argument does not by itself give grounds for preferential treatment. Indeed, preferential treatment, if any, might be better directed toward the socially disfavored condition. For example, it is plausible to suppose that it is almost always better to be intelligent than unintelligent (though during Red Guard purges of the intelligentsia and other such social upheavals, intelligence may come to have certain obvious disadvantages). But for educational purposes, it is arguable that a society that values equality should devote special resources to help the intellectually less gifted. What counts as a "special need" or, in the older terminology, a "handicap"? To say someone is "handicapped" is to say they are at a disadvantage. But disability is always relative to some purpose, and the value or disvalue of a disability must depend on the value, including the social usefulness, of the relevant power. Say one's powers of visual discrimination are limited, e.g., one is color-blind. Or suppose one lacks a power of discrimination that only a few in fact possess (tea or wine tasters or perfume sniffers, persons of fine palate and olfactory discrimination): the few can regularly note differences that those less empowered cannot, but are *most* of us thus handicapped? Is handicap necessarily a minority condition, so the norm is statistical? Is handicap necessarily a limitation of a socially important power, so lacking extraordinary powers is no handicap? Or is the value of a norm sometimes independent of the width of distribution and even of general social attitudes?

Thinking about deafness for a moment may help bring out the issues. The play (and movie) *Children of a Lesser God* makes an eloquent case for the beauty and power of signing as used by the deaf. Using sign language, one can even make points one cannot make or not make so forcefully as in, say, spoken English (the play illustrates this when "veal" on a menu is explained by poignantly combining the signs for "cow" and "baby").

While sign language is obviously different from oral speech, it nonetheless constitutes a fully structured language that can facilitate thought and interaction; and the insistence that deaf people leave it aside and learn to speak, an insistence that prevailed in institutions for the education of the deaf for a long period starting in the late nineteenth century, can be seen as a benighted prejudice (Sacks 1990). It is nonetheless arguable that whatever the power and beauty of sign language as a language, whatever its intellectual and social usefulness, not hearing remains in any case a loss—and not just because the majority hear. In a majority deaf society, there might be a common language used by all (as in the Martha's Vineyard community discussed by Sacks [32–35]), and more accommodations might be made, but still most would be missing something, whether the warning noises of an approaching vehicle or the singing of birds. There are losses in not hearing, exclusions from aspects of life. In certain social conditions the losses might be less felt, but that does not make them any the less losses. (Though one must wonder whether if *no one* had the ability, it could still appear a loss. It would surely be odd for any human to experience the inability to fly as a "loss," as a handicap. But is that simply because it is odd for humans to compare themselves to birds rather than other humans?) None of this, again, is an argument against "Deaf Pride" as a political movement. That one might rather not be deaf is no reason to fail to respect the deaf, or to discriminate against them, or to fail to make accommodations. (Sacks writes: "The deaf do not regard themselves as handicapped, but as a linguistic and cultural minority" [138 n.147; 151].) Some disadvantages may be only socially imposed, and then the language of "handicap" or "special needs" may be inappropriate, but both socially imposed and natural disadvantages may often be ameliorated. In any case, the value claimed in all the movements that call for pride may ultimately be a matter of equal human dignity and respect and so may not turn on the difference between the chosen and the given or the socially useful and socially disfavored.

Another response is to think that rather than transvaluing an identity category, one ought to question the divisions and classifications themselves. Sometimes this is a matter of pointing out the predominance of gray. Sexual preferences and sexual activities allow for all degrees of exclusivity and combination. The exclusive heterosexual, in deed and fantasy, may be as rare as the exclusive homosexual. And even who counts as "black" is, despite what might appear a simple visual criterion, by no means always obvious. Lawrence Wright, in a *New Yorker* article entitled "One Drop of Blood," brings out how troubled the category is, in an interbreeding society, even for purposes of census taking (especially when tied to the distribution of social benefits). This is before issues of cultural and self-identification are introduced to complicate matters—whether a black child adopted and brought up by white parents in a white neighborhood is somehow thereby denied the blackness conferred by "black culture." An interracial society leads to multiracial individuals. But there are other problems with the socially constructed categories of invidious discrimination than being sure who fits in them. The problem is not just the existence of degrees of gray; some would reject the categories even in the supposedly clear cases.

Foucault and some of his followers urge that a truly radical politics should emphasize resistance rather than liberation. Liberation, it is charged, involves accepting the categories of the powers that be, even when liberation insists on transvaluation (that is, asserting the positive value of the denigrated, marginalized category). Resistance questions and rejects those categories. Thus David Halperin (1995) writes:

> The most radical reversal of homophobic discourses consists not in asserting, with the Gay Liberation Front of 1968, that "gay is good" (on the analogy with "black is beautiful") but in assuming and empowering a marginal positionality—not in rehabilitating an already demarcated, if devalued, identity but in taking advantage of the purely oppositional location homosexuality has been made to occupy. (61)

The rejection of categories in this sort of "queer" politics, a politics of positionality (of opposition, contrast, resistance) rather than identity, obscures (deliberately) the identity of the group being defended. That is, it objects to identity politics by attacking the terms of identity:

> To shift the position of "the homosexual" from that of object to subject
> is therefore to make available to lesbians and gay men a new kind of
> sexual identity, one characterized by its lack of a clear definitional
> content. The homosexual subject can now claim an identity without
> an essence. (61)

But the lack of a clear essence makes the alternative politics of positionality rather unclear. In Halperin's version, "queer" politics (vs. "gay" politics) includes all sexually marginalized individuals: "anyone who is or who feels marginalized because of her or his sexual practices: it could include some married couples without children, for example, or even (who knows?) some married couples *with* children." All that unites the group is its felt marginalization in relation to social norms—a definition that seems rather too broad for an organized group politics. (Put differently, the "subject position" emphasized is perhaps too subjective, however true it may be that we are *all* gay, all women, all black, for we are all marginalized, denigrated, despised, under some heading or other some of the time.) Halperin acknowledges (64) that the vast range of sexual outlaws (including sadomasochists, fetishists, pederasts) can have diverse and divergent interests. There is another paradox here in a politics of positionality: aside from the fact that we are all somehow, in some aspect, outside the accepted norms, the supposed de-essentialized subject position requires that one feel marginalized in terms of a norm that is the norm of society or of "the others." Therefore, those norms and their understanding—objectification—reenters the picture: one's self-identity for oppositional purposes must depend on categories and norms provided from outside (at least if it is to count as "resistance" to those categories and norms), just as identity politics depends on those categories and norms before it undertakes its work of transvaluing them. Self-identification through desire may remain the best defense: "De-gaying gayness can only fortify homophobic oppression; it accomplishes in its own way the principal aim of homophobia: the elimination of gays. The consequence of self-erasure is . . . self-erasure. Even a provisional acceptance of the very categories elaborated by dominant identitarian regimes might more effectively undermine those forces than a simple disappearing act" (Bersani 1995, 5).

The appealing inclusiveness of "queer" rather than "lesbian and gay" politics becomes especially problematical when one considers the history of the extension and enforcement of rights as it has developed in the United States through legal protections for particular classifications of persons. How flexible can such legal categories be and where do they (must they) come from? Gays and lesbians have sought antidiscrimination laws and social recognition of our intimate associations. But no one that I know of has seriously proposed civil rights legislation ensuring nondiscrimination in employment and housing for sadomasochists (of course both homosexual and heterosexual). Why does that seem such an unpromising political agenda? (The notion of ensuring pedophiles the right to marry the boys they love raises further, special difficulties.) Must potential employers inquire about their employees' private sexual preferences in order to avoid unknowingly discriminating against them? (Is unknowing discrimination discrimination?) I will return to problems of "visibility" in a moment. Morris Kaplan (1997), in a recent book on *Sexual Justice,* sensibly notes, "Adding 'lesbian' and 'gay' to 'heterosexual' in the repertoire of acceptable identities in our society would be a real but limited accomplishment in the struggle for full equality" (144). Anything short of equal treatment for all is rightly condemned as "limited," but civil rights for blacks were similarly "limited." The practices of discrimination, however, make some "limited" advances more pressing than others. (Are sadomasochists regularly discriminated against in employment and housing? Who would know?)

Whose oppression matters most? Here visibility plays a role, but it is multi-faced. The possibility of invisibility can provide protection, protection that the law may deny. But the fact that one can hide one's sexual preferences, keep them private, is small consolation to those who regard those preferences as an important part of who they are, a part they do not wish to be obliged to conceal (especially given that there are advantages in being identifiable to those others who happen to share one's preferences). And of course, another side of the possibility of concealment, of passing, is the possibility of mistaken identification, of misidentification. Suppose someone was mistakenly identified as a member of a currently protected category (say of religion or race, say an Episcopalian was mistaken for a Catholic, or a very tan individual for an African American) by a potential employer or landlord and improperly discriminated against on the basis of that mistaken identification? Surely there is an intention to improperly discriminate. Would the victim have standing to sue under the statutes (given that he or she was not in fact a member of the protected category)? But then, in a world where sexual orientation was given specific protection, could anyone self-declare and then obtain legal redress? Transvestites are widely and mistakenly believed to all be homosexuals. Would a heterosexual transvestite mistakenly discriminated against as a homosexual have standing to sue under civil rights laws that protected gays but not transvestites? Again one feels the push toward the universal. Who decides who is in what category? It is worth noting that there is at the moment a movement afoot among some Orthodox Jewish rabbis to denounce certain branches of Judaism, Conservative and Reform, as not-Jewish. Again, who decides? Is it the discriminators? The issue of attempted discrimination raises the question of whether the wrong is the mistake or the treating of *anyone* as though they were a second-class citizen, mistaken identification or correct notwithstanding. The question is whether antidiscrimination legislation can ultimately be understood as protecting individuals in certain categories, or all citizens. The rationale for such legislation turns on equal treatment for all, but the protections have had to be hard won in political contests, one despised category at a time.

Kaplan, like Halperin, may wish to protect all marginalized sexual outlaws, but in practice his argument has a narrower focus when he goes beyond those who would ask for no more than mere decriminalization of gay and lesbian sexual activity. Kaplan seeks specifically to add gays and lesbians to other protected categories (racial, religious, and ethnic groups, women, the physically and mentally handicapped, workers aged forty and older) for the purposes of protection against discrimination in employment, education, and housing. He argues: "The underlying rationale of the anti-discrimination provisions of civil rights legislation is the recognition that formal legal equality is inadequate to provide for equal citizenship under conditions of popular hostility and pervasive social inequality. It is precisely the intensity and extent of the prejudice against homosexuality that justifies the claims of lesbian and gay citizens to protection against discrimination" (43). And here he must have in mind extended histories of mistreatment, which have of course depended on identification by others, the mistreaters. Kaplan insists that "the definition of protected classes does not construct personal or political identities but rather forbids employers, landlords, and other decision makers from using such categories as race, religion, or sex to *impose* an invidious identity on a person rather than treating her in terms of her individual character and qualities" (45). He is certainly right about the point of such legislation. But if it is to be effectively enforced, it must specify the protected categories in a way that enables people to identify themselves under them for purposes of protection. And that risks the sort of rigidity and fixity that Kaplan wishes to avoid. I do not see how the law, for its purposes, which are indeed important, can avoid it. Moreover, the characteristics that are most significant, and so the ones most likely to be taken to be defining, are the very ones that decision makers (the discriminators and mistreaters) might be feared to improperly use—so perhaps it is the socially constructed categories, whatever the truth may be about essential characteristics, that become the most relevant ones. (As Hannah Arendt insisted: "If one is attacked as a Jew one must defend oneself as a Jew" [Kaplan 160].) Again, it is a history of popular hostility that makes something more than formal legal equality necessary.

Kaplan and Halperin are right to see the complexity, variety, and malleability of sexual desire. What follows for politics? Kaplan writes, "A politics based on fixed identities may foreclose the openness to contestation and negotiation required by justice" (112). That is surely a risk, but perhaps progress only gets made one step at a time. So far as Kaplan argues for antidiscrimination law, the groups to be protected must be defined in ways that make their members identifiable. A politics of legal reform must require the very "fixed identities" Kaplan seems to wish to deny. Of course they need not be fixed forever, or even for a lifetime, but they must be fixed for purposes of adjudication once one emerges from behind Rawls's veil of ignorance into a world where some are identified (by others, if not themselves) as gay or lesbian and discriminated against on that basis.

It is difficult to see *what* one does differently when resisting a category rather than liberating or expressing an aspect of self seen under that category. And *who* one does it with is politically problematic. Is "queer" politics supposed to unite all who are non-mainstream sexually? The "we" here might include all sorts of folks who fit very uncomfortably with each other. Not that all gay folks are comfortable together. Our political views (like our sexual activities) cover as wide a spectrum as those of heterosexual folks. It is very difficult to see heterosexuals as a group with homogenized interests. The only reason it is easier for those who march under the banner of gay pride to be so seen is that they do have one important interest in common: sexual liberation and nondiscrimination on the basis of orientation; but they may not feel that way about all aspects of sexual expression ("sexual orientation" is doubtless the way the relevant category would be described for purposes of legislation, but what exactly would it cover?). Similarly, there are all sorts of political and social diversity among blacks, though all might agree that skin color is no proper ground for shame or discrimination. Political and social coalition among *all* racial and ethnic minorities has had a hard history, even if all might agree that skin color, place of origin, and cultural background are no proper grounds for shame or discrimination. It also might become unclear who the opposed "majority" is.

Of course there are problems with traditional identity politics, some stemming from the admitted grayness of categories. The problems of inclusion may be more serious than those raised by the 49er Faithful. What and who is *in* the category? Even a category such as race, which might appear straightforwardly biological, can be problematical; as noted, skin color may provide no sure index of anything and we may all in the end be multiracial. And again, gay behavior, desires, inclinations, and attitudes can all vary in more ways than marked even by Kinsey's categories (exclusive, occasional, etc.), and that before account is taken of the unconscious. Who are "we"? And if we think of the gay-identified as excluding the repressed or closeted homosexual, we may be focusing too much on the voluntaristic aspects of identification (like 49ers fans), where identification is self-identification. But where the political problem may arise from the identification, and stigmatization, by others, perhaps a politically relevant notion of identification must be broader (even if it risks objectification of individuals and reification of the categories of the others—after all, the struggle is with or against those very others). Even when one is not asked, and does not tell, one may be discriminated against, one's life restricted.

So far as the politics of marginal positionalities is aimed at denying privileged valuations of *either* side of dichotomies, the message may ultimately be the same as "Black is Beautiful" or "Gay is Good" or "Deaf Power." For the point, typically, is not to say black is better than white, or gay is better than straight, or deaf is better than hearing, but simply to deny the denigration of the minority position. The point is to demand political equality, equal concern, and respect.

THE NARCISSISM
OF MINOR DIFFERENCES

Freud observes that groups of individuals characteristically direct their greatest hostility toward those who, from a wider perspective, are in fact most similar to them. What is the source of this "narcissism of minor differences"? Is it an interesting but accidental sociological fact? Or is it somehow rooted in features of human psychology and the conditions for identity formation; does it bespeak a natural polarity in thought?

Freud introduces the concept in his discussion of "The Taboo of Virginity" (1918 [1917]). There the topic is male hostility to and fear of women, and is complicated by the castration complex, but Freud is already prepared to take a point about individual separation and isolation ("that it is precisely the minor differences in people who are otherwise alike that form the basis of feelings of strangeness and hostility between them" [199]) and see in it "the hostility which in every human relation we see fighting successfully against feelings of fellowship and overpowering the commandment that all men should love one another" (199). When he turns to *Group Psychology* a few years later, he returns to the idea, there tying it to wider ambivalences as well as to narcissism (1921, 101). He develops the idea most fully in *Civilization and Its Discontents* where he discusses it in terms of aggression, which in this form serves "cohesion between the members of the community" against outsiders (1930 [1929], chap. 5, esp. 114). It is this final link, to what Freud regards as instinctual aggression, that may help clarify what may also be understood as a conceptual condition of identity formation. It makes conflict our normal state—and if pride is a sin, this (rather than intellectual error, even motivated intellectual error) may be its origin.

There is an old logical principle that holds "all determination is negation" (*Omnis determinatio est negatio*), and both individuals and communities often define themselves by opposition, by contrast, that is, in terms of what they reject. Stuart Hampshire (1996) elaborates the point in relation to incompatible conceptions of the good:

> Most influential conceptions of the good have defined themselves as rejections of their rivals: for instance, some of the ideals of monasticism were a rejection of the splendors and hierarchies of the Church, and this rejection was the original sense and purpose of the monastic ideal. Some forms of fundamentalism, both Christian and others, define themselves as a principled rejection of secular, liberal, and permissive moralities. Fundamentalism is the negation of any deviance in moral opinion, and of the very notion of opinion in ethics. (13)

People are who they are at least partly (and sometimes self-consciously) in terms of what they are not. The logical point is developed in Hegel and in F. H. Bradley. It is taken even further along a metaphysical dimension by Spinoza. As Hampshire puts Spinoza's vision: "Men and women are naturally driven to resist any external force that tends to repress their typical activities or to limit their freedom. . . It is a natural necessity for each distinct entity to try to preserve its distinctiveness for as long as it can, and for this reason conflicts are at all times to be expected in the history of individuals, of social groups, and of nations, as their paths intersect" (15).

In psychoanalytical terms, the individual ego (and more specifically, the ego-ideal) is formed out of identifications and introjections, the other side of which is the rejection—typically a violent spitting out—of those characteristics one does not wish to incorporate. "At the very beginning, it seems, the external world, objects, and what is hated are identical. If later on an object turns out to be a source of pleasure, it is loved, but it is also incorporated into the ego" (Freud 1915, 136). As Norman O. Brown (1966) puts it, "The distinction between self and not-self is made by the childish decision to claim all that the ego likes as 'mine,' and to repudiate all that the ego dislikes as 'not-mine'" (142). The move from individual to group identity is explored in Freud's *Group Psychology and the Analysis of the Ego* (1921c), where his central concern is with groups, such as churches and armies, characterized by identification with a leader. The important role of unconscious mechanisms of identification via incorporation must complicate the too-simple voluntaristic picture of identity formation we started by considering in relation to the 49ers and other self-selecting groups of sports fans. As the existence of unconscious mechanisms should make clear, socially imposed identities are not the only alternative to consciously chosen identities. With unconscious mechanisms, ambivalence and aggression come to the fore. Others reject us, we reject others, and we project out "bad" and undesired aspects of ourselves while at the same time introjecting the desirable aspects of others.

Belonging to a group is tied to rejection of outsiders. Freud writes, "a religion, even if it calls itself the religion of love, must be hard and unloving to those who do not belong to it. Fundamentally indeed every religion is in this same way a religion of love for all those whom it embraces; while cruelty and intolerance toward those who do not belong to it are natural to every religion" (1921, 98). One might think that toleration and the embracing of diversity should provide a ready alternative, but history suggests vast impediments to such an alternative, and psychoanalysis sees aggression in the very mechanisms that serve to create a distinctive self or group. Freud's skepticism about demands to "love thy neighbour" and even "thine enemies" is tied to his belief in fundamental instincts of aggression (1930 [1929], chap. 5). The sources of division and ambivalence run deep, perhaps deeper even than any putative aggressive instincts. All determination is negation. An embraced identity entails a rejected identity. Even the very languages that help define the identity of certain individuals and communities (not all Frenchmen need live in France) isolate and separate at the very time they unite (the story of Quebec is but one of many, very many, examples [see Ignatieff (1993) for more]). The ambiguity that some see in pride (arrogance vs. self-respect) may have behind it a deeper ambiguity in self-love and in identity itself (rejection and isolation vs. affirmation and community).

The ambiguities and ambivalences inevitably play themselves out in identity politics as well. Identity politics is by its nature divisive: it separates and distinguishes—though of course the distinctive categories are typically provided by those who would discriminate against the minority, and the transvaluation of values is most often a form of (legitimate) self-defense. In narcissism, one rejects. In self-defense, one has been rejected. It is not enough to dismiss the imposed identities as false. New positive identities must be internalized and must be recognized. A universal identity and equality based on universal rights may be the ultimate aim, but the political question is how to get there from here. (And even a universal identity may have a price—one's distinctive ethnic, or religious, or sexual, or other identity may languish unacknowledged.)

When minorities engage in identity politics, asking for themselves what society should accord to all—dignity and respect and the equal protection of the laws—can they speak for all? When we gays and lesbians ask for antidiscrimination laws and social recognition of our intimate associations, who are "we"? Kaplan tells us that Eve Kosofsky Sedgwick "marks a vacillation, within both homophobic and emancipatory discourses, between 'minoritizing' views of homosexuality that define a distinct group with a common identity and 'universalizing' views that link homosexuality to tendencies shared by all human beings" (160). That tension is pervasive. Again I ask, who are "we"? Perhaps like the non-Jewish Danish king who put on a Star of David when the Nazis decreed all Jews must wear the star, the better to single them out for persecution, we should all be Jews in a world of anti-Semitism. But how do we get to a world where we are all in this together, where no one is oppressed?

Who are "we" for purposes of political organization and activism, for purposes of demanding nondiscrimination, and so on? In a sense, of course, "we" is everyone, every citizen entitled to equal concern and respect, and equal treatment under the law. But for purposes of the law, without denying or weakening the claims of anyone else, the adherents of gay pride can insist that experiencing same-sex desire or engaging in certain sexual practices with members of the same sex is no ground for invidious treatment, for discrimination in housing, education, or job opportunities. Perhaps one wants to say the same for other sexual minorities (and other nonsexual minorities as well). But so long as discrimination law singles out special categories for protection, one must be precise. There is not much to be gained by denying the reality of the very categories under which one is asking protection. If equal treatment for all is not enough to protect gays and lesbians, and we need to ask for specific protection, why should we be surprised if other sexual minorities need to do the same? Marginalized groups might wish to band together, but "queer" identity by itself may not do what is required.

SELF-RESPECT AND SELF-ESTEEM

The absence of sinful pride is called humility or modesty, but these apparent virtues hide their own faults and failings. Humility can give way to servility and obsequiousness—an exaggerated enhancement of the other's and a slavish devaluation of one's own worth. Modesty can lead to extremes of self-effacement, denials of one's existence and value that threaten social withdrawal or personal extinction. Poised somewhere between sinful vanity and self-destructive submissiveness is a golden mean of self-esteem appropriate to the human condition. Straying too far from it in either direction leads to active evil or passive victimization. (Lyman 135)

Aristotle's "proud" man is supposed to be a mean between the foolishly vain and the unduly humble (*Nicomachean Ethics,* 1123b–25a). (I am here following those translators who take *megalopsychia*—literally "greatness of soul"—to mean "pride." Others translate it as "magnanimity" and others still as "high-mindedness." It is the virtue "concerned with honour on the grand scale" and seems to essentially involve an ideal of pride and confident self-respect.) While the proud man's self-evaluation is supposed to be accurate (he "thinks himself worthy of great things, being worthy of them . . . he claims what is in accordance with his merits" [1123b]), and so his pride is a virtue ("Pride, then, seems to be a sort of crown of the excellences" [1124a]), Aristotle's portrait of aristocratic disdain and self-sufficiency makes him sound as though he suffers from what the later Christians regarded as the sin of pride. Aristotle's ideal great-spirited man has a lofty detachment from particular goods. He cares most for honor, yet little even for that: "at honours that are great and conferred by good men he will be moderately pleased . . . for there can be no honour that is worthy of perfect excellence" (1124a); and tends to have detachment and disdain for the world in general ("honour from casual people and on trifling grounds he will utterly despise" [1124a] and "the proud man despises justly" [1124b] and "he is free of speech because he is contemptuous" [1124b]). He strives, all in all, for "a character that suffices to itself" (1125a).

Aristotle's proud man "is the sort of man to confer benefits, but he is ashamed of receiving them; for the one is the mark of a superior, the other of an inferior" (1124b). Even today, individuals who are described as "fiercely proud" are typically being singled out as especially independent. Some find it humiliating to be indebted, especially deeply indebted. Even a gift can humiliate. This can be understood broadly in terms of a general need to repay or reciprocate in human life: a whole theory of punishment flourishes under the heading of "retribution." Insults must be repaid, so must gifts—all are debts and create a burden. There are standards of reciprocity in human relations that can be felt as burdensome. (Some of the complexities here are nicely delineated by William Miller 1993.) Of course, not accepting help (like, more obviously, not helping) can be a kind of aggression. The pride connected with independence and freedom from indebtedness can also be understood in terms of dependence (a central concern of Hegel) and power (a central concern of Nietzsche—who of course looked beyond virtue and sin). (See Neu 1996 on the unease of dependence.)

Some would distinguish between pride the sin and pride the emotion in terms of the former being a general character trait, though a person with the self-satisfied character trait might be especially liable to experience the corresponding emotion on a variety of occasions (as in Ryle's dispositional analysis of character traits such as vanity [1949, 85ff.]). As a matter of motivation, pride is expansive and goes with a tendency to display and show off (while shame is of course tied to a desire to hide, to disappear and become invisible). It is arguable that, even as a character trait, pride may not be a sin, or at least no longer a sin. Lyman suggests narcissism and pride are now a psychic necessity because of the need for individual strength in "the modern lonely age":

> The pattern of parental overestimation and excessive indulgence helps establish the psychic institution that must replace the now defunct social institutions of human conservation. Emancipation of the individual requires him to abandon his dependence on social security in favor of a hardly developed psychic self-sufficiency. The personal character appropriate to this liberating social structure is one in which pride must hold an important place. Less a sin than a necessity in the modern lonely age, pride is absolved from much of its guilt as the individual is freed from most of his constraints. (157)

The *sinful* character trait then might be equated to a kind of arrogance, as Solomon Schimmel puts it, "exaggerating our worth and power, and feeling superior to others" (1992, 29). We are back to Spinoza's understanding of pride as bias in favor of oneself and excessive self-esteem. On the other hand, Gabriele Taylor distinguishes the sin and the passion in terms of the sin involving a character trait where one's worth is taken for granted, and so one's high expectations may make particular occasions of pride the passion become relatively rare (1980, 394ff.; 1985, 36ff.). This may, like Aristotle, take the error out of the attitude. So, as sin, does the character trait necessarily involve error or not? Is a person with the character trait more or less likely to experience particular occasions of pride the emotion? Such occasions are based on particular reasons (one is "proud of this" or "because of that"). The generalized character trait of pride may need no reasons. But then "taking one's worth for granted" may be a matter of having a due regard for one's rights, may amount to self-respect. Self-respect also needs no reasons— in which case pride the character trait does *not* obviously amount to a sin, need not amount to presumptuous arrogance or anything more than self-assurance, or indeed, simple dignity.

There may be a contrast between self-esteem and self-respect that is helpful here. The pleasure that Hume discerns in pride is ultimately a form of self-approval (Davidson 1980 [1976]; Neu 1977). But self-approval is ambiguous in a way that may help explain the dual attitudes, sin to be avoided and virtue to be sought, toward pride itself (whether regarded as a character trait or a passion). We can understand the ambiguity in terms of certain contrasts between self-esteem and self-respect. Self-respect, having to do with one's rights and dignity as a person, may be noncomparative. Self-esteem, having to do with one's merits and self-valuation, may depend on the standards of value in one's society and how one compares with other members of that society. Put crudely, of self-respect one cannot have too much, of self-esteem one obviously can. Put more precisely, the idea of too much self-respect is at best problematic, while that of too much self-esteem, like those of either too little self-respect or too little self-esteem, poses no difficulty. (See

David Sachs [1981]. Cf. Rousseau's contrast of *amour de soi,* which is supposed to be natural, noncomparative, and tied to self-preservation, and *amour propre,* which is supposed to be social, comparative, and other-directed; see *Discourse on the Origin of Inequality* [1950 (1755)] and *Emile,* Book IV [1969 (1762)].) Thus a person might have low self-esteem and yet have self-respect. As Sachs puts it, "it could be categorically true of a person both that he takes no pride in anything whatever, and yet that he has his pride" (350).

So far as pride is a matter of self-respect, one must have a certain amount. This point is developed by Thomas Hill (1991 [1973]) who interprets certain forms of objectionable servility as resulting from misunderstanding one's moral rights or placing a comparatively low value on them, a lack of a certain type of self-respect, a respect that is owed one as a person, independently of special merits. That is, self-respect is a matter of appreciating one's equal moral rights as a person and (also perhaps) of living by one's own personal standards—not an issue of merits. Respect for one's merits, or esteem, is to be distinguished from respect for one's rights. Such a distinction helps clarify Edith Sitwell's attitude toward pride. While insisting it should not be confused with silly vanity or foolish obstinacy, Edith Sitwell declared: "Pride has always been one of my favourite virtues" (1962, 15). She recognizes that pride "may be a form of love" (17), and she refers to "ugly humility" (19) and notes that "A proper pride is a necessity to an artist" (21). She sees it as a form of self-defense needed by the original against inevitable attacks by the envious and untalented. Such self-confidence needs to be understood in relation to self-respect (something essential to all) and self-esteem (which can be greater than justified, but also has a "proper" level). Everyone needs self-respect and is, moreover, entitled to it. It is a condition of moral identity.

One of the errors of certain recently popular self-help psychologies is to suppose that increasing self-esteem is simply a matter of changing one's attitude rather than the more strenuous activity of changing one's life. So far as esteem depends on merit, a pride that simply depends on deciding one is "ok" whatever one does becomes like the sinful individual pride of old: one falls into unjustifiable self-satisfaction. Group credit too, or "bragging rights," does little to advance claims based on merit unless responsibility (as well as "nearness") can somehow be claimed. So far as group pride gives self-respect and asks for respect from others based on one's common humanity and equal moral rights, there is no sin, no error. But one should be careful of too simply tying the contrast between pride as sin and as virtue to the contrast of self-esteem and self-respect, for while self-esteem can be excessive (people can think too well of themselves), there is surely a "correct" or justified level of self-esteem, which might be quite high in some cases (even if not quite so high as in the case of Aristotle's great-souled man).

We have seen that nearness to self is necessary to distinguish pride from mere happiness or joy; that is, pride is self-enhancing. Taking credit for a valuable object expands our identity, enhances our self-esteem. So one can see how pride can be competitive, concerned as it is with ego-identity and its enhancement, and it is thus subject to envy and liable to fall into sinful arrogance. Arrogance may be the heart of (certain understandings of) pride the sin. It is the antithesis of the concern for equality in self-respect. It is the excessive self-esteem emphasized by Spinoza, a bias in favor of oneself that may seem more a general character trait than a particular emotion. If self-esteem is understood as based on perceived merits, then it is perhaps more like pride the emotion which is also based on particular reasons. Enough such pride amounts to conceit, the character trait of thinking too well of oneself (even if one has particular reasons). But self-respect needs no reasons and so is more like a generalized pride that is more like a character trait—but, again, it is then *not* obviously a sin, need not amount to presumptuous arrogance or anything more than self-assurance or dignity.

The cardinal (or chief) sins were in the beginning not necessarily mortal (or deadly) ones. Their importance attached to those temptations with special significance from a monastic point of view—which was the point of view of Evagrius of Pontus and John Cassian, the fathers of the seven cardinal sins in the fourth and fifth centuries. There is the familiar phenomenon of pride in one's humility. Cassian points out that "Pride is the most savage of all evil beasts, and the most dreadful, because it lies in wait for those who are perfect" (quoted in Payne, 68). The early lists sometimes had eight sins—sometimes, for example, distinguishing *vana gloria* (vainglory) from *superbia* (pride). The lists later came to serve penitential purposes with priests using them as a helpful aid in the examination of conscience for confession, and the distinction previously made between cardinal and deadly sins dropped away. As St. Thomas pointed out, a sin is called capital "simply because other sins frequently arise from it" (*De Malo* IX.2–5, quoted in Bloomfield, 88).

Pride's special importance among even the deadly sins Aquinas attributed to its general character which made it arguably the source of all sins insofar as it involves a turning away from God (1995 [1269], 314ff.). The specific sins each in their own way involve rebellion against the law of God, but such rebellion is the essence of pride as a general sin. In its more specific form, vainglory, it involves an inordinate desire for honor and renown, a special admiration of one's own excellences. And it was of course vanity rather than pride that became the focus of (the relatively godless) later French moralists. Vanity is especially concerned with public reputation. Pride is the sin of not knowing one's place and sticking to it. It is of course Faust's ambitious sin. Challenging God—going above your place.

Greek *hubris* (thinking oneself superior to the gods), like Christian pride (thinking oneself independent of God, self-sufficient), involves placing oneself above one's station. This is one of the features of pride that makes it peculiarly appropriate as the banner for political movements that seek to change the station of those in them—i.e., that seek a transvaluation of values. Both identity politics and a politics of marginal positionalities, whatever their views on whether God has died, deny that the social valuations and positions that denigrate certain groups and privilege others are ordained by God. Times have changed. The death of God would leave the concept of sin with little conceptual foothold. But even in a world where God is still believed to preside, an attack on social hierarchy need not be regarded as sin, for it is not an attack on God: social hierarchy is not a matter of natural law, is not God-given.

These political movements are challenging positions in the political world rather than a God-given order. And, as we have seen, on an individual level, the self-approval that is characteristic of pride may be ambiguous, and the different significances may be understood in terms of a contrast between self-esteem (which can be excessive and unjustified) and self-respect (which does not depend on invidious comparison and may be essential to human dignity). A politics of self-respect, where the self has a social identity, may not be so ungodly after all.

REFERENCES

Aquinas, St. Thomas (1995 [1269]). *On Evil,* trans. Jean Oesterle. Notre Dame, IN: University of Notre Dame Press.

Aristotle (1984). *Nicomachean Ethics,* in *The Complete Works of Aristotle,* Vol. II, ed. Jonathan Barnes. Princeton, NJ: Princeton University Press.

Bersani, Leo (1995). *Homos.* Cambridge, MA: Harvard University Press.

Bloomfield, Morton W. (1952). *The Seven Deadly Sins: An Introduction to the History of a Religious Concept, with Special Reference to Medieval English Literature.* East Lansing, MI: Michigan State College Press.

Brown, Norman O. (1966). *Love's Body.* New York: Vintage Books.

Davidson, Donald (1980 [1976]). Hume's Cognitive Theory of Pride. In *Essays on Actions and Events* (pp. 277–90). New York: Oxford University Press.

Elster, Jon (1983). Sour Grapes. In *Sour Grapes: Studies in the Subversion of Rationality* (pp. 109–140). New York: Cambridge University Press.

Fairlie, Henry (1978). Pride or Superbia. In *The Seven Deadly Sins Today* (pp. 39–58). University of Notre Dame Press.

Foot, Philippa (1978 [1958–59]). Moral Beliefs. In *Virtues and Vices* (pp. 110–31). Berkeley, CA: University of California Press.

Freud, Sigmund (1915). *Instincts and Their Vicissitudes. Standard Edition* Vol. XIV. London: The Hogarth Press.

Freud, Sigmund (1918 [1917]). *The Taboo of Virginity. Standard Edition* Vol. XI. London: The Hogarth Press.

Freud, Sigmund (1921). *Group Psychology and the Analysis of the Ego. Standard Edition* Vol. XVIII. London: The Hogarth Press.

Freud, Sigmund (1930 [1929]). *Civilization and Its Discontents. Standard Edition* Vol. XXI. London: The Hogarth Press.

Halperin, David M. (1995). *Saint Foucault: Towards a Gay Hagiography.* New York: Oxford University Press.

Hampshire, Stuart (1996). Justice Is Conflict: The Soul and the City. Tanner Lectures on Human Values, Harvard University, October 30–31, 1996. [unpublished ms]

Hart, H. L. A. (1968). Responsibility. In *Punishment and Responsibility: Essays in the Philosophy of Law* (pp. 211–30). New York: Oxford University Press.

Hill, Thomas E. Jr. (1991 [1973]). Servility and Self-Respect. In *Autonomy and Self-Respect* (pp. 4–18). Cambridge University Press.

Hume, David (1888 [1739]). *A Treatise of Human Nature* [THN], ed. L. A. Selby-Bigge. Oxford University Press.

Ignatieff, Michael (1993). *Blood and Belonging: Journeys into the New Nationalism.* New York: Farrar, Straus and Giroux.

Isenberg, Arnold (1980 [1949]). Natural Pride and Natural Shame. In A. Rorty, ed., *Explaining Emotions* (pp. 355–83). University of California Press.

Kant, Immanuel (1964 [1797]). *The Metaphysical Principles of Virtue,* trans. J. Ellington. Indianapolis: Bobbs-Merrill.

Kaplan, Morris (1997). *Sexual Justice: Democratic Citizenship and the Politics of Desire.* New York: Routledge.

Lyman, Stanford M. (1978). *The Seven Deadly Sins: Society and Evil.* New York: St. Martin's Press.

Miller, William Ian (1993). *Humiliation.* Ithaca, NY: Cornell University Press.

Nagel, Thomas (1979 [1976]). Moral Luck. In his *Mortal Questions* (pp. 24–38). New York: Cambridge University Press.

Neu, Jerome (1977). *Emotion, Thought, and Therapy.* London: Routledge & Kegan Paul and University of California Press.

Neu, Jerome (1996). *Odi et Amo:* On Hating the Ones We Love. In J. O'Neill, ed., *Freud and the Passions* (pp. 53–72). University Park, PA: Pennsylvania State University Press.

Payne, Robert (1960). *Hubris: A Study of Pride.* New York: Harper Torchbooks.

Rousseau, Jean-Jacques (1950 [1755]). *Discourse on the Origin of Inequality.* Trans. G. D. H. Cole in *The Social Contract and Discourses.* London: Dent (Everyman's Library).

Rousseau, Jean-Jacques (1969 [1762]). *Émile.* Trans. B. Foxley. London: Dent (Everyman's Library).

Ryle, Gilbert (1949). *The Concept of Mind.* London: Hutchinson & Co.

Sachs, David (1981). How to Distinguish Self-Respect from Self-Esteem. *Philosophy and Public Affairs,* 10, 346–60.

Sacks, Oliver (1990). *Seeing Voices: A Journey into the World of the Deaf.* New York: HarperPerennial.

Schimmel, Solomon (1992). *The Seven Deadly Sins: Jewish, Christian, and Classical Reflections on Human Nature.* New York: The Free Press.

Sitwell, Edith (1962). Pride. In Angus Wilson et al., *The Seven Deadly Sins* (pp. 15–22). New York: William Morrow & Co.

Smith, Adam (1969 [1759]). *The Theory of Moral Sentiments.* Indianapolis: Liberty Classics.

Spinoza (1985 [1677]) *Ethics,* in *The Collected Works of Spinoza,* Vol. I, ed. and trans. Edwin Curley. Princeton, NJ: Princeton University Press.

Taylor, Charles (1992). *The Ethics of Authenticity.* Cambridge, MA: Harvard University Press.

Taylor, Gabriele (1980). Pride. In A. Rorty, ed., *Explaining Emotions* (pp. 385–402). Berkeley, CA: University of California Press.

Taylor, Gabriele (1985). *Pride, Shame, and Guilt.* New York: Oxford University Press.

Walsh, W. H. (1970). Pride, Shame and Responsibility. *The Philosophical Quarterly,* 20, 1–13.

Wright, Lawrence. (1994). One Drop of Blood. *The New Yorker,* 70 (July 25, 1994), 46ff.

CHAPTER ELEVEN

In Defense of
GOSSIP

*G*ossip suffers from a bad reputation. St. Paul considered it evil, as have hundreds of other thinkers, writers, and moralists. In the following essay, written in 1995, Aaron Ben-Ze'ev argues that good gossip involves no malice. We have gotten gossip all wrong, he says. If there were no such thing as speaking your mind, life would be much more stressful than it already is.

Ben-Ze'ev characterizes typical gossip as an idle, relaxing activity whose value lies in the venture itself and not the achievement of an agenda. In this sense, gossip more closely resembles joking than rumor-mongering; in fact, they often accompany one another. Joking leavens human existence by making us laugh, by compelling us to enjoy ourselves, and not necessarily at someone else's expense. Through gossip, we acquire sensitive information about the lives of others and, in so doing, come to understand ourselves better. Further, gossip can strengthen ties between people and create a sense of solidarity within a group. True, gossip may sometimes spring from the misfortunes of other people. Ben-Ze'ev claims, though, that we usually turn away from gossip when those misfortunes strike us as undeserved or frightening.

Neither virtuous nor sinful, good gossip is perhaps best understood as flattery. When other people gossip about us, they show how much they care.

∾

AARON BEN-ZE'EV is Rector at the University of Haifa, Israel, as well as Professor of Philosophy and Codirector of the Center for Interdisciplinary Research on Emotions. Among his numerous articles and books are *Good Gossip* (1994), *The Perceptual System* (1993), and *The Subtlety of Emotions* (2000).

THE VINDICATION
OF GOSSIP

Aaron Ben-Ze'ev

Gossip is a very popular activity, yet its psychological and moral aspects have received little theoretical attention. Consequently, the public image of gossip is often confused and includes features that are neither typical nor common in gossip—in particular the maliciousness that is commonly attributed to gossip seems to be wrong. The vindication of gossip requires a different characterization of its psychological and sociological nature.

CONCEPTUAL TOOLS
FOR CHARACTERIZING GOSSIP

Two conceptual tools are important for characterizing gossip. The first is the prototypical category and the second is the distinction between intrinsically valuable activities and extrinsically valuable actions.

A distinction can be made between two major types of cognitive categories: "binary" and "prototypical." Binary categories provide a clear criterion that constitutes the sufficient and necessary conditions for membership. It is an all-or-nothing category with two basic attributes: (a) clear-cut boundaries within which the criterion's conditions are met, and (b) an equal degree of membership for all items. There are no varying degrees of membership in this category because meeting the criterion is not a matter of degree; it is either met or not met. War veterans, eligible voters, and only children are examples of binary categories. One cannot be a partial veteran, semi-eligible voter, or almost an only child. Membership in a prototypical category, on the other hand, is determined by an item's degree of similarity to the best example in the category: the greater the similarity, the higher the degree of membership. The prototypical category has neither clear-cut boundaries nor an equal degree of membership. Some items are so similar to or so different from the prototype that we have no doubt about their inclusion or exclusion; with other items the degree of similarity makes it difficult or impossible to say for sure whether they belong or not (Ben-Ze'ev, 1993; Lakoff, 1987; Rosch, 1977, 1978).

If, as I believe, various instances of gossip constitute a prototypical category, then there is no single essence that is a necessary and sufficient condition for all instances of gossip and no simple way of describing them. Accordingly, my characterization of gossip concerns typical rather than all cases. The basic features of gossip are fully manifest in typical, or paradigmatic, examples; in less typical examples, these components occur in a less developed form and some may even be absent. I consider the prototypical nature of gossip fundamental to its explanation, and since my characterization refers only to typical examples, the claim that some examples differ from the typical does not contradict my characterization but derives from it.

The use of prototypical categories may draw the criticism that there can be no counter examples to prototypical characterization, since any such example may be regarded as atypical. True, it is more difficult to confirm membership in a prototypical category than in a binary category, but the characterization is more complex. A binary category has a clear criterion that constitutes the sufficient and necessary condition for membership; accordingly, there is usually an equal degree of membership for all items. Working with binary categories is easier, but they often do not adequately represent reality. Since in fact there are usually no clear-cut boundaries between many phenomena, working with prototypical categories is often more to the point. In light of the prototypical nature of gossip, I will frequently use terms such as "usually," "typically," and "often" while characterizing gossip. A refutation of my characterization of gossip remains possible, but it could not consist of describing an isolated case that seems to be an exception to the suggested characterization; it would have to show that indeed most phenomena differ from the suggested characterization or that the conceptual analysis is inconsistent.

The second basic conceptual tool I employ in characterizing gossip is the distinction between an intrinsically valuable activity and an extrinsically valuable action (see, e.g., Aristotle, *Metaphysics*, 1048b18, 1050a23; *Nicomachean Ethics,* 1174a14). An extrinsically valuable action is a means to a certain end; its value lies in achieving this end. The criterion for evaluating this action is efficiency, namely, the ratio of benefits to costs. Time is one resource we try to save in extrinsically valuable actions. Examples of extrinsically valuable actions are cleaning the house, attending job interviews, paying bills, and the like. In an intrinsically valuable activity our interest is directed at the activity itself, not at its results. Such an activity also has results, but it is not performed to achieve these; rather, its performance is typically enjoyable as it satisfies our needs. When the value of dancing for us is in dancing itself and not in its results (although these may be beneficial), this is an intrinsically valuable activity; accordingly, we do not try to finish dancing as fast as possible. Another example may be intellectual thinking whose basic motivation is creativity or intellectual curiosity, not the ensuing money or academic publications. Moral activity, which is accompanied by the pleasure of helping other people—without regard for cost-benefit calculations—is another example of an intrinsically valuable activity.

Most human activities have both intrinsic and extrinsic value. Often the factors underlying each value conflict over how long activities should continue or how far other resources should be invested in them. In such cases, we must determine whether the activity in question is an extrinsically valuable action or an intrinsically valuable activity. De Sousa cites the examples of tourism and sex. Harried tourists who consider sightseeing as an extrinsically valuable action (or "achievement") instead of an intrinsically valuable activity want to see as many possible sights in the shortest possible time: they want "not to see, but to have seen." Similarly, many people who construe sexual activity "as the harried tourist construes sightseeing" are "taking sex for an achievement" (1987: 219). Both tourism and sex can also be done, as we know, differently—in a way typical of intrinsically valuable activities.

When people take gossip to be an extrinsically valuable action, it loses many of its important characteristics and often becomes malicious. Considering gossip to constitute a prototypical category and regarding its typical cases to be intrinsically-valuable activities are crucial for understanding gossip and its non-malicious nature. Characterizing gossip as having an intrinsic value does not mean that it has no practical results. Similarly, one may view chewing gum as an intrinsically valuable activity but still, chewing gum may have practical, positive results such as reducing one's tension or cleaning one's teeth. I do not deny that gossip has practical results or that it can be used as a means to achieve them. I argue, however, that its use as a means is parasitic with regard to its intrinsic value.

THE NATURE OF GOSSIP

A common dictionary definition of "to gossip" is "to talk (or write) idly about other people, mostly about their personal or intimate affairs." My characterization of gossip is compatible with this definition. Typical gossip is an idle, relaxing activity whose value lies in the activity itself and not the achievement of external ends. This does not imply that gossip has no consequences, but those are mostly by-products, not ends. Typical gossip is easygoing and enjoyable, with no significant intended practical results. Gossip is usually relaxing and effortless and, like games, often relieves people of daily tensions. One reason for the relaxing nature of gossip is being able to talk about what is really on your mind (Tannen, 1990: 98). People indulging in gossip do not want to deeply ponder the content or consequences of what they say. Sometimes gossip seems to be talk for the sake of talking. When people are involved in serious, practical, and purposive talk, they are not gossiping; gossip is idle frivolous talk. Thus when two psychiatrists discuss the love affairs of my neighbor, their discussion is not gossip; however, when my wife and I discuss the same information, gossip it is. The psychiatrists' discussion is not idle talk (or so they claim).

Gluckman (1963) argued that people who gossip may be idle, but gossip itself is anything but idle. He indicated that since gossip has various social functions, such as maintaining and reinforcing social norms, it cannot be regarded as idle. I would put it differently: gossip is an idle activity although the people who gossip may not be idle. I do not dispute that gossip has social functions; however, I do not think that these functions alter its idle nature. In characterizing gossip as an idle activity, I refer to its psychological nature, namely, to whether *the person who gossips* does it in order to achieve a certain means, such as maintaining and reinforcing social norms, or because this person enjoys gossiping itself (and is usually unaware of its social or biological functions). I have argued that the latter interpretation is the correct one.

It is important to distinguish between gossip and the spread of unsubstantiated rumors. When recounting a personal affair that one has witnessed, one is engaged in gossip, but the information conveyed is substantiated. Since the typical content of gossip is usually behind-the-scenes, intimate information, it is indeed hard to verify and hence it is sometimes unsubstantiated. Lack of substantiation is not however an essential element of gossip, but a by-product of the confidential nature of the information conveyed. The unsubstantiated character is more typical of rumors, indeed it forms part of their definition. Moreover, unlike gossip, spreading rumors is essentially a purposive activity of merely extrinsic value. The difference between these is similar to the difference between harried tourism and an enjoyable sightseeing. The harried tourist, like a person who spreads rumors, wishes to achieve a certain end. The "calm" traveler, like the typical gossip, is engaged in his activity because he enjoys it. Spreading rumors is often a purposive vicious action, whereas gossip is not. Oscar Wilde (in *Lady Windermere's Fan*) said, "Gossip is charming. History is merely gossip. But scandal is gossip made tedious by morality." The derogatory connotation of gossip derives by and large from the failure to distinguish gossiping from the spreading of rumors.

Sometimes gossip becomes a kind of commodity exchange: "If you wish to know about other people, tell me what you know about the people of interest to me." This case is not typical as this is a kind of purposive activity. Although typical gossip is an exchange of intimate and personal information, it does not require reciprocity. One who loves to gossip does not expect to get an equal amount of information in return (although this person would be glad to hear unknown intimate information about other people). We engage in gossip because we delight in and value the activity itself.

Gossip resembles joking as both are intrinsically valuable activities. That is, both gossip and joking are essentially social activities that strengthen interpersonal bonds—we do not tell jokes and gossip to ourselves. As popular activities that evade social restrictions, they often refer to topics that are inaccessible to serious public discussion. Gossip and joking often appear together: when we gossip we usually tell jokes and when we are joking we often gossip as well. Both gossip and telling jokes involve an element of surprise, although this is more important in joking. In gossip the informational content is primary, whereas in joking the crucial element is the form in which this content is presented. The two activities sometimes involve disguised insults, but those are not typically their main focus. Jokes are often about fictional characters, whereas gossip deals with real people and, accordingly, more often damages reputations. Consequently, though people readily express their pleasure in joking, they are more reluctant to confess pleasure in discussing other people's affairs. Gossip seems to fulfill functions, which are not less basic than those fulfilled by joking, and yet jokes have received much greater scientific attention than gossip (Morreall, 1994).

Heidegger condemns gossip as too trivial to aid genuine understanding of the more profound aspects of human life (1962: 212–213). To be sure, gossip does not address highly sophisticated, profound, and serious issues, but this should not damn it altogether. A great deal of literary fiction deals with issues similar to those discussed in gossip, but no one takes this to be a profound flaw of such literature. One cannot and should not wrestle always with serious issues, and gossip is a sort of communication all people can share. Furthermore, I would deny that gossip involves no genuine understanding. Informal talk about trivial and particular issues furnishes an alternative perspective that may in fact shed light on matters that are sometimes misunderstood in serious, abstract discussions. One should not stipulate that human beings must choose between either gossip or the serious discussion of abstract ideas—as if the love of gossip reflected a corresponding hatred of serious matters. Gossip is but one among many types of discussion and should be examined against the spectrum of other types. With such comparison, the moral evaluation of gossip becomes more positive.

GOSSIP AS A MEANS FOR SATISFYING NEEDS

Gossip satisfies two basic needs: the need to know about other people and the need to be associated with other people.

As an intrinsically valuable activity, gossip satisfies the need to acquire information about the personal and intimate aspects of other people's lives. Such knowledge satisfies our curiosity and may be valuable in understanding our own lives (Collins, 1994). Although intimacy plays an important role in our lives, we remain quite ignorant how it works in other people's lives. Gossip is an enjoyable way to gather information that is otherwise hard to obtain. Moreover, intimate and personal aspects often reveal more about the personalities of other people than does their public behavior. This need to acquire knowledge of intimate and personal aspects of other people's lives occupies a central role in gossip because there are very few other ways to satisfy this need. Candid and open self-description is rare and limited to very few close friends. Literature, of course, may partially fulfill such a need, but it does not refer to "real" people who share our lives. Gossip satisfies a personal curiosity concerning people who are of particular interest to us. The results of a statistical survey showing that the incidence of intercourse among average British couples is higher than that of most other Western couples, including, surprisingly, that of French and Italian couples, is not a typical subject of gossip; the number of times each week our neighbor meets with her lover is.

Gossip also satisfies the tribal need, namely, the need to belong to and be accepted by a unique group. (One meaning of "gossip" is indeed "being a friend of.") The sharing of intimate and personal information and the intimate manner of conveying this information contribute to the formation of an exclusive group with intimate and affectionate ties between its members. Gossip functions crucially in establishing intimacy and in this sense satisfies the tribal need. Like friendship, gossip is a kind of sharing (though a quite superficial one). If friendship leads to gossip, gossip also leads to friendship (Heilman, 1973: 153). Tannen (1990) argues that "not only is telling secrets evidence of friendship; it *creates* friendship" (98), and adds that telling secrets is a privilege and even an obligation among friends. People can be deeply hurt when they find out that a friend failed to inform them about confidential intimate events. Moreover, "Small talk is crucial to maintain a sense of camaraderie when there is nothing special to say" (102).

People who are aware of the friendly character of gossip may use it to make new friends. Behaving toward someone the way friends do indicates our wish to consider that person a friend. Similarly, giving someone confidential information conveys our confidence in this person. Such a use of gossip to make friends belies its intrinsically valuable nature, but one can use gossip in making new friends only because gossip typically has intrinsic value as a friendly activity that strengthens social bonds. Perhaps the tribal need is not really satisfied unless intimate information is exchanged; only such information indicates intimate relations.

Like many other kinds of need-satisfying activities, gossip is enjoyable. The teller and the listeners delight in the activity of gossip and not in its results. Really good gossip is usually not just a piece of information but an anecdote, a narrative with a beginning, middle, and end. It is interesting, even to strangers. The pleasure derived is often that of a good story. Most people like to gossip now and then: it is a form of social communication that usually revolves around information not yet widely known and therefore intriguing. The information, which is sometimes negative, generally concerns people who are not there to hear it and includes both a description and an evaluation of their behavior. (As George, in the television series *Seinfeld,* said: "I'm much more comfortable criticizing people behind their backs.") Participants appear to share the same standards of right and wrong. And although adherence to such standards is often superficial, even the mere appearance of common moral standards establishes intimacy among the participants.

GOSSIP AS A MEANS
FOR CONVEYING INFORMATION

The suggested characterization of gossip as an intrinsically valuable activity accords well with its other features. This is true, for example, of the type of communication used in gossip, the content of the conveyed information, the similarity of gossip to literary fiction, and its enjoyable nature.

The two major forms of communication typical of gossip are private conversations and public communication by the media. The former is more typical since gossip is usually intimate not only in the type of information conveyed, but also in the type of communication employed.

The limited size of the audience suits the often confidential nature of the information and is compatible with the need to belong to an intimate and exclusive group. This sense of belonging to an exclusive group and of being a source of and one of the few recipients of exclusive information may boost the teller's as well as the listener's ego. And whereas active gossips often convey intimate information to many people, they usually do so not by addressing a large audience but through series of conversations with individuals or small groups. Gossips may indulge their hobby whenever possible and have little concern for the time spent doing so. Gossip has been called verbal chewing gum; Aldous Huxley described a gossip as a professional athlete—of the tongue.

Gossip conveys interesting information about sex, violence, money, vices and virtues, and foibles. These themes, of much concern to us individually, are also the focus of gossip columns (Levin and Arluke, 1987). Those who engage in dissemination of gossip in the media, however, take it as a purposive action of extrinsic value. Gossiping is not an idle and easy activity for columnists whose living depends on it. Professional gossips may enjoy their work in the same way that other people enjoy their extrinsically valuable work, but their enjoyment will usually differ from that of the nonprofessional gossip. Through the public media we learn the intimate and personal details of celebrities' lives. We become familiar with these celebrities and more easily identify with them, as we vicariously share their pleasures and come to believe that our own little world is not much less valuable than theirs. Furthermore, the immoral behavior of famous people, reported in gossip columns, enhances our self-respect. Celebrity gossip also allows us to draw comfort from other people's misfortune; our own small problems pale in comparison to the severe misfortunes of other people. As Levin and Arluke aptly say: "Misery loves miserable company—especially when the miserable are rich, famous, and apparently successful" (1987: 37).

The objects of gossip fall into three major groups: (a) people in our immediate surroundings, (b) famous people, and (c) people whose intimate and personal lives are unique. The common feature of all three groups is our interest, though that interest varies from group to group. Whereas we are usually interested in the ordinary, everyday activities of famous people, we are characteristically interested in the nonordinary activities of ordinary people. The more remote an ordinary person is from us, the more unusual her activity must be in order to be of interest to us.

Insofar as gossip does not require intellectual knowledge of the abstract but awareness of the specific, it is similar to literary fiction (and as we shall see below, also to emotions). As Tannen says, "When people talk about the details of daily lives, it is gossip; when they write about them, it is literature." Gossip also resembles anthropology, "the academic discipline that makes a career of documenting the details of people's lives" (Tannen, 1990: 97). Some gossip develops like folktales that are "told and retold year after year and time after time with all the freshness of a new report" (Heilman, 1973: 163; see also Spacks, 1985). Kierkegaard argues that gossips would be in despair if there were a law "which did not forbid people talking, but simply ordered that everything that was spoken about should be treated as though it had happened fifty years ago" (1962: 71–72). It is true that gossip is mainly concerned with new information about people who are still around. Even so, this cannot be used (as it is in Kierkegaard's claim) as a weapon to condemn gossip. The curiosity satisfied by gossip differs in important respects from intellectual, scientific curiosity, but this difference *in itself* is irrelevant to the moral evaluation of gossip.

The enjoyable and interesting elements in gossip stem not merely from acquiring novel information, but also from the content of this information. Like jokes, gossip often includes irony and unexpected features. Thus the sexual life of a priest, or even of our next-door neighbor, makes juicier gossip than the exploits of a prostitute. Likewise, the romance between a very old woman and a very young man is more delectable fare than that between two people of a similar age. This gap between reputation or conventional behavior and actual behavior is what makes gossip interesting.

WHO GOSSIPS?

The claim that gossip satisfies basic human needs is compatible with the observation that most (and probably all) people engage from time to time in gossip and enjoy it. Some people engage in this activity much more than others, however: the gossipmongers. Gossipmongers often have a strong need either for repeated evaluation of their own personal and intimate life or for further social relationships. An excessive preoccupation with the intimate and personal affairs of others may be substitute for "real action"; talk about others may not be as gratifying as interaction with them, but sometimes it is the only available option. Gossipmongers are generally considered those who tell gossip and not those who listen. But the tellers usually do not invent the information they convey; accordingly, gossipmongers are also listeners who receive novel information about other people that can serve as a basis for their own self-evaluation. Furthermore, in typical gossip sessions many participants respond to novel information by providing other information in return. Gossipmongers may have a stronger need to be accepted by and belong to an exclusive group, for, being a purveyor of novel information, the person not only belongs to the group, but becomes its center of attention. Having exclusive knowledge enhances gossipmongers' status in the group, though in the long run they find that they are no longer trusted with confidential information (Heilman, 1973: 16). In addition to the respect gained by conveying interesting behind-the-scenes information, gossipmongers, who often have a low self-image, may gain some respect by conveying information which is slightly damaging to others. Lowering the evaluation of others may seem to them to somehow increase their own. There is indeed some evidence that individuals who are anxious about themselves tend to spread gossip about other people (Rosnow and Fine, 1976; see also Levin and Arluke, 1987).

Society evaluates gossipmongers negatively not because of evil in gossip's essential nature, but because of the excessive preoccupation of gossipmongers with this activity. This preoccupation often distorts the basically harmless and enjoyable character of gossip. When gossip becomes a constant occupation, and harmless or merely embarrassing information is not abundantly available, the purveyor can easily slip into hurtful revelations.

A quantitative increase in the time one spends on gossip may result in a qualitative difference in the type of activity involved. This possibility underlies the Jewish prohibition against all forms of gossip, including that between husband and wife; the assumption apparently being that loose talk may easily become loose living. Just as sins of the heart may lead to vicious activities, idle talk about sex may turn into loose sexual conduct. To a certain extent this fear is justified, though the same can be said of literature, movies, and most other forms of communication and cultural expression. Furthermore, one may assert that this kind of talk in fact substitutes for forbidden activities, thus reducing the likelihood of actually indulging in these activities. Gossip is a safe way to feed on activities in which, for reasons of security or safety, we normally do not engage (Spacks, 1985).

The typical gossipmonger is intelligent, with a good memory and an ability to discern connections between events. Gossips are quite realistic people; their extensive knowledge of embarrassing events prevents them from being naive. Gossips are often quite sensitive, curious, social-minded, and involved. Although incessant gossipers seem to have quite a few positive features, they are wasted on superficial matters and distorted by their excessive occupation with the superficial issues typical of gossip. The opposite of gossipmongers, excessive nongossips, often have little interest in other people, not only concerning their intimate and personal life, but other aspects as well. (Needless to say, there is no clear-cut distinction between excessive nongossips and "normal" nongossips, nor between "normal" gossips and excessive ones.)

Do women gossip more than men? Research indicates that both women and men spend a similar amount of time in idle conversations but that the topics differ: women tend to talk more about other people, whereas men dwell more on sports, politics, and weather. In this sense women more often discuss topics typical of gossip. This difference may be explained by traditional cultural expectations: feminine activities were supposed to be confined to family and friendship networks whereas masculine activities were supposed to involve more distant relationships. Indeed, there is evidence that women adapt more to the needs of others and cooperate more than men do (Hochschild, 1983: 165; Levin and Arluke, 1987; see also Nevo et al., 1994; Spacks, 1985). Traditionally, many men "have little use for small talk, since they believe talk is designed to convey information" and hence should have "significant content, be interesting and meaningful" (Tannen, 1990: 104) Men were supposed to maintain their manhood by not being involved too much in close relations (which are typical of gossip). Just as "real" men should not cry and should be reticent about their emotions, "real" men should not concentrate unduly on their personal and sentimental affairs. Influenced by this traditional image, men often doubt that they can benefit from a candid discussion with their peers; hence the topics of their relaxing, enjoyable conversations are less personal. Nevertheless, these idle conversations provide the benefits typical of gossip: they are relaxing, enjoyable activities that express a form of friendship. Because such conversations do not provide the access to intimate knowledge about others that enables one to understand oneself better, it may also be true that the friendship that evolves from these conversations is less intimate. Perhaps the sex-difference in topics of idle conversations stems not from a lack of masculine interest in issues typical of gossip, but from the pressure on men to eschew personal and sentimental matters. Gossiping about the intimate and personal matters of other people easily leads to discussing these issues in one's own life.

Is gossip a culture-dependent phenomenon? In the same way that there are differences among the sexes concerning the type and extent of gossip, differences may exist among cultures. However, since gossip fulfills some basic needs, we might expect to find it in some form in all cultures, although the extent and type of gossip may vary. It seems that the more exclusive and intimate the society is, the more pervasive and important gossip and the more important its role in this society (Gluckman, 1963). However, some form of gossip is to be found in every society. One indication for this is that children—who are supposed to be less influenced by cultures—gossip practically from the time they learn to talk and to recognize other people (Fine, 1977).

GOSSIP AND EMOTIONS

Both emotions and gossip express a personal concern toward other people. Emotions and gossip are concerned with people who are of interest to us, namely, those who are psychologically close to us and those who may be in somewhat unusual circumstances. Both emotions and gossip express our interest and involvement in the lives of other people, albeit in a more profound way in the case of emotions. In the same way that abolishing emotions means abolishing both negative and positive emotions, abolishing gossip would mean abolishing all types of conversations about other people. Emotions and gossip express our sensitivity toward other people; abolishing them would lead to our indifference toward other people. I would rather live in a society whose members have positive and negative attitudes toward me than in a society whose members are indifferent to me. Caring about someone does not always mean showing a positive attitude toward that person's deeds.

Like gossip, emotions constitute a sort of sincere communication all people share. What both require is not knowledge of the abstract, but awareness of the specific. The specific and the concrete are quite meaningful elements in both emotions and gossip. Informal talk about trivial and particular issues furnishes an alternative perspective which may in fact shed light on matters that are sometimes misunderstood in serious, abstract discussions. Similarly, emotional knowledge provides us with an understanding often missing from intellectual thinking. Yet, unlike gossip, emotions are directed at issues which are perceived by us to be quite significant.

One important difference between emotions and gossip concerns the practical nature of emotions and the nonpractical nature of gossip. Gossip is typically relaxing and effortless, since it relieves us of daily tensions; emotions are typically tense and require most of our resources, since they deal with changes with which we are not sure how to cope. Due to their intense nature, emotions are relatively brief, whereas gossip is a relaxing activity that can go on for quite a while.

I would now like to briefly discuss the comparison people often make between gossip and the emotion of pleasure-in-others'-misfortune (for detailed discussions of that emotion, see Ben-Ze'ev, 2000: chap. 12; Portmann, 2000).

The joy of gossip is often thought to resemble the pleasure we take in the misfortune of others. Both gossip and pleasure-in-others'-misfortune are severely condemned on moral grounds as malicious—indeed, their practice often makes us feel uncomfortable. Despite their prevalence, a great deal of confusion characterizes our attitude toward them. A significant distortion is perceiving extreme instances as typical and common instances. Owing to this mistaken identification the two states are often perceived to be malicious.

In describing pleasure-in-others'-misfortune, two features are not disputable: our pleasure and the other's misfortune. I have suggested three additional typical characteristics: (a) the other person is perceived to deserve the misfortune, (b) the misfortune is relatively minor, and (c) we are passive in generating the other's misfortune (Ben-Ze'ev, 2000: 355–361).

If the misfortune is grave, our pleasure often turns into pity. When a person's misfortune seems deserved, we often feel that justice has been done, and the more deserved the misfortune, the more justified the pleasure. Typically, one of the greater contributions to the pleasure we take in others' misfortune is the feeling that the failure of our competitor is due not to our own wicked behavior, but to inexorable fate. It is as if justice has been done in the spirit of the Talmudic saying: "The tasks of the righteous get done by others."

Do the characteristics typical of pleasure-in-others'-misfortune— namely, the subject's pleasure, the object's misfortune, the perceived minor and deserved nature of the object's misfortune, and the subject's passivity—typify gossip as well? Although the subject's pleasure is not as essential to gossip as to pleasure-in-others'-misfortune, it is certainly typical. Whereas in pleasure-in-others'-misfortune we cannot be sad, in gossip we may at times be sad, albeit rarely. The subject's passivity is typical also of gossip: we do not usually gossip about our own activities. It may be less accurate to describe the object's situation in gossip as misfortune. Like pleasure-in-others'-misfortune, gossip is often associated with envy; both are usually directed at those whose general fortune is comparable or better than ours. Those who enjoy better fortune are of more interest to us because we would like to imitate them. In gossip the typical misfortune is more likely a social failure related to embarrassment rather than to shame. The violation of social norms presumably gives other people the legitimacy to talk about it, and in this sense, the object of gossip (as that of pleasure-in-others'-misfortune) seems to deserve to have his intimate life made the topic of other people's conversations.

Gossips often envy the objects of their gossip. What underlies gossip and envy is a constant comparison with others, but in envy this comparison is accompanied by a concern over the unequal, inferior position of the agent (Ben-Ze'ev, 2000: chap. 10); in gossip this concern is less important. Despite the negative attitude toward the object that is often present in envy and gossip, both attitudes frequently involve some kind of admiration for certain aspects of the object.

IS GOSSIP MORALLY NEGATIVE?

Despite the prevalence of gossip and pleasure-in-others'-misfortune, both are condemned on moral grounds. A major reason for this is the inclination to take extreme cases as typical and common for the whole category. Quite often extreme cases constitute the public image of the category and are mistakenly *perceived* to be both typical and frequent because like other abnormalities, they are more noticeable than the typical or common. For example, the public image of male jealousy includes the picture of a husband killing his wife for her infidelity. Yet it is obvious that murder is neither the common nor the typical behavior in jealousy. Surveys have revealed that between 37 percent and 50 percent of the respondents reported past extramarital affairs. Yet far less than 0.01 percent of the U.S. male population commits murder in response to adultery (Hupka, 1991: 258–59).

The distorted public image that results in confusing extreme with typical cases also appears in the identification of gossip with malicious activity. Pleasure-in-others'-misfortune is not sadistic by nature; nor is gossip inherently malicious. Gossip is engaged in for pleasure, not for the purpose of hurting someone, and though gossip may inflict some damage on its subject's reputation, such damage is usually minor (Jaeger et al., 1994; Levin and Arluke, 1987). Many people cannot really enjoy themselves while explicitly knowing that their activity is very harmful to others. As Kant observes, "We feel pleasure in gossiping about the minor misadventures of other people; we are not averse . . ." (1963: 218); moreover, the damage sometimes caused by gossip is usually a by-product, not an end. And when gossip does inflict significant damage to other people, the gossipers themselves do not usually consider the damage to be significant. The idle nature of gossip implies not merely the absence of declared purpose, but the lack of concern for such a purpose.

Nor is it true that the information conveyed in gossip is totally negative. One study suggests an even distribution of negative and positive information in gossip, and almost half of the information was found to be neither clearly negative nor clearly positive. Furthermore, when the information was negative, it often concerned minor misfortunes (Levin and Arluke, 1987). Levin and Arluke show that even gossip columnists usually do not convey information meant to harm or destroy a celebrity. In fact, most of the information that appears in gossip columns is favorable. Little wonder that gossip columnists receive much of their information from the celebrities themselves or from their press agents. When these columns include negative information, it almost never refers to the violation of major social norms and is often associated with happy or hopeful conclusions. Thus, criminal activities or a celebrity's connections with criminals are rarely reported in these columns. Similarly, although many stars have been known to be gay, gossip columnists have mostly kept silent, fearing permanent harm to the actor's career. Levin and Arluke (1987) argue that these columns have focused on folkway, not moral standards, and on eccentricity rather than on deviations.

Contrary to its popular reputation, then, gossip is not basically concerned with detraction, slander, or character assassination. Negative information may be remembered better, and hence the illusory impression of its dominance. In some cases gossip may indeed involve exaggerated or distorted information, but usually gossip does not deliberately convey false information. Sometimes gossip is the only way to acquire accurate information, and often gossip is more accurate and more complete than "official" information. Although information conveyed informally may be inaccurate, so too is the news conveyed by the media. Gossip is not essentially an activity of telling lies, and there is no reason that it should be morally condemned on these grounds. If indeed gossip mainly conveyed false information, most people would not find it interesting. (The relation between the truth-value of the information conveyed in gossip and its moral evaluation is not simple. On one hand, true information does not distort the character of the object; but, on the other hand, intimate and personal information may hurt more when it is true, as one cannot refer to it as merely unsubstantiated rumors. Moreover, truthful information may be partial, e.g., when one takes things out of their context, and hence distorted after all.)

Gossip may also have some positive by-products. It may help to sustain the moral values of a community where people fear becoming a target for gossip. This is especially true of small communities or of famous people. Gossip may also provide lower classes with a socially acceptable outlet for frustration and anger (Spacks, 1985).

CONCLUSION

I do not wish to claim that gossip is a virtue (cf. De Sousa, 1994), but nor are its typical cases malicious. To gossip is to assert the right to be informed about other people's affairs, though one may condemn the way the information is acquired. Gossip seems less immoral if the information about the object is not pejorative, if by relaying the information in telling it the subject does not (significantly) hurt the object, and if the telling has some justification. Since the suggested characterization of gossip is compatible with these factors, typical cases of gossip are not strongly negative from a moral viewpoint.

No doubt, gossip has a bad reputation. I believe, however, that this reputation is more in the nature of an unsubstantiated (and even malicious) rumor than of reliable judgment. Although the moral condemnation is not entirely groundless, it applies, for the main part, to nontypical cases of gossip and is not justified with respect to typical gossip, which is mostly harmless. Aristotle's emphasis upon the right proportions is relevant here. Distorting the subtle proportion of typical gossip may indeed be harmful. But the fact that excessive and distorted gossip is harmful does not establish the intrinsic malicious nature of typical gossip, just as the fact that excessive eating is harmful does not imply an intrinsic evil in eating. Much of the negative press gossip has received stems from the confusion of extreme and excessive instances with typical and common instances. I argue that the extreme case, which many people take to be the prototype of gossip, is neither essential to nor common of gossip.

If my claim that typical gossip satisfies basic human needs and is mostly harmless is correct, then gossip cannot be very bad from a moral viewpoint. It may even have some positive moral values. As an old high-school teacher of mine used to say: "gossip is not a morally negative activity; after all, it expresses an interest in other people's lives." Indeed, the exchange of relatively insignificant details about daily life sends a message of caring. The noticing of details, so typical of gossip, "shows caring and creates involvement" (Tannen, 1990: 114–15). Gossip usually does not, however, express a genuine concern for other people's problems. The interest, we may say, is merely focused on the interesting, light aspects of other people's lives. Gossip is not a virtuous activity; I have tried to show that it is not vicious either.[1]

NOTES

1. This paper was originally published in R. E. Goodman and A. Ben-Ze'ev (eds.), *Good Gossip* (Lawrence: University Press of Kansas, 1994). This is a somewhat revised version of the original paper. I thank University Press of Kansas for the permission to use the original paper. Michael Strauss, to whom I owe a great intellectual debt, has introduced me to the important distinction between an intrinsically valuable activity and extrinsically valuable action. I am grateful to Lisa Frank, Robert Goodman, William Lycan, Cynthia Miller, and Amelie Rorty for helpful comments. The work on this paper began while I was on sabbatical leave at the Center for the Philosophy of Science at the University of Pittsburgh. The hospitality and support of the center is gratefully acknowledged.

REFERENCES

Ben-Ze'ev, A. (1993). *The perceptual system: A philosophical and psychological perspective.* New York: Peter Lang.

Ben-Ze'ev, A. (2000). *The Subtlety of the Emotions.* Cambridge, Mass.: MIT.

Collins, L. (1994). "Gossip: A Feminist Defense." In Goodman and Ben-Ze'ev (eds.), *Good Gossip.*

De Sousa, R. (1987). *The Rationality of Emotions.* Cambridge: MIT Press.

De Sousa, R. (1994). "In Praise of Gossip: Indiscretion as a Saintly Virtue." In Goodman and Ben-Ze'ev, *Good Gossip.*

Fine, G. A. (1977). "Social components of children's gossip." *Journal of Communication,* 27, 181–185.

Gluckman, M. (1963). "Gossip and scandal." *Current Anthropology,* 4, 307–316.

Goodman, R. E., and Ben-Ze'ev, A. (eds.) (1994). *Good Gossip.* Lawrence: University Press of Kansas.

Heidegger, M. (1962). *Being and time.* New York: Harper and Row.

Heilman, S. C. (1973). *Synagogue life.* Chicago: University of Chicago.

Hochschild, A. R. (1983). *The Managed Heart: Commercialization of Human Feeling.* Berkeley: University of California Press.

Hupka, R. B. (1991). "The motive for the arousal of romantic jealousy: Its cultural origin." In P. Salovey (ed.), *The Psychology of Jealousy and Envy.* New York: Guilford Press.

Jager, M. E., Skleder, A. A., Rind, B., and Rosnow, R. L. (1994). "Gossip, gossipers, gossipees." In Goodman and Ben-Ze'ev, *Good Gossip.*

Kant, I. (1963). "Jealousy, Envy, and Grudge." In *Lectures on Ethics. New York:* Harper and Row.

Kierkegaard, S. (1962). *The Present Age.* New York: Harper and Row.

Lakoff, G. (1987). *Women, Fire, and Dangerous Things.* Chicago: University of Chicago.

Levin, J., and Arluke, A. (1987). *Gossip: The Inside Scoop.* New York: Plenum.

Morreall, J. (1994). "Gossip and Humor." In Goodman and Ben-Ze'ev, *Good Gossip.*

Nevo, O., Nevo, B., and Derech-Zehavi, A. (1994). "The tendency to gossip as a psychological disposition: Constructing a measure and validating it." In Goodman and Ben-Ze'ev, *Good Gossip.*

Portmann, J. (2000). *When Bad Things Happen to Other People.* London: Routledge.

Rosch, E. (1977). "Human categorization." In N. Warren (ed.), *Advance in cross-cultural psychology.* London: Academic Press.

Rosch, E. (1978). "Principles of categorization." In E. Rosch and B. B. Lloyd (eds.), *Cognition and categorization.* Hillsdale: Erlbaum.

Rosnow, R. L., and Fine, G. A. (1976). *Rumor and gossip: The social psychology of hearsay.* New York: Elsevier.

Spacks, P. M. (1985). *Gossip.* New York: Knopf.

Tannen, D. (1990). *You Just Don't Understand.* New York: Ballantine Books.

CHAPTER TWELVE

In Defense of
LUST

*A*sk any advertising executive, or simply look at the cover of this book: Sex sells. Lust, the food of sex, can help us understand what it is to be human. Granted, not every human inclination can be called good—think of aggression toward fellow humans, for instance. Lust, however, deserves praise for brightening the dreary horizon and inspiring us to pull the very best out of ourselves that we can.

There is such a thing as too much of a good thing, particularly with lust. Contemporary employers increasingly worry about the time employees spend furtively visiting pornographic Web sites at work. And parents complain about unwillingly exposing children to a barrage of films, television programs, and music videos flaunting sexual images. Lust resists nearly every social attempt to contain it, it seems.

Is lust so bad? What would life without lust look like? Psychiatrists now consider the lack of lust a telltale sign of depression, something everyone wants to avoid. Lust cheers and sustains us with the confirmation that some people really can bring us joy.

Does lust lead to sex? Sometimes, no doubt, it does. But just as desiring money does not bring you money, appreciating the human form does not bring you company. Adam and Eve were not forbidden to look at the fruit on the tree, only to eat it. The pleasure we derive from looking around us can lighten the burden of existence.

The Internet has transformed communication in many ways, only one of which is the usage of the word "chatting." Although not all chat rooms are erotic, the word "chat room" has taken on a richly sexual connotation. Does erotic chatting (the only kind I discuss here) qualify as a harmless exercise of the moral imagination or as a sexual activity? Or perhaps both? Even it we considered chatting a sexual activity, it could hardly be worse than flipping eagerly through pornographic magazines.

Lust gave birth to chatting, at least the kind that goes on in erotic Internet spaces. In my view, chatting does not amount to adultery or betrayal of a romantic partner. In an essay written in 2000, I argue that defending chatting pays tribute to the life-giving zest of lust. Lust can uplift us as it fills us with a renewed sense of how nice it is to be alive.

∾

JOHN PORTMANN's book *When Bad Things Happen to Other People* (2000) was nominated for Phi Beta Kappa's Ralph Waldo Emerson Prize. He studied philosophy at Yale and Cambridge and now lectures at the University of Virginia.

CHATTING IS NOT CHEATING

John Portman

*Do you know what it is as you pass to be
loved by strangers?
Do you know the talk of those
turning eye-balls?*
—*Walt Whitman,* "Song of the Open Road" *(1856)*

A triumph of human imagination, the Internet has expanded and facilitated communication. Lust, an age-old focus of human imagination, now enjoys a new stage on which to triumph.

The Internet simplifies life in ways many people have noticed. It complicates life as well, though, particularly with regard to sexual morality. Anonymous dirty talk over the Internet presents what may seem to be a new moral puzzle: Is it sex? Does it amount to betrayal if your boyfriend, girlfriend, husband, or wife logs on to an erotic chat room? Your mother or father? Your son or daughter? A priest, nun, rabbi, or minister? No. The Internet has not given us a new way to *have* sex but rather an absorbing new way to *talk about* sex. Distinguishing between flirting and infidelity will show that talking dirty, whether on the Internet or on the phone, does not amount to having sex.

I make a case for the moral acceptability of anonymous dirty talk, which is no better or worse than viewing pornography. Along the way, I suggest that reflection on the erotics of the Internet usefully exposes the largely intuitive and pre-articulate anxiety with which most of us approach the topic of sex.

WAYS OF FLIRTING

Probably as long as *Homo sapiens* have been around they have been having dirty thoughts. Like some Greeks before them, many ancient Jews (Genesis 20:2 and Leviticus 18) and Christians suffered through lust as if it were a curse. Famously, Jesus taught that the man who lusted after a woman in his heart had already committed adultery (Matthew 19:9). When, some two thousand years later, Jimmy Carter confessed in a *Playboy* interview to having lusted after women other than his wife, Americans took the news badly. Carter lost the 1980 presidential election.

What's so bad about lust? Certainly it can lead to bad consequences, but so can love, charity, mercy, and a host of other decidedly laudable motivations. We might place the blame on how lust affects our relations to others, but Plato objects to how lust affects our relation to *ourselves*. The true philosopher doesn't concern himself with sexual pleasure, according to Plato, who refers to sexual desire as a disease of the personality. Plato counsels us to sublimate sexual energy in intellectual pursuits.[1]

Many Jewish and Christian thinkers have endorsed Plato's denunciation. Aquinas and Luther, among other theologians, regarded lust as a consequence of self-love or pride. Augustine, perhaps the greatest Christian theologian of all time, struggled to describe just how lust contorted him: "Surely I have not ceased to be my own self . . . and yet there is still a great gap between myself and myself . . . Oh that my soul might follow my own self . . . that it might not be a rebel to itself."[2]

Lust prevents us from being who we really are, Augustine says. He cultivates an athletic ideal, one in which we become strong enough to surmount lust as a champion hurdler mechanically leaps over obstacles in his path. Augustine's reflections leave us to wonder whether he understood the harmful effects of repressing sexual desire (Freud made a career out of detailing these effects). Missing from Augustine is the idea that lust completes us (however temporarily), fills us with a vivid sense of being alive, propels us along the way to self-fulfillment. (The zeal with which religious figures such as St. Teresa of Avila, St. John of the Cross, or St. Jerome have sought God approximates lust, it may sometimes seem.) Lust, like the playfulness of children or the treasures of the Louvre, lights up a rainy day.

Not surprisingly, dirty thoughts can terrorize those who condemn lust. Hemingway's short story "God Rest You Merry, Gentlemen" introduces a sixteen-year-old boy whose fear of lust drives him to castrate himself. Some parents in Arabia and Egypt subject their daughters to clitorectomy in order to prevent lustful desires or succumbing to passion. And in the autobiographical *Confessions*, Augustine mentions a monstrous thought that came to him during a religious ceremony, a thought he viewed as properly punishable by death. That thought seems to have been about sex, possibly even about sex in church.

At the dawn of a new century, there is considerably less public fear of dirty thoughts than there used to be. In the 1990s the American press trumpeted the singer Madonna's confessing to fantasies of having sex in a Catholic church (her 1989 video "Like a Prayer," set in a church, stirred controversy upon its release).[3] And in that same decade, Americans largely forgave President Bill Clinton his now-famous marital misdeeds.

Even now, though, some conservative religious people will still insist that sex ought to be procreative, not merely recreational (as in adultery). As late as 1972, one of the better-known philosophers in the West insisted that this view is a necessary step if one is morally to oppose petting, prostitution, sodomy, and "homosexual intercourse."[4] People who morally object to dirty thoughts will naturally (and reasonably) object to talking dirty (in person) and chatting dirty (over the phone or on the Internet). My thoughts will do nothing to dissuade them. Here I address what must be the overwhelming majority of people who see some moral leeway in dirty thoughts and indeed dirty talk.

∾

On the Internet, dirty talk passes as "chatting" (which is not to say that all chat rooms are erotically oriented). As if chatting were not already ambiguous enough, some people have taken to referring to it as "phone sex." What is phone sex? Do you need a phone for it? Will a chat room do? Is phone sex any different from what we call "talking dirty"?

For at least a decade before the advent of the Internet, pornographic magazines and subway advertisements (ubiquitous in Paris) offered the telephone numbers of professionals (in the sense that they got paid) available to explore sexual fantasies. A business transaction, this call entailed a fee, charged to your phone bill, based on time spent talking. You paid, and the pro profited.

By "phone sex," people seem to mean talking dirty on the phone. You may have a private phone conversation with an amateur you have "met" in a chat room, or you may call a "pro" and pay for his or her services, as advertised on the Internet or elsewhere. In any event, you do not meet, although you may have seen a photograph of him or her (or think you have—you may have exchanged pictures on the Internet, but he or she may have submitted a photo of someone else). "Phone sex" involves another person in a way that solitary sprints through porno-graphic magazines do not.

Is this talk a way of having sex? The idea that words can seduce others, or might serve as a kind of foreplay, has been around for centuries. Poets from around the world have left us shining examples. With Freud came the idea that talking might be equivalent to sex itself. Certainly talking dirty falls within the realm of sexual harassment—it is not something a manager can do at work to subordinates, for example (although technically, the dirty talk must be unwelcome, severe, and protracted in order to win a lawsuit against an employer). The idea that "phone sex" is a "gateway drug" that will escalate to something much bigger and more dangerous does not seem obvious, though. Chat rooms are journeys that needn't lead to physical contact with another. Of course, they sometimes do.

What people call "phone sex" isn't really sex at all. Of crucial importance is the lack of touching (despite AT&T's commercial invitations to "reach out and touch someone"). Thinking of dirty talk over the phone as sex confuses moral evaluation. The verbal innovation "phone sex," clever as it may sound, ought to be abandoned. We already have a perfectly apt way of describing this activity: talking dirty. Anyone wishing to emphasize the phone's role in dirty talk would do better to speak of phone flirting. Flirting may or may not lead to sexual contact, but flirting itself is not sex.

Neither is voyeurism sex. Ogling pornographic images, either in an old-fashioned magazine or on the Internet, is a kind of voyeurism. It is not sex. Most of us are soft-core voyeurs to some extent (not just the prosaic husband with "a wandering eye"). Depending on the configuration of the shower room, lesbian, gay, and bisexual people can hardly avoid becoming voyeurs each time they wash off at the gym. Looking into other people's windows, what a peeping Tom does, is hardcore voyeurism. Although a peeping Tom can get into trouble with the law, what he or she does is not sex. People who talk dirty in Internet chat rooms are a new kind of peeping Tom—typing Toms, we might call them. They are not having sex.

Whatever else flirting may be, it is not sex. Patting someone on the bottom or giving a hug may sometimes arouse us; neither amounts to sex, though. And what about dancing? Is that sex? Indeed, there is such a thing as "dirty dancing"—even a movie by that title. Flirting and dancing have long troubled religious leaders because of the confusing dynamic that these activities inaugurate. We want to insist that waltzing with the boss's husband or the boss's wife can be morally innocent, despite the close physical contact involved. Dancing, like flirting, is not sex.

It might be thought that flirting is intentional, that is to say that we flirt only if we intend to do so. But this view misses the ease with which we can hide behind our roles as sales clerks, waiters, and entertainers. We can flirt even when we pretend we are just doing what's expected of us. We can deceive others, even ourselves, about what we intend.

Waiters and sales clerks routinely report that flirting with customers is good for business. It is hard to deny that flirting becomes us. The stodgy butler from Ishiguro's celebrated novel *The Remains of the Day* ruminates on his refusal to flirt and the colorless, lonely existence to which it has led: "Perhaps it is indeed time I began to look at this whole matter of bantering more enthusiastically. After all, when one thinks about it, it is not such a foolish thing to indulge in—particularly if it is the case that in bantering lies the key to human warmth."[5] Flirting can build rapport with others. We understand what it means, for example, to dress for success in the workplace or to keep up with fashion trends when going to parties. We may find ourselves flirting by wearing clothing that fits our bodies closely or exposes a certain amount of leg, chest, or arm. We might wonder, What is the difference between the sight of a woman's cleavage emerging from an expensive French gown and the chat room journey of someone who never intends to have sex with anyone he meets in cyberspace? It may well be that flirting amounts to self-centered bragging or exhibitionism: "Look how beautiful I am," fashionably dressed people may be saying. Flirting may sometimes ask nothing more of others than admiration.

In contrast to flirting, it is possible to engage in another suspect kind of activity all by yourself: masturbation. Involving no mutuality, masturbation is known as a distinctly inferior form of sexual activity. In his early writings, Karl Marx derided what he took to be Hegel's extravagantly theoretical books through a mean analogy: Hegel is to "real" philosophy what masturbation is to "real" sex. Those who view anonymous cyberchatting as a new way of having sex would presumably conclude that chatting is a disappointing and even embarrassing substitute for a higher pleasure.

Long-standing opposition to pornography is rooted in an ancient fear of (male) masturbation. (Most moral thinking about masturbation has ignored female masturbation.) Chatting will likely (and reasonably) offend anyone who objects to pornography, in part because of the alleged link between pornography and masturbation.

Vilification of masturbation, or, onanism, stretches back over two thousand years. Modern people often find the received reasons for condemning masturbation hilarious. Ancient Greeks and Romans, for example, thought of semen as costly horsepower. Ejaculation robbed a man of a vital fluid without which he could not roar or soar. As recently as a hundred years ago, some religious thinkers in the United States insisted that unused semen was reabsorbed by the body and then harnessed as energy. Proper religious devotion was impossible without the tremendous energy supplied by conserved semen. Frequent intercourse in a marriage was therefore discouraged and masturbation vilified (soldiers in the ancient world were cautioned against any ejaculations at all). Rabbinical Judaism and Roman Catholicism have long condemned the sin of Onan. The film *Monty Python's The Meaning of Life* even includes a musical send-up of Catholic reverence for semen called "Every Sperm Is Sacred."[6] To the extent that chatting, like pornography, induces masturbation, it is not surprising that a cultural tide of objection rises up to greet this cyber-innovation.

∽

Men fantasize about sex roughly twice as frequently as women, according to studies in Japan, the United Kingdom, and the United States. Men are more likely to fantasize about strangers as well, which means that chatting might tempt men more than women.

But if Oscar Wilde is correct that women fall in love with their ears and men with their eyes, then the textual, nonpictorial world of chat rooms might appeal more to women than men. Some recent fiction (such as Sylvia Brownrigg's *The Metaphysical Touch,* Jeanette Winterson's *The Powerbook,* and Alan Lightman's *The Diagnosis*) prominently feature women chatting. We are sure to see a steady stream of novels involving chatting in the near future, and these works may challenge the very idea that chatting appeals more to one gender than the other.

Women may risk more in chatting or flirting. Culture and law have long been men's domains. It is hardly surprising that religious and secular cultures both reflect a masculine bias. To be sure, there are words for men who "get around": We call them a Don Juan, a Casanova, a Lothario. We call women other names, names that should not be repeated in polite society. For millennia, fathers and husbands have made it difficult for their daughters and wives to flirt. The Internet makes it easier for anyone with access to cyberspace to flirt. As long as women remain economically dependent on men, though, they will risk more in chatting (assuming, of course, that those on whom they depend consider chatting cheating).

Flirting requires a certain comfort level with uncertainty. As the popular saying "flirting with disaster" indicates, we are on our way somewhere when we flirt. We have not arrived, nor will we necessarily. Augustine, who cast greater aspersion on sex than perhaps any other Western thinker, started out as an adventurous young man. His famous plea to God "Give me chastity and continence—but not yet" plays off of flirting. Augustine had not yet embraced the ideal moral life and so, his reasoning goes, did not deserve any credit for the desire. By the same reasoning, we do not deserve blame for flirting with attractive people.

We sustain our notion of fidelity by banishing uncertainty and policing its attendant complications, such as devouring porn magazines, a night at Chippendale's or a topless bar, and everyday flirting. We may understandably fear ambivalence once we have made a romantic commitment. Nonetheless, the idea that better or deeper erotic fulfillment lies elsewhere may nag at us. Through flirting, we enjoy uncertainty. Our comfort level with uncertainty (and love is notoriously unstable) drives our moral evaluation of online dalliances.

WAYS OF CHEATING

Strangers in the Net, exchanging glances, strangers in the Net, what are the chances? They'll be sharing love, before the night is through? The chances of falling in love on-line may not be any worse than in the street.

Yet, as always, a person intent on remaining faithful to a spouse or partner must be careful to avoid crossing a certain line. Whatever else a monogamous commitment may entail, it forbids sex outside the couple.

As I have acknowledged, some people certainly do believe that talking dirty is a form of having sex.[7] In some arenas (such as the office), talking dirty qualifies as sexual harassment, but, as I have said, I don't think it makes sense to call this sex. I hold on to the notion, admittedly old-fashioned, that sex entails skin-to-skin contact. Peeping Toms may get into real legal trouble, but it doesn't make sense to say that voyeurism amounts to having sex. Like sexual harassment, voyeurism implicates the active party but not necessarily the passive one.

Ranking sexual misdeeds requires talent and time. Our legal system can help. "Adultery" signifies penile-vaginal penetration and applies to the illicit sexual activity of two or more people, at least one of whom is married. Only married people can be guilty of adultery: if an unmarried woman engages in vaginal intercourse with a married man, he is guilty of adultery, whereas she is guilty of fornication. "Fornication" is to unmarried people what "adultery" is to the married, which is not to say that married people can't fornicate. "Sodomy" applies to both the married and the unmarried and involves anal and/or oral sex. Because they cannot legally marry, gay and lesbian couples can in principle never be guilty of adultery, only of fornication or sodomy. In the highly publicized Monica Lewinsky case, President Clinton (a married man) was guilty of fornication and Lewinsky was guilty of sodomy.

Moral distinctions loom behind such legal ones. There is nothing legally wrong with serial monogamy, for instance. Lots of people in their late teens and twenties devote themselves in earnest to a sexual relationship that they claim has long-term potential. After the breakup, another relationship begins and then ends. The cycle continues. Morally speaking, such serial monogamy may not seem very different from fornication. And yet most of us will feel there has to be some difference between promiscuity and failing to carry through on good intentions.

It is important to recognize these distinctions as culturally conditioned. Not everyone agrees with American mores (not even in America).

Throughout much of Asia, for example, married men have openly taken concubines with apparent impunity:

> A traditional Chinese or Japanese man could be branded as adulterous only if he slept with the wife of another man. This was taboo. Illicit sex with a married woman was a violation against the woman's husband and his entire ancestry. In China these lawbreakers were burned to death. If a man seduced the wife of his guru in India, he might be made to sit on an iron plate that was glowing hot, then chop off his own penis. A Japanese man's only honorable course was suicide. In traditional Asian agricultural societies, only geishas, prostitutes, slaves, and concubines were fair game. Sex with them was simply not considered adultery.[8]

Not surprisingly, extramarital sex in traditional East Asian cultures was strictly off limits to women, always. What is nonetheless interesting here is the notion that morality (like immorality) has a limit. Adultery doesn't signify *all* sex with someone other than your spouse, just some. This is roughly analogous to the idea that on the third Friday of every month, husbands and wives may morally have sex with anyone they like. If the analogy seems arbitrary, it is because so little of cultural practice is transparent to people who live beyond it.

And so the identity of the person one courted or bedded has figured into the ways other cultures have defined adultery. That identity counts for little in America, where *all* sex with someone other than your spouse qualifies as adultery. Where does cyberflirting fit into this schema? Legally, Internet flirting (what typing Toms do) does not fall into any of our three categories (adultery, fornication, or sodomy). And yet many people will maintain that chatting threatens, or could threaten, monogamous unions. If chatting did represent a kind of cheating, then it would have to be acknowledged as a genuinely new one. I do not think there is anything new under the sun.

Despite the criticism heaped upon Bill Clinton in the wake of his "rationalizations" of sexual adventures (or nonadventures, as he insisted) in the White House, still it remains that most of us agree there is a difference between all-out adultery, hanky panky, and just talking about one or the other. I am not claiming that we should think of the ethics of virtual flirting on a case-by-case basis but that we should think of chat rooms as intrinsically morally ambiguous—neither wholly bad nor wholly good.

Another way of thinking about online fidelity is to ask whether a virgin is still a virgin after chatting. In strict religious terms, certainly not.[9] He or she has affronted modesty—"sinned against purity," as Catholic theologians say. Nowadays it is hard to imagine such a view commanding much agreement, even among Catholics. It is still important to remember that rules in a given religion or society go far toward shaping cultural attitudes, though. We can tell something important about Catholicism, for example, from the fact that its greatest moral theologian of the past century maintained that fantasizing about someone else during sex (with your spouse) was a grave moral sin.[10]

Even virgins may burn with lust. The people whom chatting helps most are those committed to celibacy or monogamous relationships. We should expect these people to become the most ardent defenders of imaginative possibilities wrought by the Internet. An obvious advantage to chat rooms is that they keep people out of bars and clubs: away from actual (as opposed to virtual) adulterous possibilities, and away from sexually transmitted diseases as well. This is hardly a moral defense, admittedly.

A good way of defending chatting in the context of committed relationships (whether straight, gay, or religiously committed) is as a temporary "fix"—not unlike a sleeping pill or an antidepressant. Chatting can help you through the inevitable tough times in a relationship aiming at permanency.

Chatting is dangerous to the extent that it absorbs some of the energy required to make a couple a success. A double life carried out in veiled Internet spaces resembles the closet against which most gay and lesbian people develop a sense of self-identity. Chat rooms can become a new closet of sorts (at base, any deep secret can). Double lives can exhaust us, and the Internet can become a demanding mistress indeed, even an addiction. Until chat room adventures start taking up more time than the relationship from which they are a distraction, this danger has nothing to do with the moral acceptability of courting strangers in cyberspace.

While perhaps not the moral ideal, chat room adventures should not be considered adultery or infidelity. The possibility of deceit lurks here, as it does in so many other places. We may pretend to our spouses or spouse equivalents that we would not, could not, even look at another man or woman. There is no question that Romeos and Juliets would be guilty of deceiving their partners if they entered a chat room after having declared they couldn't even conceive of doing so. How many among us pretend never to notice attractive strangers? How many of us feel threatened when our partners do notice attractive strangers (or familiars, for that matter)? Chiding chatters may reveal more personal insecurity than moral concern. In any event, it seems the only durable moral objection to chatting is deceit. There might be a good practical objection as well: that chatting will inure us to erotic pleasure with our spouses. If the mind could be so easily dulled by the computer screen, then chatting might in fact threaten a sexual tie to a spouse or spouse equivalent.

Some people are better at flirting than others, and some people are better at fidelity than others. Those who excel at flirting may strike us as cruel if they insist on pointing out our inferior charms and relative unattractiveness. And those who excel at fidelity might strike us as cruel if they were to demand perennial center stage in the thoughts of their spouses or spouse equivalents.

PENETRATION VENERATION

Why should penetration serve as the pivotal criterion for infidelity? Precision is a ready answer. It may seem impossibly difficult to ascertain what someone wants from flirting. She bats her eyelashes and he thinks he has a chance. Then she declines his invitation for a drink, and he furiously demands an explanation. She maintains that he misunderstood her attempt at civil conversation. Or another scenario: Eager to show her interest, she requests help repairing her car. He agrees to try. She cries when he leaves without having asked to see her again. Intentions and desires may sometimes drive our behavior, but others may quite understandably fail to see our motives.

Penetration is another story. A penis in a vagina or someone else's tongue in your mouth can be readily felt or observed. Even if we are under the influence of drugs or alcohol, we will almost certainly realize that penetration is taking place. Act and motive overlap, and so penetration lends itself to the certainty lacking in flirting.

Both formally in the law and informally in the streets, we have long venerated penetration as a reliable threshold for whether sexual intercourse is taking place. Two thousand years ago, for instance, the poet Ovid lamented his impotence. In a poem included in the "Amores" series, he wrote: "Although I wanted to do it, and she was more than willing, / I couldn't get my pleasure part to work./ She tried everything and then some. . . ."[11]

Ovid piques our curiosity through the terseness of this last line. Despite the diligence of his partner, Ovid tells us that: "She left me, pure as any Vestal virgin / polite as any sister to her brother."[12] He leaves us to wonder how seriously Vestal virgins took their profession and also how well he knew his sister. Ovid's coquettishness aside, we should take him at his word here. He apparently believed that he had not had sex with this woman, who so exerted herself and with whom he tried "everything and then some." Anne Fausto-Sterling has woven this notion into a description of male identity. "Of course, we know already that for men the true mark of heterosexuality involves vaginal penetration with the penis. Other activities, even if they are with a woman, do not really count."[13] Other writers have used penetration as a dramatic psychological threshold. Entering another person may excite fear, a fear that even marriage may not dislodge:

> Among couples who come to a sex-therapy clinic, the prevalence of
> the madonna/whore or saint/sinner phenomenon is astonishingly

high. It wears a proverbial coat of many colors and designs, and so has many disguises. A classic example is that in which the period of romance and courtship was intensely positive for both partners. They engage in much above-the-belt activity and some heavy petting of the genitals to the point of climax, but no genital union itself. They don't actually say that they are saving the dirty part of sex until after they are legally married. Their own explanation is that they are applying their own moral standards by postponing actual penovaginal penetration.

Once they are legally married, they gradually reach the discovery that they can't have ordinary sexual intercourse. He blames himself for ejaculating too soon and for not being able to arouse her to have much active desire or enthusiasm for his penis. She goes along with his self-blame and keeps both of them blinded to the fact that she has a paralyzing fear of having anything actually penetrate into the cavity of her vagina. For her that would be as degrading as being a whore.[14]

Johns Hopkins psychobiologist John Money draws our attention to a primitive fear of one of the most sensitive boundaries of all—that between our bodies and the outside world. Religious anxiety blossoms on this boundary. This is how sex writer Lisa Palac recounts her furtive sexual debut while a Catholic high school girl in 1970s Chicago:

Just before the big moment, I admitted that I didn't *exactly* know what to do. "Just open your legs and rock," he told me, which sounded remarkably like a Foghat song. It was over in minutes. Afterwards, I was extremely disappointed and felt sick with guilt. I kept torturing myself with the mantra "I am not a virgin I am not a virgin," which was stupid because I'd done practically everything else—as many other girls in my class had done—yet none of that constituted sex. It wasn't sex until he put it in.[15]

Penetration veneration finds itself covertly transmitted through the celebration of modesty in this confession. Later recounting one of her first online erotic encounters, Palac tells us of the terrible guilt she felt after the fact. She warned her chat man: "'If you tell anyone what we just did, I'll never speak to you again!'" She added, "I felt so uncontrollably *Catholic*. I shouldn't have had cybersex on the first date. Big sin. I should have waited. It would have meant more to me if I'd waited!"[16]

Ironic chuckles aside, Palac contradicts herself. Her dirty talk, which in this case eventually progressed from the Internet to the telephone, was not sex, even on her own terms. But vestiges of Catholic school modesty surfaced and prompted guilty feelings.

Carnal contact cannot by itself distinguish flirting from cheating. Unlike exhibitionism or rape, flirting plays off of negotiation. We do not force ourselves on others in flirting; we toy with the exploration of another's opinion of us. It would be too simplistic to reduce flirting to sexual playfulness, though. The ancient Greeks and Romans were notoriously playful sexually. Ascetic Jews and then Christians challenged this playfulness and replaced it with *gravitas,* a high moral seriousness. It is difficult to ally flirtatiousness with either side of this divide. For the sexually playful will pursue flirting until sex, which is to say that the flirting is actually foreplay. The morally serious will swear off flirting generally but smile on a scripted version of chaste romance. Who, then, flirts?

Technically speaking, gregarious people who do not really intend to have sex are just flirting (using penetration as the criterion here). Of course, it is often difficult to predict whether any spirited conversation or eye exchange will lead to full-fledged physical contact. But people who know what they want will see the sense of setting foreplay off from flirting. Seduction can be a game that consciously starts with words and glances. Flirting is an end unto itself—a way of showing someone else that we know "how to play the game" or, perhaps, a test in which we prove to ourselves that we are still attractive. Happily (or even not so happily) married people flirt with colleagues and cocktail party strangers, and it is perfectly acceptable for them to do so. Chatting is the technological celebration of flirting. Adulterous impulses lurking in protected cyberspaces will likely lead to penetration; curiosity, playfulness, or boredom, however, will just end in chatting.

The problem with penetration veneration, to which I myself fall victim, is that we end up saying that a man who receives anonymous fellatio has had sex, whereas two close friends who spend a night cuddling naked in bed have not. Even this position is easier to accept than the idea that typing amounts to having sex, though. In the second scenario, we might applaud whatever moral motivation prevented the two friends from consummating their passion. The first scenario, meaningless as it might have been, lacks this moral motivation.

Penetration veneration molds the mind of many a Westerner, sometimes to quite surprising effect. In *Been There, Haven't Done That,* recent Harvard graduate Tara McCarthy, also Catholic, tells us that she is a virgin, despite having been "touched, kissed, poked, prodded, rubbed, caressed, sucked, licked, bitten—you name it."[17] Reflection on this so-called virgin's way of seeing the world should remind us that sex, despite all the advertising it gets, is neither transparently obvious nor wholly intuitive. If it accomplished nothing else, the media coverage of the Monica Lewinsky scandal made clear the extent to which people can differ over the question of when sex begins and flirting ends.

In a sea of ambiguity, penetration emerges as the best single criterion of cheating we may expect to find.

INFIDELITY ONLINE?

Nothing prompts divorce so often as infidelity. We can't stand it when our partners go astray—"go astray" may mean sex, lying about having had sex, or both. Many of our most engaging plays and novels have relied on infidelity as a plot device.

Who cares about the ethics of cyberchatting? Many if not most couples naturally do, as well as those who worry about the moral health of the communities they inhabit. The sex lives of strangers have something to do with us, after all. Our children may someday attend school or play soccer with their children, and we want those meetings to be as constructive as possible. Our fear of lust affects our children, our neighbors, and our laws.

Moral evaluation of chatting colors the ways couples interact with one another as well as what we think of our teachers, colleagues, priests, and rabbis. It should go without saying that in order to care about the ethics of chatting, you first have to care about something else: fidelity, "sins against purity," or trust. I consider fidelity a moral ideal, one I certainly endorse.

We can remain agnostic as to whether or how often chatting will lead to a face-to-face encounter. My goal here is to isolate chatting from attendant activities and ask whether there is something intrinsic to chatting itself that qualifies as betrayal (of a promise to a lover or to God), as opposed to an exercise of the imagination (whether we can betray others though the free use of our imagination is a question I do not take up here). I have presented penetration as the decisive test of whether someone has cheated, while indicating the unsettling underside of flirting. I concede that a whole-hearted person, a saint of heroic integrity, would consistently avoid flirting of any sort.

Is cyberchatting the moral equivalent of talking to someone in a bar, then? Anonymous chatting is morally superior to the extent that it is less likely to lead to physical contact. Is Net naughtiness, even when it becomes a habit, morally worse than an actual (and physical) one-night stand? No. Net naughtiness enhances the sexual imagination. It teaches as it titillates. Giving into lust and allowing ourselves to chat may provide the illusion of flying over personal limitations that reduce our attractiveness to others. So much of human industry (for example, cosmetics, fitness, fashion, and real estate) comes down to this goal that we really should look sympathetically on chatting. Moreover, we may deepen our sense of who we are and what we want from anonymous chatting. Net naughtiness challenges the sexual uniformity many take monogamy to impose. It shows us that something like sexual diversity is possible without shattering monogamous bonds.

Net naughtiness strains traditional ideas about what a person is. Are the faceless strangers we meet online real people? Can we hurt their feelings? Can they have us arrested? They understand that we do not know who they are; presumably they cannot be slighted by us over the Internet in the way that they can in person. Given the way the Internet depersonalizes human contact (even as it increases the opportunities for locating other people), it is hard to say whether chatting involves another human being in the way that even a one-night stand does. How thinly can we stretch our notion of a person? Very thin indeed, chatting shows us. Those we chat with may seem no more human than the characters who populate the fiction we read.

In the course of defending it, I have recognized the danger of chatting. If it is true that "women are more forgiving and less upset if no emotional involvement accompanies their husband's affair,"[18] then extensive chatting might seem more threatening than a one-night stand. Pen pals or Net pals might seem to develop an emotional attachment to one another over time, an attachment unlikely to begin in a one-night stand. Time, or duration, has a lot to do with both the psychological and moral evaluation of chatting. A night of passion is for many fuming spouses easier to forgive than a cultivated attachment. Chatting certainly can fray our commitments to others, no less than our quest for self-fulfillment.

In sum, the Internet has given lust a new outlet. Fantasy life has always been possible, and pornography already abounded in ancient Greece and Rome (despite Plato's disapproval). Being human just got more exciting—and more complicated. The Internet and the phone may threaten fidelity, chastity, even integrity—but no more so than old-fashioned pornography. Chat rooms may in the long run facilitate fidelity, insofar as they can in themselves satisfy an active imagination.

A pleasure both simple and complex, chatting captures nicely the undying tension between trust and lust. Making room for chatting in a monogamous relationship honors both the promise of sexual exclusivity and the titanic power of the imagination.

NOTES

Pamela Karlan, Jerome Neu and Anthony Ellis graciously provided comments on this essay, which Daniel Ortiz especially enriched.

1. Edith Hamilton and Huntington Cairns, eds., *The Collected Dialogues of Plato,* trans. Lane Cooper et al. (Princeton, New Jersey: Princeton University Press, 1961), pp. 64, 82, 402–405, 485.

2. Augustine, *Confessions,* Trans. R. S. Pine-Coffin, (Baltimore: Penguin Books, 1961),10.30.41–42.

3. This, despite the allowance of the highly influential eighteenth-century Roman Catholic theologian St. Alphonsus Liguori that having sex in a church or a public place might be allowed in a case of "necessity." See Peter Gardella, *Innocent Ecstasy: How Christianity Gave America an Ethic of Sexual Pleasure* (New York: Oxford University Press, 1985), p. 18.

4. G. E. M. Anscombe, "Contraception and Chastity," *The Human World* 7 (1972), p. 22.

5. Kazuo Ishiguro, *The Remains of the Day* (New York: Vintage, 1990), p. 245.

6. *Monty Python's The Meaning of Life* (Celandine Films, 1983), starring Graham Chapman, John Cleese, Terry Gilliam, Eric Idle, Terry Jones, Michael Palin, Sydney Arnold, and Guy Bertrand. Kasy Moon provided the correct reference here.

7. "You can meet someone on-line. You can fall in love on-line. You can even consummate that love on-line." Paco Underhill, *Why We Buy: The Science of Shopping* (New York: Simon & Schuster, 1999), p. 212.

8. Helen Fisher, *Anatomy of Love* (New York: W. W. Norton, 1992), pp. 79–80.

9. Bernard Häring, *The Law of Christ,* trans. Edwin G. Kaiser (Westminster, MD: Newman Press, 1966), vol. III, p. 306.

10. Ibid., pp. 375–376.

11. Quoted in Elizabeth Abbott, *A History of Celibacy* (New York: Scribners, 2000), p. 354.

12. *Ibid.*

13. Anne Fausto-Sterling, "How to Build a Man" in Vernon A. Rosario (ed.), *Science and Homosexualities,* (New York: Routledge, 1997), pp. 219–225. Quoted in Robert A Nye, ed., *Sexuality* (New York: Oxford University Press, 1999), p. 238.

14. John Money, *The Destroying Angel* (Buffalo, NY: Prometheus Books, 1985), p. 127.

15. Lisa Palac, *The Edge of the Bed: How Dirty Pictures Changed My Life* (Boston: Little, Brown, 1998), p. 20.

16. Ibid., p. 106.

17. Tara McCarthy, *Been There, Haven't Done That: A Virgin's Memoir* (New York: Warner Books, 1997), p. 3.

18. David M. Buss, *The Evolution of Desire: Strategies of Human Mating* (New York: Basic Books, 1994), p. 155.

CHAPTER THIRTEEN

In Defense of
PROMISCUITY

*W*ho would dare defend promiscuity, or casual sex? After all, having sex isn't like changing shirts, is it? Surely sex is a moral activity, hence a very serious one.

Elizabeth Anscombe (1919–2001), a Cambridge University professor and influential moral philosopher, denied that there was even such a thing as casual, non-significant sex. Miss Anscombe, as she preferred to be called, drew a distinction between sexual acts which were capable of being genuine marriage acts and those sexual acts which were not. Contraceptive intercourse within marriage was the latter (as, in her view, were masturbation and homosexual sex) and therefore offended morality more than straightforward adultery or fornication (presumably without contraception).

Anscombe had converted to Roman Catholicism in 1940. Devoutly religious, she held that modern philosophy fundamentally misunderstood ethics; she taught that notions like "moral obligation," "moral duty," "morally right," and "morally wrong" mean nothing without the idea of a law-giving God to back them up.

Part of what makes Miss Anscombe interesting is that she dared to step where most other philosophers fear to tread. In a pamphlet entitled "Contraception and Chastity" (1975), she lamented the consequences of contraception: "you might as well accept any sexual goings-on, if you accept contraceptive intercourse." For Anscombe (as for all Catholics who follow the pope on this matter), a legitimate sexual act must be of the "procreative type," as she put it. If you use contraception, you are having sex for pleasure, or perhaps just to express love. Once you allow sex merely for pleasure or love, though, it becomes much more difficult to oppose sex between two men or two women. Allowing contraception within marriage might eventually lead to social acceptance of promiscuity, and would even, she warned, legitimize gay sex. Anscombe has a powerful point here. However, the majority of people who oppose gay rights today probably think that birth control is just fine.

In the following essay from 1986, the British philosopher Anthony Ellis probes sexual morality. There is indeed such a thing as "casual sex," he urges us to see, and it need not always be considered immoral.

∾

ANTHONY ELLIS was Senior Lecturer in Moral Philosophy and Chair of the Moral Philosophy Department in the University of St. Andrews, Scotland, before becoming Professor of Philosophy in Virginia Commonwealth University. He was also cofounder and first Academic Director of the Centre for Philosophy and Public Affairs in St. Andrews. He is currently editor of the journal *Philosophical Books*.

CASUAL SEX

Anthony Ellis

*There is no such thing as a casual, non-significant
sexual act; everyone knows this.*
—(Anscombe 1976: 148)

I shall distinguish *casual* from *non-significant*.

We have an intuitive idea of what is meant by casual sex. But it is
not true that everybody knows that there is no such thing. On the
contrary, nearly everybody knows that there is such a thing. The only
question is about whether it is morally acceptable.

In the ordinary understanding, whether a sexual act is casual or not
depends upon the relationship between the partners, not upon the
motive, manner, or consequences of the act. Most people would find it
odd to be told that a happily married couple had indulged in casual sex
with each other; the oddness would not be removed by the explanation
that they had done it for fun, or out of lust, or whatever. A sexual act
could not be casual, in the ordinary sense, if the partners had an
(intendedly) long-term and exclusive commitment to each other in
which sexual activity was a component. Roughly (it is in any case only a
rough idea) we can say that casual sex is sex between partners who have

no deep or substantial relationships of which sex is a component. Thus, friends can have casual sex: their friendship may not be deep; if it is deep, then it may still be true that sex is no part of what makes it the relationship that it is. If sex becomes an essential part of their relationship, then they are no longer just friends (but lovers) and their sex is no longer casual sex. The paradigm case is sex between people who are only casually acquainted, or related only by some other sort of relationship, such as a professional one. Sex between strangers is the most extreme example, but probably the rarest.

The idea of *non-significance* is harder to get hold of. The claim that there is no such thing as a non-significant sexual act could mean different things.

It might be said that one cannot have a conception of what a sexual act is that makes no use of moral vocabulary. It is clear that there are such concepts. (Though there are fewer, in my view, than is often thought. *Contract,* for instance, is not one, since it requires only a legal vocabulary, and this is true of many of the putative instances of such concepts.) Whether the concept of a sexual act is such a concept is not easy to be clear about. If we assume that a full understanding of the sexual act will involve the notion of *procreation,* and thus of *parent* and *child,* then it begins to look plausible. But of course we cannot assume this. For one thing, it is not clear that we have any licence here for going beyond *progenitor* to that of *parent,* and it is not at all clear that *progenitor* is a moral concept. And some people think that *parent* is not a moral concept. More important, even if we could show that the concept of a sexual act were such a concept, very little of any relevance to our present interests would follow. Even if a full account of sexual acts must employ some moral vocabulary, it would not follow that every sexual act will engage the sort of issue that requires this vocabulary. Any given sex act may, in the event, do so of course; but then *any* action of any sort may raise moral issues. One might admit that sexual acts are more likely to do this than are many other sorts, but unless we were unjustifiably pessimistic about foreseeing the consequences of sexual acts specifically this would not suggest to us that all sexual acts are morally significant.

A related claim might be that a full description of the place of sex in our lives must make some reference to moral matters. This is no doubt true, but is again of no interest. A complete account of the place of games in our life will require some reference to morality, but this does not show that every piece of play is morally significant in any interesting way. And again, we could agree that sex is more likely to raise serious moral issues than are games.

Something else that might be meant by the claim would be that sexual acts are, as a class, one of the things that invest our lives with significance. (I do not mean just enjoyment.) This may be true: indeed, I shall later argue that it probably is true, and that this in turn might be the result of our not being too casual about sex (rather than the other way round). But this is not obvious. And it does not imply that there is no such thing as a non-significant sexual act. I shall return to this.

Something quite different that the claim could mean would be this: that there is always a moral presumption against the act, a presumption that can be overridden if and only if certain conditions obtain. This is the view that most people take about, say, lying; and certainly, some people hold this view of sexual acts. But it is not an attractive view, at least if it is spelled out in one way. That way would be to say that the act, in itself, is simply morally wrong, but that it may become permissible, or required, if the good that can be achieved by it is sufficiently great. As I have said, some people hold this view, but I have no wish to discuss it.

Something quite different again that could be meant would be this: it might be held that the sexual act is of a sort such that any instance of it must be either positively good or positively bad, unlike most of what we do which is of neutral value. Some people might think that there are no such acts; and certainly the issue is a difficult one. But it is not implausible to claim that there are such acts: one might think this about divine worship, for instance. However, any such claim would have to be explained and defended. In the case of sexual acts, this will not be easy. One might claim that the function of the sexual act is to procreate, or to express love, and that any such act, properly performed, is intrinsically good. But if the act is performed recklessly of this proper function then it becomes bad. I shall not discuss this view; there are familiar objections to this style of thinking. And I do not see how else one could plausibly try to defend this claim.

II

I take it that sexual acts may be good, bad, or neutral, right, wrong, or indifferent. It does not follow that casual sex may not always be wrong or bad. That is the claim I wish to discuss.

A particular act may be morally unacceptable in three different ways.

First, it might have, on balance, bad consequences, and this may be enough to make it wrong for someone to do it.

Second, whatever its consequences, it may issue from a bad or inappropriate motive.

Third, though it may have, on balance, good consequences, and issue from a good motive, it may be unacceptable as being an act of a certain sort. It is wrong to commit murder, and it would not be made right merely by the fact that the act produced, on balance, good consequences and proceeded from a good motive. (Or so it is generally, and plausibly, thought).

Many actions of the third type are wrong or bad because the type itself is specified partly in terms of consequences which it is impermissible to bring about. Thus to *murder* someone is, in part, to do something that has his death as a consequence. But it need not be consequences that make actions of a certain type wrong or bad. It may equally be the circumstances or the manner in which the act is performed. But if an action type is claimed to be morally unacceptable in itself, then some explanation should be available. We are not forced to answer that it just is wrong when somebody asks why murder is wrong. We can say something about the evil of death, the innocence of the victim, and so on.

If someone claims that casual sex is a wrong type of act, independently of its motive or consequences, then he must give us some explanation of *why* it is wrong. I have already dismissed (without argument) one sort of such explanation: it might be said that casual sex is necessarily divorced from its proper function. This is the most common type of such explanation. Sometimes people say that what is wrong or bad about casual sex is that it is an exploitative relationship: but this, strictly, is to characterize its motive, and I shall deal with it later. And indeed, it is hard to see what could plausibly be said about the act itself to explain why it is always wrong or bad. The partners may be acting freely, in full knowledge of what they are doing, violating no one's rights, deceiving no one. Unsurprisingly, then, most attempts to show that casual sex is morally unacceptable focus either on motives or consequences, or both. In the first half of the remainder of this paper I shall consider the question of the possible motives that casual sex might express, and in the second half its consequences.

III

A common view is that, standardly, the motive behind casual sex is lust, and lust is a bad motive.

It is worth pointing out that casual sex may be the result of all manner of motives, some of them, as motives, good and others bad. One may do it out of kindness, or a desire to hurt, or as a way of earning money, for instance. Many people would condemn casual sex even when its motivating force was not lust but some motive in itself morally admirable, so *their* objection to casual sex would not simply reflect an objection to *lust*. (Of course, they might object to that too.)

Some people think that whereas lust is an unacceptable attitude in casual relations, it is acceptable in non-casual ones. Others think it unacceptable in any relationship whatever; this seems to be the view of the present pope, for instance, who holds that a man who lusts after his wife commits adultery with her in his heart. The wording is provocative, but the basic thought is clear.

To discuss lust, then, is not the same thing as to discuss casual sex. But it is not implausible to think of lust as the standard motive for casual sex and so I shall devote most of my discussion to it.

What *is* lust? I shall define it, initially, simply as the desire for sexual activity for its own sake. This may manifest itself as an undirected yearning simply for sexual activity as such, or, at the other extreme, a desire precisely focussed on a particular person and which could not be satisfied by sexual activity with anyone else. Such a precisely focussed desire does not, of course, *preclude* sex with anyone else, and may be *dissipated* by it; but that is quite different. (Such dissipation is, I would guess, the most usual result of masturbation, which rarely satisfies the desire which motivates it. Hence, no doubt, the sense of futility which, as D. H. Lawrence observed, is a standard accompaniment of masturbation.)

Lust is, in its logical structure, like the desire for food. One may simply be hungry, and will then find desirable food that is placed in front of one even when one had previously had no thought of this particular food (though not just any food will do); or one may just fancy some particular food whether one is hungry or not (and only that food could satisfy that desire, though some other food may dissipate it).

Let us speak, then, of undirected and directed lust.

Is there any reason to think of *directed* lust as morally objectionable? Some people think that it is intrinsically the desire to *use* somebody, that it involves regarding them as a means rather than an end, and that it is therefore necessarily an exploitative attitude. This is because it is not the woman[1] in herself one is interested in; rather, she is simply a means to one's own pleasure.

It is easy to see that this alleged contrast amounts to nothing. If the allegation is that the woman is being regarded merely as a mechanical device for producing pleasurable sensations, then this reveals a total ignorance of the phenomenology of sex. This is simply not what lust is. (I do not deny that there *is* such a way of regarding people, but, unlike lust, it is very rare.) It is a very striking fact that the face is a vitally important element in the object of lust. Anyone who doubts this can, I think, verify it by the most superficial inspection of pictorial pornography—from some of the Tate Pre-Raphaelites to contemporary popular erotic photography. This is a symptom of the fact that lust is an attitude to a *person,* as such. In its most common form it is the desire to have a reciprocal relationship with another person.[2] It is worth emphasizing the word "reciprocal." Lust is not the desire to have sex with someone whatever her attitude may be; it involves the desire that she herself should have that same attitude.

If, on the other hand, the allegation amounts to this: that one wants a sexual relationship with the woman merely for the pleasure of it, then this is no doubt true but is quite innocuous. For this does not involve regarding the woman as a means. To want to do something with someone (to on a picnic or a mountain climb, say) simply because one would enjoy it does not involve using them as a means to one's enjoyment. (Or it does, simply in virtue of a decision to employ the notion in that way; but then it is completely mysterious why anyone should think it objectionable to use someone as a means to one's own pleasure.)

What it is to use someone as a means is not in fact easy to say. We use people, such as bus conductors, all the time. Kant's prohibition (Kant 1785) was on using someone as a means *only*. This must mean something like the following: being prepared to ignore or override his needs, desires or will when one ought not. And *when* ought one not to do this? We do not need to answer that question to see that, whatever the answer, lust need not involve such a preparedness. Of course, it may: so may any desire. To think that lust is intrinsically, or even characteristically, prone to this vice is not, in my view, worldly wisdom but something considerably less attractive.

A related objection is that lust is morally distasteful because it is a response to only one aspect of a person; it may be thought that this has the implication that it is not really true that lust is, as I expressed it above, an attitude to a person as such.

The objection can take many forms. The most popular is that lust involves only a desire for the woman's *body,* and so involves no attitude to her as a *person.* It is easy to see that this is wrong. For one thing, it may be that other aspects of a person than her body arouse sexual desire; indeed, it is commonplace that this is so. One may be aroused by the awareness of a flirtatious manner, or a vivacious personality, or a wanton character, or simply by being the object of lust oneself.

Secondly, and most importantly, the particular contrast between the body and the person that is being used here is confused. One does not have to take any very controversial view about the so-called mind-body problem to see this. We may say, minimally, that our only access to people is through their bodies. And our attitude to a human body (and to most animal bodies) is not simply the attitude to a physical object. A human body is, for us, a *human*. Hence the importance of the face, which is expressive of most of what is human in us, including sexuality. And when someone is sexually aroused by a body then this perception is immediately surrounded by a sense of the body as the body of a person, and by thought of the more general sexual relationship that the satisfaction of this desire would require.

It may be that there are cases where this is not so, where the desire for the body is just the desire for a physical object satisfying certain physical conditions. I very much doubt it, in fact, but such deviations would be in any case, in one sense, of no interest. Compare necrophilia. Necrophilia is not like this in fact, since the necrophiliac lusts after a corpse, which (to him as to others) is not merely a physical object, but a dead person; still, it runs counter to all that I have said so far. It is lust that precisely is not aimed at even the most minimal sort of human relationship; and it certainly exists. But the most significant fact about necrophilia for our purposes is that the normal person finds it unintelligible. Of course, psychiatrists and others try to articulate what they take to be the motives of the necrophiliac. Most of these thoughts strike me as crude and predictable, but that is not to the point; even if we did have some understanding of the motivation of necrophilia, it is a motivation that most of us do not share—it is not that we share the motivation but have stronger inhibitions than the necrophiliac. Such phenomena throw no light on normal sexual motivations, save by contrast, and it is in that sense that they are of no interest.

Lust, then, is not, in the way required by the objection, the desire merely for a body. But the objection may take another form. Someone may say that the relationship aimed at in lust is merely a partial one, even though it involves more than the mere body. When one wants merely a sexual relationship with someone, then that is all one wants; but there is much more to a person than that. A sexual interest, then is an interest in only a *part* of the person and is therefore not an attitude to a person as such.

In one obvious sense this is true. If one lusts after someone there will be much about her life that one has no interest in. She may be, perhaps, a talented chess player, and this fact may not engage with one's attitude to her at all. It is a mistake to think that her sexual life can be separated from everything else about her, since sex has all sorts of connections with the rest of one's life. But it is true that, as far as one's lust goes, much of her life will be of no interest.

I have put the point as harshly as I can, but it is, even so, hard to see what could be found objectionable here. After all, most (at least) of our relationships with people are partial in this way. There is much about the life of my friends in which I have no interest. A friend may have a passion for golf, say, in which I have no interest at all, and this may not engage in any way with my relationship with him. ("May not," since equally, in a different case, it may.) Of course, circumstances may arise in which friendship requires that I *take* an interest; it may be that on some occasion he simply wishes to talk to someone about a particularly enjoyable game that he has played. But equally, such circumstances may not arise.

Not only is it the case that our relationships are generally like this. It is plausible to think that they *ought* to be. Even the most intimate relationship should be conditioned by the thought that one's friend or whatever has a life independent of oneself, and the most natural, perhaps inevitable, way in which this expresses itself is in one's friends having some part of their lives in which one has no interest.

However *this* may be, there is no reason to lay a demand on sexual relations which other relations, casual and non-casual, do not satisfy. I may, for instance, enjoy playing chess with someone, or music; and I may, at some point, simply desire to play some music with that person. No one objects to this on the ground of its being the desire to have a relationship with only a part of a person. I may have no great interest in other aspects of her life, but so long as I am prepared to take the appropriate sort of interest should the occasion arise, then this is perfectly acceptable.

The point can be put differently, and less provocatively. When I say that one may wish to have a particular sort of relationship with someone, and have no interest in other aspects of her life, then the phrase "have no interest" is ambiguous. It may simply mean that my interest is not actively engaged by these aspects in themselves. Or it may mean that I simply do not care about these aspects, whatever they may be, and that I have no intention of meeting any demands they may come to place upon me. The latter attitude is, of course, reprehensible, but there is no reason to think it characteristic of, let alone intrinsic to, lust. The former attitude is indeed intrinsic to lust, and to most of the desires that we have about other people; but there is nothing unacceptable about it.

Many people have thought that it is in the nature of lust to make one careless of the needs and desires of the person one lusts after (the latter attitude) because it is such a dominatingly powerful motive. There is nothing much to say about this except that it is clearly false. Lust comes in every degree of strength. In some people it can be overmastering, and lead to callousness and cruelty. But all of this is true of many motives. No one objects to the desire for material well-being simply on the ground that it can become greed and lead to deceit, theft and murder. Why lust has been thought specially prone to corruption in this way is, in my view, a question for historians, and I have no desire to speculate on it here.[3] Even if it were true it would not, of course, show that lust is *intrinsically* vicious.

I have tried to suggest that there is nothing morally objectionable about what I earlier called *directed* lust. What should be said of undirected lust?

At first glance it may seem that this is more obviously morally unappealing. Here, one's lust is not aroused by the particular person; one simply has an undirected yearning which eventually focusses on somebody. But it might have been someone else; and whilst it is true that just anyone would do, one's attention is not focussed on the object of one's lust in the same way as in directed lust. In directed lust, only *this* person can satisfy one's desire. (Of course, undirected lust may *become* directed lust.)

To be the object of undirected lust is not, clearly, particularly flattering. (Which is not to say that it is demeaning.) But this has nothing to do with morality. More relevantly, a sexual relationship motivated in this way seems to be, given the way things go, more vulnerable to lack of candour and one-sidedness. But that is not intrinsic to the motive, merely a corruption which the motive is prone to lead to; and it need not do so.

About the motive itself, we should say what I have already said about directed lust; it is morally neutral. Parallels are not uncommon in the rest of our lives. One might fancy a game of golf and go to the golf club simply to find someone to play with. Not just anyone will do, but equally it is not that one wants a round with just *this* person. All of this is consistent with respecting one's partner and one's relationship with him in every way that is morally required. If sex is different in any relevant way then this has to be shown, and I do not think it can be.

I have spoken so far of lust, and have tried to suggest that there is nothing objectionable about this attitude to people. But of course there are other motives that can lead to casual (or indeed to non-casual) sex. About these, there seems to me to be very little of a philosophical, or even of a very general, sort to say.

Plainly, some of these are bad. One can want to have sex with someone merely to hurt them, or gain power over them. Such things can occur in almost any sort of relationship, casual and non-casual alike, and it is clear what is to be said about them. Some of them can, of course, even occur in a loving relationship, since none of us is perfect. This is not to deny that some of them, even in the form of temporary outbursts, are not compatible with a loving relationship—I would contrast here, for instance, the desire to hurt and the desire to have power over someone—but this is a point about the nature of love, not about sex, which is no more prone to such corrupt motivations than is any other human relation.

Other motives, it seems to me, are just plainly good. One can want to have sex with someone as an act of kindness, say.[4] It may be that this is often misguided but, if that is so, it is not to the point here.

About other motives, it seems to me that there can be serious and respectable dispute, partly because we do not have a proper moral grasp of the motive itself, and partly because we do not know much about how the motive in itself interacts with the attitudes to the sexual acts that it leads to. Take prostitution, for instance. It is clear that this is generally morally tawdry in the extreme. But that, it seems to me, does not follow immediately from the fact that one of the motives involved (not necessarily the main one) is material profit. It would need an enormous argument to show that this motive corrupts everything it touches; it touches most of what people do, since most people spend most of their time (as I am now) earning a living. But perhaps it could be shown. If, instead, it is specially prone to corrupt sexual relationships, then this also has to be shown. And it may be possible to show it, perhaps by showing that, characteristically anyway, prostitution will involve deception about the sort of "relationship" that is being paid for. Or worse than that may characteristically be involved. But in any case none of this would tell us anything about casual sex as such.

About the motives to casual sex there is no general moral judgement to be made. Sometimes they are good, sometimes they are bad.

IV

We say that some acts are wrong, even if they can proceed from good motives, on the ground that they tend to lead to consequences which are, on balance, bad. Could this be said of casual sex?

"Tends to" here could cover a number of different possibilities. It could mean no more than that casual sex *often* leads to consequences which are undesirable on balance (for brevity, I shall from now on assume this qualification). Though this is no doubt true, it is uninteresting, since very many things that it is not wrong to do often lead to undesirable consequences.

More strongly, "tends to" could mean (1) that casual sex *normally* leads to undesirable consequences, (2) that it *always* does so, or (3) that it *necessarily* does so.

We must also make another distinction. Casual sex is, in Western society, not the norm. It is not especially common, and it is very generally thought to be morally unacceptable. It is, of course, indulged in frequently by particular people and is common in some subgroups of society, but in these cases it exists against a background in which it is not the norm. When we ask about the morality of casual sex we need to know whether we are asking about the morality of particular acts of casual sex against a background in which it is not the norm, or about the morality of its being, hypothetically, the norm.

As things are at present in Western society, I do not think it can be shown that casual sex necessarily, always, or normally leads to undesirable consequences.

To show that casual sex necessarily leads to undesirable consequences would surely be impossible. It would have to be shown that it *always* does so, and that things simply could not be any different. This is very hard to show for any type of act whatever. One can always think of deep changes in the psychology of human beings, or in social structures, which would alter the value of the consequences being envisaged. One can also think of changes sufficiently deep to take away any possibility of forming sensible judgements about what, in those circumstances, would be desirable and undesirable.

Could it be shown that casual sex *always* leads to undesirable consequences? Again, this would be difficult to believe: indeed, it is generally agreed that this cannot be shown to be so for type of act whatever.

The most promising possibility is that we might show that, as things are, casual sex normally leads to undesirable consequences. This would be enough for the conclusion that casual sex is morally wrong, as such judgements are normally understood. At its weakest, we could infer from this judgement that normally, we ought not to do it; this would leave open the possibility that on those occasions when we could foresee that the consequences would not be undesirable then the act would be permissible. More strongly, however, it might be possible to argue that the chances of (correctly) foreseeing all of the relevant consequences are sufficiently low for it to be the case that, though the act only *normally* leads to undesirable consequences, we should nonetheless *always* refrain from it. I do not intend to try to decide between these two possibilities.

Can it be shown that casual sex normally leads to undesirable consequences?

People sometimes appeal to the fact that casual sex leads to disease and unwanted pregnancies; and this objection need not be paternalistic, since these things can affect society at large. But I take it that it is clear what we should say about this. As long as these risks are present, then precautions should be taken against them; and those precautions will often amount simply to abstention. But there is a sense in which this requirement is not specifically a part of sexual morality. Disease and unwanted pregnancy are medical problems, and if there is no other objection to casual sex then the first response to those problems should be to seek a medical solution.

Sometimes it is said that indulgence in casual sex trivialises one, makes one shallow. If this is true in some sense or other, it is worth knowing, though it is not immediately clear that it is a moral objection. (In general, there is no moral objection to doing that which harms only oneself.) The real problem is in knowing what exactly the claim is supposed to mean, and what evidence there is supposed to be for it. It ought to mean that indulgence in casual sex will have discernible effects in one's life (if only in one's sexual life), presumably making one less able to take seriously things that are serious (which might adversely affect others). There seems to be no evidence that this is true, and much evidence that it is false.

Does it *need* evidence? It may be thought that it is just obvious that if one indulges in casual sex then one will become unable to take sex in general seriously, lose the capacity to have sex as an essential element in a deep and intimate relation, say. But this is not obvious. It is not *a priori*. There is no contradiction in the idea of someone being able, in different contexts, to regard the same thing both casually and seriously. (We can laugh at jokes about death; and this phenomenon does not need the crude and ponderous explanations it is often given.) The claim has to be one about psychological effects, and as such it seems, as I have said, to be false.

It seems clear, in fact, that we cannot make any general claim about the personal consequences of casual sex. We do not have the evidence. And indeed, we have no real reason to think that there *is* anything very general to be said beyond this: casual sex has attendant risks; it can also be enjoyable. (And perhaps just as the pleasure in casual sex is less than many people expect, so the risks are less than many people fear.)

Casual sex, as I have said, is not the norm in Western society. Against this background I have said that there is no reason to think that it will generally lead to undesirable consequences. But we may also raise the question: what if casual sex were completely normal? That is to say, what if there were no presumption that sex should largely be confined to couples who have a serious relationship in which sex is a component? One reason, though not the only one, for asking this is that it may be thought that this would be a bad state of affairs, and that indulgence in casual sex as things are tends to lead to this state of affairs. This would, of course, be a different sense of "tends to" from those I distinguished earlier. I shall return to the question whether casual sex has this tendency. For now, I shall address myself to the question whether it would be a good or bad thing if casual sex were the norm.

The question is hard to think about, since we have no experience of a life sufficiently like our own in which casual sex is entirely normal. Those groups and individuals for whom it is normal practise it against a background in which it is not normal, and it is not easy to know what it would be like otherwise. But a plausible thought is that there would be losses and gains.

The major gain, presumably, would be that there would be more, and more varied, sex. In itself, that must be a good. But the gain should not be exaggerated. The excitement of casual sex at present derives in part from the fact that it is not the norm, and it seems very likely that the greater amount and variety of sexual experience would be to some extent offset by this experience being less exciting and enjoyable.

The likely loss is even harder to be clear about, but it is plausible to think that if we were completely casual about sex then we should have lost one of the elements in our life that gives it significance.

As things are, our sexual relationships are one of the things that make our lives significant. They are, as one might say, a vehicle for human value. It is easy to think that this is why we hedge them round with ceremony and restrictions, but the truth, in my view, is pretty well the other way around: it is because we treat them in this way that they can be significant in the way that they are.

Let us take a parallel. Children create in their lives relationships which, in their exclusiveness and intensity, are like sexual relationships in infusing their lives with significance. And these relationships generally have as an essential element a particular place where only these children go, or a particular thing that only these children do. Two children might have, for instance, a tree house, and only they go there. They may never have said explicitly that this is how things are to be, never have entered into any agreement; this relationship simply grows, and the tree house is part of it. Sometimes, children think that the enjoyment they derive from these relationships can be generalized: the more people with whom I play in the tree house the more fun I shall have, obviously. So we can imagine that one day one of the children takes another child to the tree house, and after that it can never be the same again. They can still play there, of course; they now play there with other children and so their play can be more varied and perhaps more relaxed. But something significant will have been lost. Their relationship may survive, of course, but only because there will be other things in their lives that play this sort of role.

Sex, it seems to me, plays a role like this in our lives. It is not the only thing that does so, but it is peculiarly fitted for the role. And clearly, it could not play that role if we were completely casual about it. So if we were completely casual about sex something that we value would be lost. And it would not be as easy to replace as a children's tree house.

So there would be a loss and a gain. Would the gain outweigh the loss? I do not think we know the answer to that question. We have too little idea of what the possibilities we are trying to envisage would actually be like. And in any case, the loss and the gain seem to be along different dimensions, and we have no clear idea how to weigh one against the other.

I want to turn, finally and briefly, to a question I postponed a moment ago. Can it be said that, as things are, casual sex tends to lead to a state of affairs in which we would be completely casual about sex? That is, can it be held that each act of casual sex makes it more likely (even if only to a very small degree) that such a state of affairs will eventually obtain? Difficult and technical issues are involved in this question, which I cannot go into here,[5] but it seems to me that we should be sceptical about this claim. It is clear that many practices and attitudes can survive some degree of non-compliance perfectly securely, and this seems to me to be true of our attitudes to sex. For one thing, those attitudes are not simple; they leave room for casual sex in many circumstances, or at least find it easy to condone it. For another thing, they are very deep. They are shared, if only at an emotional level, by many of those who think there is no objection to casual sex. And there is in any case no reason to think that most people have any settled desire to be more casual about sex, nor even that they have a latent desire that could be awakened by the experience of it. Indeed, since there has always been some significant degree of casual sex there is good reason to think this is not the case. We should conclude, then, that our attitudes to sex are not in fact threatened by indulgence in casual sex as things now are. And in that case there seems to be no moral objection to it.

NOTES

I am grateful to Alice Anne Ellis, David Cockburn, and John Haldane for helpful discussion of this issue.

1. For brevity, I shall speak of men's lust for women.
2. Thomas Nagel has described this aspect of sexual desire (Nagel 1969).
3. A crude, but nonetheless beguiling, thought is that this idea characteristically has its source in people whose own sexual lives have been repressed, and its home in societies whose official morality is formed by such people.

4. H. A. Williams caused something of a stir in 1962 when he suggested in his article "Theology and Self-Awareness" that a casual sexual relation might be "an act of charity which proclaims the glory of God" (Williams 1962: 81).
5. The problem of how we are to understand the contributions made by a single act to an outcome which requires the joint action of a number of agents has been much discussed in the utilitarian tradition. The best recent treatment is by Derek Parfit (Parfit 1984: 67–86).

REFERENCES

Anscombe, E. (1976) "Contraception and Chastity" in Ed. Bayles.

Bayles, M.D. (ed.) (1976) *Ethics and Population*. Cambridge, Mass.: Schenkman.

Kant, I. (1785) *Grundlegung zur Metaphysik der Sitten* (translated by Beck. L.W. (1959) as *Foundations of the Metaphysics of Morals*. New York: Bobbs-Merrill).

Nagel, T. (1969) "Sexual Perversion" in *The Journal of Philosophy* LXVI.

Parfit, D. (1984) *Reasons and Persons*. Oxford: The Clarendon Press.

Vidler, A. R. (1962) *Soundings*. Cambridge: Cambridge University Press.

Williams, H. A. (1962) "Theology and Self-Awareness" in Ed. Vidler.

The editor is grateful to Cora Diamond for a helpful discussion on Elizabeth Anscombe.

CHAPTER FOURTEEN

In Defense of
PROSTITUTION

*A*ugustine once asked: "What can be more sordid, more void of modesty, more full of shame than prostitutes, brothels, and every evil of this kind? Yet remove prostitutes from human affairs, and you will pollute all things with lust; set them among honest matrons, and you will dishonour all things with disgrace and turpitude." Well over a thousand years later, prostitution is widely outlawed and condemned.

In a richly documented article from 1979 (from which this except is taken), David A. J. Richards tries to establish that there are no good moral arguments for criminalizing consensual adult commercial sex. In this necessarily narrow excerpt from an extensively reasoned essay, Richards takes aim principally at Immanuel Kant, perhaps the single most influential moral philosopher since Aristotle. Richards examines Kant's argument (in the *Foundations of the Metaphysics of Morals* from 1784) that the commercial sale of sex is intrinsically immoral for the same reason that the sale of body parts is shameful. Richards argues that commercial sex is no more the sale of sexual organs than is the sale of a mover's muscles or a model's beauty or a lawyer's legal talent. Respect for autonomy demands providing people with the choice to sell their sexual services.

Beyond that, Richards asserts: "Many women have traditionally found in prostitution a useful escape from limited, oppressive, and parochial family and career lives." What complicates thinking about the morality of prostitution is insistence that prostitutes loathe their work. If Richards is correct, such loathing does not always occur. This insight will no doubt redouble the efforts of opponents to keep prostitution criminal—both legally and morally.

Perhaps the most interesting prostitution takes place not on seedy street corners but in corporate hallways, Hollywood back rooms, and university offices. We will never succeed in preventing attractive people from discreetly exchanging sex for professional or personal promotion.

Richards, as a legal scholar, principally takes aim at the *criminal* law. But if he can undermine the *moral* assumptions on which the criminal law to some important extent rests, he will have succeeded. And so his essay pertains as much to moral philosophy as it does to legal theory.

Note: All original footnotes (over a hundred) have been omitted from this excerpt in order to make the text more fluid and accessible.

∾

DAVID A. J. RICHARDS holds a Ph.D. in Moral and Political Philosophy from Oxford University and a J.D. from Harvard. The Edwin D. Webb Professor of Law at New York University, he teaches both criminal law and constitutional law. Richards was a founder of NYU's internationally distinguished Program for the Study of Law, Philosophy, and Social Theory, of which he is currently director. He is the author of numerous books and articles, including *Conscience and the Constitution* (1993) and *Identity and the Case for Gay Rights* (1999).

from

COMMERCIAL SEX AND THE RIGHTS OF THE PERSON

David A. J. Richards

COMMERCIAL SEX AND THE ALIENATION OF MORAL PERSONALITY

At the root of this argument is the idea of intrinsic moral limitations on the range of human conduct that may be justly subjected to the economic laws of the marketplace. The argument, derived from the father of modern moral theory, Immanuel Kant, is that commercial sex is immoral per se because it involves the sale of the body, which is the foundation of personal integrity, and thus the root of ethical relationships. Kant put the argument in Augustinian terms of objections to the intrinsically degraded nature of sexual appetite per se as an appetite for another person's body. Kant's words are striking: "Sexual love makes of the loved person an Object of appetite; as soon as that appetite has been stilled, the person is cast aside as one casts away a lemon which has been sucked dry." The only legitimate sexuality for Kant is in conventional marriage, where there is reciprocal equality, each party having full rights in the person and the body of the other. Commercial sex, in particular, is forbidden for the same reason that a person "is not entitled to sell a limb, not even one of his teeth." Indeed:

> to allow one's person for profit to be used by another for the satisfaction of sexual desire, to make of oneself an Object of demand, is to dispose over oneself as over a thing and to make of oneself a thing on which another satisfies his appetite, just as he satisfies his hunger upon a steak. But since the inclination is directed towards one's sex and not towards one's humanity, it is clear that one thus partially sacrifices one's humanity and thereby runs a moral risk. Human beings are, therefore, not entitled to offer themselves, for profit, as things for the use of others in the satisfaction of their sexual propensities. . . . To let one's person out on hire and to surrender it to another for the satisfaction of his sexual desire in return for money is the depth of infamy. The underlying moral principle is that man is not his own property and cannot do with his body what he will. The body is part of the self; in its togetherness with the self it constitutes the person; a man cannot make of his person a thing, and this is exactly what happens in *vaga libido*. This manner of satisfying sexual desire is, therefore, not permitted by the rules of morality.

The integrity of the person rests on the integrity of the body; accordingly, the sale of the body is the alienation of moral personality, a kind of moral slavery. Charles Fried's recent references to prostitution in a discussion of the sale of body parts suggests a reintroduction of this argument, although without Kant's Augustinian view of sexual appetite as intrinsically degraded, nor Kant's view that only marital sex is legitimate. Fried does seem to follow Kant in arguing that, in a society where distributive shares are just, the commercial sale of sex is intrinsically immoral for the same reason that the sale of body parts is shameful.

This moral argument is sometimes put in Marxist terms that prostitution represents the ultimate capitalist degradation of personal relationships. Since personal sexual love is conceived by Marx as the model for non-alienated personal relationships, prostitution, degrading love into commerce, cuts to the heart of morality. In similar ways, some contemporary feminists regard prostitution as the ultimate symbol of woman as a degraded sex object, making sexuality a capital asset exploited in impersonal business terms. These arguments seem to depend on the underlying Kantian argument about the alienation of moral personality.

Initially, it is important to see and be puzzled by the fact that the argument proves too much. Commercial sex is condemned as a sale of body parts, but this is, of course, not actually true. Commercial sex is no more the sale of sexual organs than is the sale of a mover's muscles or a model's beauty or a lawyer's legal talent. It is a gross misdescription to call commercial sex, on the one hand, a "sale," and, on the other, to denominate the latter as "services." Both the one and the other are most accurately described as services. So construed, the condemnation of commercial sex as a service would surely require the condemnation of others as well. If it is argued, for example, that commercial sex in some way degrades the talents of the prostitute because the prostitute is emotionally alienated, the same arguments could be made, perhaps more strongly, about other forms of service that our economy not merely tolerates but encourages. Prostitutes clearly perform an important social service; many people find with them a kind of personal release and solace not otherwise available to them; and many prostitutes perform complex supportive and even therapeutic roles for their patrons in addition to sexual services. It is difficult to regard such services as intrinsically degraded: the work is not more emotionally detached than much other contemporary work, and may be less so. It is often well and fairly paid, and the needs served are deep and real. Many forms of factory work in the United States unnecessarily involve repetitive boring tasks that create an emotionally alienated work force and, in a plausible sense, degrade capacities for committed and engaged work. Many people in highly remunerated service professions engage in boring, sometimes socially wasteful work that they know sacrifices their better talents and that leads to deep alienation and emotional detachment. If prostitution is to be criminalized as degraded work, much other work in the United States, a fortiori, would have to be criminalized. We are not prepared to do so in the latter case because of considerations that apply to prostitution as well: in a society committed to equal concern and respect for autonomy people are entitled to make choices for themselves as to trade-offs between alienation, social service, and remuneration. We certainly can criticize these decisions, but we do not regard criminalization as an appropriate expression of our condemnation.

It is impossible to see how sexual services can be distinguished from other cases. The suggestion, for example, that highly remunerated professional services require effort and training, but that prostitution does not, obviously will not do. Many forms of service other than commercial sex call for comparably little effort and training; yet, we do not criminalize them on that ground. In any event, why should years of training make any difference, if the work itself is empty, alienated, and socially unproductive?

However, let us assume arguendo that it is possible to distinguish commercial sex from other forms of service, and even to regard it as a kind of sale of the body like the sale of body parts. Kant's argument, nevertheless, rests on an indefensible interpretation of the relation of moral personality to the body. Kant identifies the person with the body, and then argues roughly as follows:

1. It is always wrong to alienate moral personality.
2. Prostitution is the sale of the body.
3. The person and the body are the same.
4. It is always wrong to engage in prostitution.

The crucial assumption is the third, on the basis of which Kant associates prostitution with a kind of moral slavery.

Kant's identification of moral personality with the body in his discussion of sexual morality is remarkably inconsistent with what he says elsewhere about autonomy as the basis of moral personality. In his central statements of ethical theory, moral personality is described in terms of autonomous independence—the capacity to order and choose one's ends as a free and rational being. By comparison, in his sexual morality discussion, the body acts as an absolute and inexplicable limit on autonomous freedom. It is impossible to square these views. Indeed, the deeper theory of autonomy, Kant's central contribution to ethical theory, requires the rejection of the rather parochial and unimaginative views of moral personality applied in his consideration of sex. Autonomy, in the fullest sense, rests, as we have already seen, on persons' self-critical capacities to assess their present wants and lives, to form and act on wants and projects, and to change them. Autonomy occurs in a certain body, occasioning a person self-critically to take into account that body and its capacities in deciding on the form of his or her life. The existence of certain capacities or physical traits, as opposed to others, will importantly shape basic decisions on work and love. But the embodiment of autonomy does not limit the exercise of autonomy in the way Kant supposes. Kant means to be making the quite valid point about autonomy-based ethics that it is immoral to abdicate one's autonomy, or one's capacity for self-critical choice about the form of one's life. All forms of slavery are thus forbidden because they involve such a surrender of basic autonomy and of the human rights that express and facilitate such autonomy. But Kant conflates this valid moral idea with the quite unrelated idea that one's body parts are not alienable. It is a flat non sequitur to assume that such alienations are alienations of moral personality. The self-critical capacities of autonomy may validly be exercised by the sale or donation of blood or, within limits, other body parts. The extension of the argument to commercial sex is equally mistaken. Voluntarily engaging in commercial sex cannot reasonably be supposed to be the same thing as the forbidden moral slavery of alienating moral personality. Indeed, there is something morally perverse in condemning commercial sex as intrinsic moral slavery when the very prohibition of it seems to be an arbitrary abridgement of sexual autonomy.

Kant's argument would be perceived as the non sequitur that it is if it were applied to other forms of commercial service. Certainly the form of Kant's argument renders dubious the whole idea of the marketplace and the role of personal services in it, as if there were some moral impediment to rendering services on equitable terms. There are moral limits on the range of activities to which the market properly applies; slavery and ceratin kinds of services are correctly forbidden. But the market sensibly operates in making commercially available to willing buyers those willing to offer their services on terms equitable to both parties. Sexual services are not, in moral principle, any less worthy of being in the marketplace than are any other valued services. Rendering such services is no more harmful to the seller or buyer than many other personal services conventionally available and may, in some cases, be less so.

In this connection, Kant, followed by Marxists and recent feminists, argues that in the sexual area there is a unique evil in treating another person as an object, and that commercial sex is the most degraded example of such objectification. Sexual relations of all kinds do, of course, involve making the sex partner the object of one's sexual interests, but it is a rather silly equivocation on the notion of sex object to conflate this uncontroversial truth with the moral claim that sex necessarily treats the partner as a nonperson. In many human relationships, we take other persons as the "objects" of our endeavors, but this grammatical truth says nothing about the morality of our endeavors, which may be highly humane and morally sensitive. In having sex, our partner is the object of our sexual interests, but the moral character of the intercourse will depend on many background factors. Among lovers, the morality of the intercourse may depend on exquisite issues of awareness of and sensitivity to giving and receiving reciprocal pleasure. Among non-lovers, the moral issues may center on issues of the nature of mutual understanding. In commercial sex, presumably a subcase of non-lovers, a crucial issue will be the fairness of the bargain, determined by the nature of the service and the money paid. There is no reason why the morality of a sexual relationship may not, like any other commercial service, be judged in this way. Kant argues that the only just reciprocity for sex can be marriage, and Marx similarly suggests that the only just equivalence can be mutual love. Kant's arguments, as we have seen, are mistaken; and Marx appears to invoke the model of romantic love, which we have seen to be an improper measure of legally enforceable morality. In general, commercial sex involves a valued service and may be given in a fair bargain. The buyer receives a kind of attention not secured elsewhere, and the seller receives fair payment. In neither case is there any evidence that the parties in question are disabled or rendered incapable of love elsewhere. If one thinks of the prostitute as an unloved sex object, the alleged symbol of sexually exploited women carried to its immoral extreme, the crucial difference becomes clear: the prostitute demands and exacts a fair return, as an autonomous person should, for service rendered.

It is not difficult to understand how Kant, so powerful in his statement of abstract universalistic ethics, could be so time-bound in his casuistry of sex; he assumes, as the foundation of his discussion of sexual morality, the Augustinian model of sexuality. Thus, when Kant argues that we do not have a property right in our sexuality, he is not only making the confused argument about alienating moral personality just discussed, but he is echoing Augustine's quasi-theological argument that our sexuality is the property of God which we may employ only on His marital, procreational terms. Accordingly, Kant isolates sex from autonomy in the way conventional for his period. But there is no reason to continue this mistake today. If the religious overtones of the subject caused Kant to miss the implications of his own ideas, there is no reason for us irrationally to isolate sex for ad hoc treatment. Such isolation blinds us to the reality of our sexual and social lives, encouraging us to see degradation in commercial sex when there may be better examples of the degradation of work elsewhere in our society, to see in prostitution loveless waste where, in fact, there may be fair service, and to support as national dogma romantic love which may be a sentimental mask for exploitative self-sacrifice.

PATERNALISTIC ARGUMENTS AGAINST PROSTITUTION

Even if no other moral argument on behalf of criminalization can be sustained, it may still be argued that undertaking particular conduct is sufficiently irrational for an agent that there is moral title to interfere on paternalistic grounds. Such forms of argument in defense of prohibitions of commercial sex, however, are radically inappropriate.

Let us begin with a consideration of the proper scope of paternalistic considerations in general, and then turn to the special problems raised by the application of these considerations to basic life choices. We have discussed the moral point of view in terms of a structure of reasons expressing mutual concern and respect, universalization, and minimization of natural fortuity, and have employed a contractarian model to articulate these ideas. This model would clearly justify a principle of paternalism and explain its proper scope and limits. From the point of view of the original position, the contractors would know that human beings would be subject to certain kinds of irrationalities with severe consequences, including death and the permanent impairment of health. They would, accordingly, agree on an insurance principle against certain of these more serious irrationalities in the event they might occur to them. There are two critical constraints on the scope of such a principle. First, the relevant idea of irrationality cannot itself violate the two constraints of morality imposed on moral contractors: ignorance of specific identity and reliance only on facts capable of empirical validation. In particular, possibly idiosyncratic personal values cannot be smuggled into the content of "irrationality" that defines the scope of the principle. Rather, the notion of irrationality must be defined in terms of a neutral theory that can accommodate the many visions of the good life compatible with moral constraints. For this purpose, the idea of rationality must be defined relative to the agent's system of ends, which are, in turn, determined by the agent's appetites, desire, capacities, and aspirations. Principles of rational choice require the most coherent and satisfying plan for accommodating the agent's ends over time. Accordingly, only those acts are irrational that frustrate the agent's own system of ends, whatever those ends are. Paternalistic considerations, then, only come into play when irrationalities of this kind exist (for example, the agent's jumping out the window will cause his death, which the agent does not want but which he falsely believes will not occur). Second, within the class of irrationalities so defined, paternalistic considerations would properly come into play only when the irrationality was severe and systematic (due to undeveloped or impaired capacities, or lack of opportunity to exercise such capacities) and a serious, permanent impairment of interests was in prospect. Interference in irrationalities outside the scope of this second constraint would be forbidden in large part because allowing people to make and learn from their own mistakes is a crucial part of the development of mature autonomy.

When we consider the application of paternalistic considerations of these kinds to the choice of engaging in commercial sex, we face the question how to assess the rationality of this kind of choice. Again, the idea of rationality employed here takes as its fundamental datum the agent's ends. In this context, principles of rational choice call for the assessment of choices of occupation in terms of the degree to which each choice satisfies the agent's ends over time. This is because choices of occupation determine a number of subchoices having effects throughout the agent's life, and indeed may determine the duration of that life. Since the agent's ends over time are often complex and difficult to anticipate with exactitude, a number of such choices may be equally rational. Nonetheless, there is a coherent sense to the application of rationality criteria to such choices. Some such choices are clearly irrational if they frustrate every significant end which the agent has and available alternatives do not. Such choices, if they satisfy the stringent constraints of the principle discussed above, may be the proper object of paternalistic interference.

One radically inappropriate form of paternalistic interference is that which is grounded in the substitution of the interferer's own personal ends for the ends of the agent. This fails to take seriously the fundamental datum of paternalism, that the agent's ends are given and that the agent acts irrationally only when his or her action frustrates them. This error is a frequent problem in the paternalistic assessment of basic choices such as that of occupation, for in this context people find it all too natural facilely to substitute their own personal solutions for the kinds of imaginative understanding of the perspectives of others required properly to examine these matters. The temptations to such paternalistic distortions are particularly strong in cases in which conventional moral judgments mistakenly condemn certain conduct. The idea of human rights may, in part, be understood as a prophylaxis against such abuses.

The assertion of paternalistic arguments sometimes marks a period of transvaluation of values in matters of certain kinds of life choice. Certain conduct traditionally believed to be morally wrong may no longer justifiably be so regarded. In such a context, the last stand of traditional moralists, after they are compelled to concede the lack of moral foundations for their views, is to retreat to paternalistic arguments that covertly mask the discredited traditional morality. This is quite natural. People attach deep significance to traditionally sanctioned life choices such as marrying and having children. For many, such decisions are of metaphysical import and invoke the person's deepest ideology and philosophy—the kind of choice associated with what many naturally think of as the "meaning of life." Given the personal significance that they may have found in such traditional moral judgments, their imaginations systematically fail them when they try seriously to consider whether it could be a rational life choice to adopt a traditionally condemned occupation. Nevertheless, such views cannot be sustained in terms of rationality criteria and, indeed, can be seen to rest on deep moral confusions which contradict the ultimate values of human rights.

No good argument can be made that paternalistic considerations would justify the kind of interferences, either in choices to render sexual services commercially or to use such services, that are involved in the criminalization of prostitution. Indeed, in many cases such choices seem all *too* rational. It is important, first, to understand that people are not always full-time prostitutes or are full-time prostitutes only for certain periods of their lives, after which they lead more conventional lives. For many, prostitution is engaged in for limited financial and social purposes and is abandoned when these purposes are achieved. These purposes are not irrational. Prostitutes have been described as the highest paid professional women in America. There is no evidence that prostitution itself is necessarily an unpleasant experience for the prostitutes, or that, in general, it disables them from engaging in other loving relationships; indeed, there is some evidence that prostitutes, as a class, are more sexually fulfilled than other American women. Many women have traditionally found in prostitution a useful escape from limited, oppressive, and parochial family and career lives. Prostitution, for them, is not adopted exclusively for economic reasons but because its urban life style affords a kind of social and cultural variety, color, glamor, and range of possibilities that would not have been available to them otherwise. In periods when women had no substantial access to social and economic mobility and the jobs available to them were underpaid and servile, the case for prostitution was rationally powerful. With greater social and economic opportunities for women today, presumably the case for adopting this life is not as strong, but that is not to say that it is not still one of the number of ways in which people may rationally advance their ends. At the least, there is no good case for its irrationality, let alone the kind of irrationality required to bring paternalistic considerations into play.

It is important to see that the traditional arguments for the irrationality of rendering commercial services are typically based on mistaken distortions of the facts. It is as if the extant moralistic condemnation of prostitution inexorably shaped the reading of the facts so as to confirm that the putatively immoral conduct was personally irrational as well. Older accounts of prostitutes, for example, claim that they are mentally deficient and have much shortened life spans because of the horrors of their work. Psychiatrists have commonly supplied a psychiatric makeweight to the moral condemnations by claims that the prostitute is mentally ill or, at least, neurotic. None of these claims has been sustained by careful empirical research observing sound scientific methods. Typically the older claims rested on the limited sample of people whom the researcher mistakenly believed to be typical of the research population at large. For example, a psychiatrist might mistakenly infer from the class of prostitutes who seek therapeutic help that all prostitutes need therapeutic help. In fact, some recent studies indicate that classes of prostitutes may be happier and healthier than other women. In any event, the class of prostitutes whose life is most harsh, that of the streetwalker, is precisely the class affected most directly by criminalization. There is reason to believe that much of the harshness of their lives would be ameliorated by decriminalization.

I do not wish to romanticize the facts of the life of a prostitute. Many accounts forcefully show how difficult and costly an occupation it can be, but many recent accounts of women's traditional role show how difficult and costly that life can be as well. It is as much a mistake to romanticize the life of the traditional woman as it is to romanticize the life of the prostitute. When we look at these lives unsentimentally, without the distorting myths that obscure American perception of these matters, we cannot regard either as necessarily rational or irrational. Rather, we must look with care and imagination at how people autonomously make such choices, often between lesser evils or lesser disadvantages. When we do so, we can see that there is no ground whatsoever to believe that prostitution is, for a mature adult, irrational in the way required to justify paternalistic interference.

In similar fashion, the conventional arguments about the intrinsic irrationality of using commercial sexual services are misplaced. Recent studies of patrons of prostitutes how that patrons rationally secure thereby forms of sexual release, comfort, and even therapeutic understanding. In a period where the most advanced sex therapy often employs paid third parties to help a couple solve their sexual problems, the role of a prostitute as a kind of therapist is a natural one. Certainly, some patrons are able to achieve with prostitutes the natural and fulfilling expression of sexual tastes and fantasies that they cannot indulge in their marriages or central personal relationships. It is a species of dogmatism to assert that these people do not in this way more rationally advance their ends; to the contrary, the use of prostitutes is all *too* rational. Of course, in using prostitutes, a person does not cultivate the higher capacities of sensitivity, taste, and testing that the romantic love tradition celebrates. But such ideals are not without internal critical flaws and, in any event, are not a just basis for legal morality. Even the initiate of the mysteries of romantic love may, on occasion, need a recreational respite from the rigors of his or her path. Commercial sex may thus facilitate the pursuit of this ideal. Compared to the rigors of the frustrations and idealizations of romantic love, prostitution has virtues of its own: the understanding is unsentimentally clear, the reciprocal bargain fair, and the terms are met. Some would say that the best of romantic love does not quixotically repudiate such virtues. Rather, the best in romantic love is realized when the relationship is most realistic, fair, and reciprocal, for then the idealization of the beloved is not a distorting fantastic myth endowed with the egocentric expectations of one's childhood but the celebration of realistic virtues more intensely felt because they meet unique, totally individual needs of a kind that mutual love comfortably discloses. If so, romantic love and commercial sex may, at their best, express common moral virtues.

The radical vision of autonomy and mutual concern and respect is a vision of persons, *as such,* having human rights to create their own personal lives on terms fair to all. To see people in this way is to affirm basic intrinsic limits on the degree to which, even benevolently, one person may control the life of another. Within ethical constraints expressive of mutual concern and respect for autonomy, people are free to adopt a number of disparate and irreconcilable visions of the good life. Indeed, the adoption of different kinds of life plans, within these constraints, affords the moral good of different experiments in living by which people can more rationally assess such basic life choices. The invocation of inadequate moral and paternalistic arguments of the kind we have discussed violates these considerations of human rights, confusing unreflective personal ideology with the moral reasoning that alone can justify the deprivations of liberty by criminal penalty. At the least, such arguments fail to take rights seriously, and thus fail to take seriously the separateness of other persons, their different situations, perspectives, interests, and ideals, and their right to build a life with integrity from such individual materials.

COMMERCIAL SEX,
HUMAN RIGHTS, AND MORAL IDEALS

So far, we have considered a number of negative arguments directed at showing why various moral arguments condemning commercial sex are mistaken. Let us now constructively consider the affirmative case for allowing commercial sex, that is, for the existence of rights of the person that include the right to engage in commercial sex. In this way, we can clarify the scope and limits of this right, and address in more systematic fashion the relation of this right to the personal ideals, frequently invoked previously, that the state allegedly has no right to enforce.

Let us reconsider the view of sexual autonomy that emerged in our discussion of romantic love and its relation to the contractarian analysis of human rights. We argued that human sexuality is marked by its powerful role in the imaginative life and general development of the person, and that the neutral theory of the good, expressive of the values of equal concern and respect of autonomy, required toleration of a number of different visions of the role of sexuality in human life. In the contractarian model, we express these ideas by saying that the choice in the original position is choice under uncertainty: rational people in the original position have no ways of predicting that they may end up in any given situation of life and they must decide only on the basis of facts capable of interpersonal empirical validation. By definition, none of the contractors knows his or her own age, sex, native talents, particular capacity for self-control, social or economic class or position, or the particular form of his or her personal desires. Each contractor will be concerned not to end up in a disadvantaged situation with no appeal to moral principles to denounce deprivations that may render life prospects bitter and mean. To avoid such consequences, the rational strategy in choosing the basic principles of justice would be the "maximin" strategy.

As we have suggested, the contractors in the original position would regard self-respect as the primary good. Accordingly, their aim would be to adopt principles that would ensure that people have the maximum chance of attaining self-respect. Sexual autonomy, the capacity to choose whether or how or with whom or on what terms one will have sexual relations, would be one crucial ingredient of this self-respect; it is one of the forms of personal competence in terms of which people self-critically decide, as free and rational agents, what kind of person they will be. Because contractors in the original position are assumed to be ignorant of specific identity and to take into account only those facts subject to general empirical validation, they may not appeal to special religious duties to procreate in order to override sexual liberty; nor may they appeal to any taste or distaste for certain forms of the physical expression of sexuality in order to override the interest in sexual autonomy; nor may they appeal to concepts of love that illegitimately smuggle in covert premises or prejudices incompatible with respect for the myriad paths to sexual fulfillment. As we have seen, self-respect in the fulfillment and expression of one's sexuality is compatible with a number of modes. Sexual love is one of these modes; romantic love is one highly special form of it. But meaningful sexual fulfillment takes other forms as well. From the point of view of the original position and the values of equal concern and respect for autonomy that it expresses, there is no form of sexual expression that can be given preferred status, for a large and indeterminate class of forms of sexual intercourse is compatible with autonomous self-respect. Accordingly, subject to qualifying moral principles shortly to be discussed, the contractors would, in order to secure the values of sexual self-respect, agree to a principle of obligation and duty, defining correlative human rights, requiring that people be guaranteed the greatest equal liberty of autonomous sexual expression compatible with a like liberty for all.

The contractarian model would, of course, also yield qualifying moral principles relevant to understanding the limits of this human right. Thus, on contractarian grounds, one may easily derive principles forbidding killing or the infliction of harm or gratuitous cruelty. These principles would be accepted because they protect basic interests. Such moral principles are relevant to sexual expression; sexual partners should not inflict serious and irreparable bodily harm on one another, even if such harm is consensual. On the other hand, these principles would not justify prohibition of forms of consensual sexual conduct, including commercial sex, which are not harmful. Similarly, moral principles of fidelity can be derived from the original positions, requiring that mutual undertakings, voluntarily and maturely entered into, be observed faithfully. Such principles, again, do not justify general prohibition of forms of consensual sexual conduct, or commercial sex in particular; they justify, at most, only specific constraints on breaches of fidelity, such as breach of contract, or fraud and deception. A principle of consideration can also be derived from the original position, requiring that persons not impose upon others unnecessary annoyance and disturbances. This principle would justify time, place, and manner restrictions on prostitution and its solicitation, but certainly not a complete prohibition.

In addition, the contractarian model justifies, as we have seen, a moral principle of paternalism in certain carefully delimited circumstances. This principle does not justify an absolute prohibition on consensual sexual conduct in general or commercial sex in particular. However, it is important to notice here that the imperative of sexual autonomy would not apply to persons presumably lacking rational capacities—young children, for example—since the value of autonomous sexual expression turns on the existence of developed capacities of rational choice. Accordingly, the sexual commerce of quite young children may be forbidden, just as sexual intercourse with and by them may be limited in various ways. One would need, of course, to determine the appropriate age of majority for those purposes based on available psychological data. The most that can be said here is that the principle of paternalism would not sustain an unrealistically old age at which sexual nonage is ended.

Finally, principles of distributive justice would be agreed to in the original position that would require a certain form of the distribution of wealth, property, status, and opportunity. Sometimes it is suggested that prostitution is appropriately criminalized in order to advance the more just distribution of the goods required by such principles of distributive justice, on the grounds that prostitution is mainly a temptation to the poor and a symptom of poverty. Of course, on grounds of distributive justice, people should have more equal job opportunities than they currently have. Certainly better job opportunities should, for example, be available to racial minorities and women. But it does not follow that high-income job opportunities that currently exist for poor people should, on grounds of justice, be ended. If one wishes responsibly to ameliorate the situation of racial minorities who are a disproportionate number of the women arrested for prostitution, decriminalization, not criminalization, is the just course, for it would remove the moral stigma and the consequent unjustified self-contempt that they experience, the various ancillary evils that criminalization fosters, and the uniquely degrading exposure to the American criminal justice system that their more advantaged call-girl sisters in large part avoid. In addition, responsible moral concern for whatever economic disadvantages streetwalkers suffer would take the form of regulations to ensure them economic fairness, including forms of union organization. Criminalization, in contrast, fosters the economic exploitation that it is fallaciously assumed to remedy. . . .

CHAPTER FIFTEEN

In Defense of
DESPAIR

$\mathcal{G}$enerally, sin stretches around pleasures we ache to experience. Like prostitution and suicide, despair represents an important exception.

An overlooked but serious sin, losing all hope may well terrify us. We know despair afflicts others; maybe something like it has even plagued us in the past. We don't want anything to do with despair, unless our jobs as physicians, judges, or social workers (to name just a few examples) necessitate it. Should we ever find ourselves sinking in it, though, we expect compassion.

Yet Catholic theology singles out despair as superlatively sinful because in it, someone rejects God. In despair, a person decides not to trust God, not to believe that God can fix any problem. Despair combines blasphemy and pride together. In despair, a person turns her back on God, which is the worst thing someone can do—even worse than murder, for example. Murderers are often sorry about what they've done—they seek redemption. In despair a person refuses redemption.

Whereas the seven deadly sins can all be forgiven, despair cannot. This isn't fair, Joyce Carol Oates argues in the following essay from 1993, and amounts to kicking someone when she is down. Precisely

when we most need comfort, the law locks us up and throws away
the key.

∼

JOYCE CAROL OATES, Roger S. Berlind '52 Professor in the Humanities at Princeton University, is the author of numerous works,
including *Blonde* (2000); *Broke Heart Blues* (1999); *My Heart Laid
Bare* (1998); *The Collector of Hearts* (1998); *We Were the Mulvaneys*
(1996); *Zombie* (1995); and *What I Lived For* (1994), the last of which
was nominated for the Pulitzer Prize. A winner of the National Book
Award (1970), she is a member of the American Academy of Arts and
Letters.

DESPAIR: THE ONE UNFORGIVABLE SIN

Joyce Carol Oates

What mysterious cruelty in the human soul, to have invented despair as a sin! Like the seven deadly sins, despair is a mythical state. It has no quantifiable existence; it is merely part of an allegorical world view, yet no less lethal for that. Unlike other sins, however, despair is by tradition the sole sin that cannot be forgiven; it is the conviction that one is damned absolutely, thus a repudiation of the Christian Saviour and a challenge to God's infinite capacity for forgiveness. The sins for which one may be forgiven—pride, anger, lust, sloth, avarice, gluttony, envy— are all firmly attached to the objects of this world, but despair seems to bleed out beyond the confines of the immediate ego-centered self and to relate to no desire, to no thing. The alleged sinner has detached himself even from the possibility of sin, and this the Catholic Church, as the self-appointed voice of God on earth, cannot allow.

Religion is organized power in the seemingly benevolent guise of the sacred, and power is, as we know, chiefly concerned with its own preservation. Its structures, its elaborate rituals and customs and Scriptures and commandments and ethics, its very nature, objectify human experience, insisting that what is out there in the world is of unquestionably greater significance than what is in here in the human spirit. Despair, surely the least aggressive of sins, is dangerous to the totalitarian temperament because it is a state of intense inwardness, thus independence. The despairing soul is a rebel.

So, too, suicide, the consequence of extreme despair, has long been a mortal sin in Catholic Church theology, for it is equivalent to murder. Suicide, the most willful and the most defiantly antisocial of human acts, has an element of the forbidden, the obscene, the taboo about it. While thinkers of antiquity condoned suicide, in certain circumstances at least—in the "Meditations" Marcus Aurelius wrote, "In all that you do or say or think, recollect that at any time the power of withdrawal from life is in your hands"—the church vigorously punished suicides in ways calculated to warn others and to confirm, posthumously their despair. Stakes were driven through hearts, bodies were mutilated, and the dead were denied burial in consecrated soil. Ever purposeful, the Catholic Church could confiscate goods and lands belonging to suicides.

Yet how frustrating it must be, the attempt to outlaw and to punish despair! Isn't "despair" a malady with which we label people who seem to have decided that life doesn't interest them, just as "narcissism" is the charge we make against people who aren't nearly so interested in us as we'd hoped they would be?

Despair as a sin is a political phenomenon in which, in our time, it's extremely difficult to believe. As a state of intense inwardness, however, despair seems to us a spiritual and moral experience that cuts across superficial boundaries of language, culture and history. No doubt, true despair is as mute and unreflective as flesh lacking consciousness; but the poetics of despair, particularly from the pen of Emily Dickinson, has been transcendently eloquent:

The difference between Despair
And Fear—is like the One

Between the instant of a Wreck—And when the Wreck has been—
The Mind is smooth—no Motion—
Contented as the Eye
Upon the Forehead of a Bust—
That knows—it cannot see—

This condition, this stasis of the spirit, in which life's energies are
paralyzed even as life's physical processes continue, is the essence of
literary despair. The world goes its own way, and the isolated consciousness of the writer splits from it, as if splitting from the body itself. This
state of keenly heightened inwardness has always fascinated the writer,
whose subject is after all the imaginative reconstruction of language. The
ostensible subject out there is but the vehicle, or the pretext, for the
discoveries to be made in here in the activity of creating.

Literary despair is best contemplated during insomniac nights, and
perhaps most keenly savored during adolescence, when insomnia can
have the aura of the romantic and the forbidden, when sleepless nights
can signal rebellion against a placidly sleeping—unconscious—world.
At such times, inner and outer worlds seem to merge; insights that by
day would be lost define themselves like those phosphorescent minerals
that are coarse and ordinary in the light but yield a mysterious
glimmering beauty in the dark. Here is the "Zero at the Bone" of which
Dickinson, our supreme poet of inwardness, wrote, with an urgency
time has not blunted.

My first immersion in the literature of despair came at a time of
chronic adolescent insomnia, and so the ravishing experience of reading
certain writers—most of them, apart from Dickinson and William
Faulkner, associated with what was called European existentialism—is
indelibly bound up with that era in my life. Perhaps the ideal reader is
an adolescent: restless, vulnerable, passionate, hungry to learn, skeptical
and naive by turns, believing in the power of the imagination to change,
if not life itself, one's comprehension of life. The degree to which we
remain adolescents is the degree to which we remain ideal readers, for
whom the act of opening a book can be a sacred one, fraught with psychic

risk. For such a reader, each work of a certain magnitude means the assimilation of a new voice—that of Dostoyevsky's Underground Man or that of Nietzsche's Zarathustra—and the permanent altering of one's own interior world.

Literary despair, as opposed to real despair, became fashionable at midcentury, when there was a flood of rich English translations of European writers of surpassing originality, boldness and genius. Misleadingly linked by so-called existentialist themes, these highly individual writers—among them Dostoyevsky, Kafka, Kierkegaard, Mann, Sartre, Camus, Pavese, Pirandello, Beckett, Ionesco—seemed to characterize the very mission of literature itself: not to uplift, still less to entertain, but to penetrate to the most inward and intransigent of truths.

Despair at the randomness of mankind's fate and of mankind's repeatedly demonstrated inhumanity was in a sense celebrated, as if we might transcend those terrors through the symbolic strategies of art. Then it was thought that no fate, however horrific—and the graphically detailed execution of the faithful officer in Kafka's great story "In the Penal Colony" and the ignominious execution of Joseph K. in Kafka's "Trial" were classic examples—could not be transmogrified by the very contemplation of the horrific fate, or redeemed, in a sense, by the artist's visionary fearlessness.

It is not just that despair is immune to the comforts of the ordinary— despair rejects comfort. And Kafka, our exemplary artist of despair, is one of our greatest humorists as well. The bleakness of his vision is qualified by a brash, unsettling humor that flies in the face of expectation. Is it tragic that Gregor Samsa is metamorphosed into a giant cockroach, suffers, dies and is swept out with the trash? Is it tragic that the Hunger Artist starves to death, too finicky to eat the common food of humanity? No, these are ludicrous fates, meant to provoke laughter. The self-loathing at the heart of despair repudiates compassion.

I would guess that my generation, coming of age at the very start of the 60's, when the national mood was one of intense political and moral crisis, is the last American generation to so contemplate inwardness as a romantic state of being; it is the last generation of literary-minded young men and women who interiorized the elegiac comedy of Beckett's characters, the radiant madness of Dostoyevsky's self-lacerated God-haunted seekers, the subtle ironies of Camus's prose.

I doubt that contemporary adolescents can identify with Faulkner's Quentin Compson in "The Sound and the Fury," someone who moves with the fatedness of a character in a ballad toward his suicide in the Charles River. "People cannot do anything that dreadful they cannot do anything very dreadful at all they cannot even remember tomorrow what seemed dreadful today," Quentin's alcoholic father tells him, as if urging him to his doom. Even tragedy, in Faulkner's vision of a debased 20th-century civilization, is secondhand.

That this is a profound if dismaying truth, or an outrageous libel of the human spirit, either position to be confirmed by history, seems beside the point today, in a country in which politics has become the national religion. The literature of despair may posit suicide as a triumphant act of rebellion, or a repudiation of the meanness of life, but our contemporary mood is one of compassionate horror at any display of self-destruction. We perceive it, perhaps quite accurately, as misguided politics, as a failure to link in here with out there.

For Americans, the collective belief, the moral imperative, is an unflagging optimism. We want to believe in the infinite elasticity of the future: what we can will, we can enact. Just give us time! —and sufficient resources. Our ethos has always been hard-core pragmatism as defined by our most eminent philosopher, William James: truth is something that works. It is a vehicle empowered to carry us to our destination.

Yet there remains a persistent counterimpulse, an irresistible tug toward stasis and toward those truths that, in Melville's words, will not be comforted. At the antipode of American exuberance and optimism there is the poet's small, still, private voice, the voice of individual conscience; the voice, for instance, of Dickinson, who, like Rainer Maria Rilke and Gerard Manley Hopkins, mined the ideal vocabulary for investigating those shifting, penumbral states of consciousness that do, in the long run, constitute our lives. Whatever our public identities may be, whatever our official titles, our heralded or derided achievements and the statistics that accrue to us like cobwebs, this is the voice we trust. For, if despair's temptations can be resisted, surely we become more human and compassionate, more like one another in our common predicament.

> There is a pain—so utter—
> It swallows substance up—
> Then covers the Abyss with Trance—
> So Memory can step
> Around—across—upon it—
> As one within a Swoon—
> Goes safely—where an open eye—
> Would drop Him—Bone by Bone.

Dickinson's poem must be one of the most terrifying ever written, yet, in the way of all great art, it so eloquently transcends its subject that it is exhilarating.

CHAPTER SIXTEEN

In Defense of
SUICIDE

*L*ike the voluntary choice to earn money or gain favors through prostitution, the decision to end it all supposedly comes down to autonomy, or self-rule. Our actions often affect people around us, to be sure, but shouldn't we enjoy authority over ourselves?

Religious and secular law have long criminalized suicide. In various Western countries, a person who unsuccessfully attempted suicide could be prosecuted in court. In various religions, persons who succeeded in the attempt were denied a sacred burial.

One of the most revered moral thinkers of antiquity, Seneca, condones suicide. In fact, he even recommends it when quality of life has sunk unbearably: "To such a life, as you are aware, one should not always cling. For mere living is not a good, but living well. Accordingly, the wise man will live as long as he ought, not as long as he can." His argument, recorded in the following essay from around 63 A.D., sounds remarkably similar to the plea of contemporary proponents of euthanasia.

Why should we admire dying people who bravely confront a terminal diagnosis? Wouldn't it make more sense to admire dying people who, as Seneca puts it, cheat death and kill themselves before a disease or threatening condition will? Why should we surrender self-control instead of seizing it? Life can become gruesomely painful or bleak, and constant suffering may make us envy the dead. Seneca's moral views are generally conservative by today's standards, and yet he finds perverse the idea that *any* life is better than death.

Note: In order to make the text more fluid and accessible, I have omitted the footnotes from Seneca's essay.

∾

SENECA (4 B.C.–65 A.D.), one of the most insightful moralists of the ancient world, outlived Jesus, his contemporary. Not long after beginning a career in politics and law in Rome about the year 31 A.D., the emperor Caligula tried to have him killed. Next, in 41 A.D., the emperor Claudius banished Seneca to Corsica on a charge of adultery with the princess Julia Livilla, the emperor's niece. Seneca was allowed to return to Rome eight years later, thanks to the efforts of the emperor's wife. He became praetor in 50, married rich, established his power, and became tutor to the future emperor Nero. Seneca retired in 62 A.D. and proceeded to write some of his best philosophical works. When political enemies denounced him in 65 A.D., he was ordered to commit suicide and met death calmly.

ON THE PROPER TIME TO SLIP THE CABLE

Seneca

translated by Richard M. Gummere

After a long space of time I have seen your beloved Pompeii. I was thus brought again face to face with the days of my youth. And it seemed to me that I could still do, nay, had only done a short time ago, all the things which I did there when a young man. We have sailed past life, Lucilius, as if we were on a voyage, and just as when at sea, to quote from our poet Vergil,

> Lands and towns are left astern,

even so, on this journey where time flies with the greatest speed, we put below the horizon first our boyhood and then our youth, and then the space which lies between young manhood and middle age and borders on both, and next, the best years of old age itself. Last of all, we begin to sight the general bourne of the race of man. Fools that we are, we believe this bourne to be a dangerous reef; but it is the harbour, where we must some day put in, which we may never refuse to enter; and if a man has reached this harbour in his early years, he has no more right to complain than a sailor who has made a quick voyage. For some sailors, as you know, are tricked and held back by sluggish winds, and grow weary and sick of the slow-moving calm; while others are carried quickly home by steady gales.

You may consider that the same thing happens to us: life has carried some men with the greatest rapidity to the harbour, the harbour they were bound to reach even if they tarried on the way, while others it has fretted and harassed. To such a life, as you are aware, one should not always cling. For mere living is not a good, but living well. Accordingly, the wise man will live as long as he ought, not as long as he can. He will mark in what place, with whom, and how he is to conduct his existence, and what he is about to do. He always reflects concerning the quality, and not the quantity, of his life. As soon as there are many events in his life that give him trouble and disturb his peace of mind, he sets himself free. And this privilege is his, not only when the crisis is upon him, but as soon as Fortune seems to be playing him false; then he looks about carefully and sees whether he ought, or ought not, to end his life on that account. He holds that it makes no difference to him whether his taking-off be natural or self-inflicted, whether it comes later or earlier. He does not regard it with fear, as if it were a great loss; for no man can lose very much when but a driblet remains. It is not a question of dying earlier or later, but of dying well or ill. And dying well means escape from the danger of living ill.

That is why I regard the words of the well-known Rhodian as most unmanly. This person was thrown into a cage by his tyrant, and fed there like some wild animal. And when a certain man advised him to end his life by fasting, he replied: "A man may hope for anything while he has life." This may be true; but life is not to be purchased at any price. No matter how great or how well-assured certain rewards may be, I shall not strive to attain them at the price of a shameful confession of weakness. Shall I reflect that Fortune has all power over one who lives, rather than reflect that she has no power over one who knows how to die? There are times, nevertheless, when a man, even though certain death impends and he knows that torture is in store for him, will refrain from lending a hand to his own punishment; to himself, however, he would lend a hand. It is folly to die through fear of dying. The executioner is upon you; wait for him. Why anticipate him? Why assume the management of a cruel task that belongs to another? Do you grudge your executioner his privilege, or do you merely relieve him of his task? Socrates might have ended his life by fasting; he might have died by starvation rather than by poison. But instead of this he spent thirty days in prison awaiting death, not with the idea "everything may happen," or "so long an interval has room for many a hope" but in order that he might show himself submissive to the laws and make the last moments of Socrates an edification to his friends. What would have been more foolish than to scorn death, and yet fear poison?

Scribonia, a woman of the stern old type, was an aunt of Drusus Libo. This young man was as stupid as he was well born, with higher ambitions than anyone could have been expected to entertain in that epoch, or a man like himself in any epoch at all. When Libo had been carried away ill from the senate-house in his litter, though certainly with a very scanty train of followers,—for all his kinsfolk undutifully deserted him, when he was no longer a criminal but a corpse,—he began to consider whether he should commit suicide, or wait death. Scribonia said to him: "What pleasure do you find in doing another man's work?" But he did not follow her advice; he laid violent hands upon himself. And he was right, after all; for when a man is doomed to die in two or three days at his enemy's pleasure, he is really "doing another man's work" if he continues to live.

No general statement can be made, therefore, with regard to the question whether, when a power beyond our control threatens us with death, we should anticipate death, or await it. For there are many arguments to pull us in either direction. If one death is accompanied by torture, and the other is simple and easy, why not snatch the latter? Just as I shall select my ship when I am about to go on a voyage, or my house when I propose to take a residence, so I shall choose my death when I am about to depart from life. Moreover, just as a long-drawn-out life does not necessarily mean a better one, so a long-drawn-out death necessarily means a worse one. There is no occasion when the soul should be humoured more than at the moment of death. Let the soul depart as it feels itself impelled to go; whether it seeks the sword, or the halter, or some draught that attacks the veins, let it proceed and burst the bonds of its slavery. Every man ought to make his life acceptable to others besides himself, but his death to himself alone. The best form of death is the one we like. Men are foolish who reflect thus: "One person will say that my conduct was not brave enough; another, that I was too headstrong; a third, that a particular kind of death would have betokened more spirit." What you should really reflect is: "I have under consideration a purpose with which the talk of men has no concern!" Your sole aim should be to escape from Fortune as speedily as possible; otherwise, there will be no lack of persons who will think ill of what you have done.

You can find men who have gone so far as to profess wisdom and yet maintain that one should not offer violence to one's own life, and hold it accursed for a man to be the means of his own destruction; we should wait, say they, for the end decreed by nature. But one who says this does not see that he is shutting off the path to freedom. The best thing which eternal law ever ordained was that it allowed to us one entrance into life, but many exits. Must I await the cruelty either of disease or of man, when I can depart through the midst of torture, and shake off my troubles? This is the one reason why we cannot complain of life: it keeps no one against his will. Humanity is well situated, because no man is unhappy except by his own fault. Live, if you so desire; if not, you may return to the place whence you came. You have often been cupped in order to relieve headaches. You have had veins cut for the purpose of reducing your weight. If you would pierce your heart, a gaping wound is not necessary; a lancet will open the way to that great freedom, and tranquillity can be purchased at the cost of a pin-prick.

What, then, is it which makes us lazy and sluggish? None of us reflects that some day he must depart from this house of life; just so old tenants are kept from moving by fondness for a particular place and by custom, even in spite of ill-treatment. Would you be free from the restraint of your body? Live in it as if you were about to leave it. Keep thinking of the fact that some day you will be deprived of this tenure; then you will be more brave against the necessity of departing. But how will a man take thought of his own end, if he craves all things without end? And yet there is nothing so essential for us to consider. For our training in other things is perhaps superfluous. Our souls have been made ready to meet poverty; but our riches have held out. We have armed ourselves to scorn pain; but we have had the good fortune to possess sound and healthy bodies, and so have never been forced to put this virtue to the test. We have taught ourselves to endure bravely the loss of those we love; but Fortune has preserved to us all whom we loved. It is in this one matter only that the day will come which will require us to test our training.

You need not think that none but great men have had the strength to burst the bonds of human servitude; you need not believe that this cannot be done except by a Cato,—Cato, who with his hand dragged forth the spirit which he had not succeeded in freeing by the sword. Nay, men of the meanest lot in life have by a mighty impulse escaped to safety, and when they were not allowed to die at their own convenience, or to suit themselves in their choice of the instruments of death, they have snatched up whatever was lying ready to hand, and by sheer strength have turned objects which were by nature harmless into weapons of their own. For example, there was lately in a training-school for wild-beast gladiators a German, who was making ready for the morning exhibition; he withdrew in order to relieve himself,—the only thing which he was allowed to do in secret and without the presence of a guard. While so engaged, he seized the stick of wood, tipped with a sponge, which was devoted to the vilest uses, and stuffed it, just as it was, down his throat; thus he blocked up his windpipe, and choked the breath from his body. That was truly to insult death! Yes, indeed; it was not a very elegant or becoming way to die; but what is more foolish than to be over-nice about dying? What a brave fellow! He surely deserved to be allowed to choose his fate! How bravely he would have wielded a sword! With what courage he would have hurled himself into the depths of the sea, or down a precipice! Cut off from resources on every hand, he yet found a way to furnish himself with death, and with a weapon for death. Hence you can understand that nothing but the will need postpone death. Let each man judge the deed of this most zealous fellow as he likes, provided we agree on this point,—that the foulest death is preferable to the fairest slavery.

Inasmuch as I began with an illustration taken from humble life, I shall keep on with that sort. For men will make greater demands upon themselves, if they see that death can be despised even by the most despised class of men. The Catos, the Scipios, and the others whose names we are wont to hear with admiration, we regard as beyond the sphere of imitation; but I shall now prove to you that the virtue of which I speak is found as frequently in the gladiators' training-school as among the leaders in a civil war. Lately a gladiator, who had been sent forth to the morning exhibition, was being conveyed in a cart along with the other prisoners; nodding as if he were heavy with sleep, he let his head fall over so far that it was caught in the spokes; then he kept his body in position long enough to break his neck by the revolution of the wheel. So he made his escape by means of the very wagon which was carrying him to his punishment.

When a man desires to burst forth and take his departure, nothing stands in his way. It is an open space in which Nature guards us. When our plight is such as to permit it, we may look about us for an easy exit. If you have many opportunities ready to hand, by means of which you may liberate yourself, you may make a selection and think over the best way of gaining freedom; but if a chance is hard to find, instead of the best, snatch the next best, even though it be something unheard of, something new. If you do not lack the courage, you will not lack the cleverness, to die. See how even the lowest class of slave, when suffering goads him on, is aroused and discovers a way to deceive even the most watchful guards! He is truly great who not only has given himself the order to die, but has also found the means.

I have promised you, however, some more illustrations drawn from the same games. During the second event in a sham sea-fight one of the barbarians sank deep into his own throat a spear which had been given him for use against his foe. "Why, oh why," he said, "have I not long ago escaped from all this torture and all this mockery? Why should I be armed and yet wait for death to come?" This exhibition was all the more striking because of the lesson men learn from it that dying is more honourable than killing.

What, then? If such a spirit is possessed by abandoned and dangerous men, shall it not be possessed also by those who have trained themselves to meet such contingencies by long meditation, and by reason, the mistress of all things? It is reason which teaches us that fate has various ways of approach, but the same end, and that it makes no difference at what point the inevitable event begins. Reason, too, advises us to die, if we may, according to our taste; if this cannot be, she advises us to die according to our ability, and to seize upon whatever means shall offer itself for doing violence to ourselves. It is criminal to "live by robbery"; but, on the other hand, it is most noble to "die by robbery." Farewell.

POSTSCRIPT

Over four centuries ago, the Italian statesman Machiavelli exhorted others to study the road to hell in order to avoid it. A century later the English poet John Milton, author of *Paradise Lost*, wrote that we must dissect evil if we wish to understand goodness.

This sounds like altogether astute advice, assuming of course that everyone wants to be a genuinely good person. A guide that taught people how to get away with wrongdoing might be dangerous, if those who used the guide wanted to gain an advantage over their law-abiding neighbors.

This book risks showing us how to justify iniquity. But it does not aim to do that. In questioning just what is so wrong about sin, the essays of these philosophers suggest that sin might have limits we haven't fully grasped.

Like the apple in the Garden of Eden, a convenient rationalization for our misdeeds beckons us. There's something in the wisdom of these philosophers most of us yearn to absorb. Like Machiavelli, though, we don't want to die trying.

The struggle between innocence and experience ends shortly after education begins. Experience, the inevitable victor, generally strengthens us—a moral education makes it more, not less, likely that we will do the right thing.

ABOUT THE CONTRIBUTORS

Aaron Ben-Ze'ev is Rector at the University of Haifa, Israel, as well as Professor of Philosophy and Codirector of the Center for Interdisciplinary Research on Emotions. Among his numerous articles and books are *Good Gossip* (1994), *The Perceptual System* (1993), and *The Subtlety of Emotions* (2000).

George Eliot was the pseudonym for Mary Ann Evans (1819–1890), the celebrated English author of *Daniel Deronda* and *Middlemarch*, among other works. A writer of uncommon intelligence, she challenged social conventions and wrote novels that deftly explored the moral complexities of human interaction. A champion of Victorian rationalism, she simply refused to smile on religious belief.

Anthony Ellis was Senior Lecturer in Moral Philosophy and Chair of the Moral Philosophy Department in the University of St. Andrews, Scotland, before becoming Professor of Philosophy in Virginia Commonwealth University. He was also cofounder and first Academic Director of the Centre for Philosophy and Public Affairs in St. Andrews. He is currently editor of the journal *Philosophical Books*.

Jane English was a faculty member in the Department of Philosophy at the University of North Carolina at Chapel Hill when she died climbing the Matterhorn in 1978. Prior to the fatal accident, she published several well-received articles and edited both *Sex Equality* (1977) and *Feminism and Philosophy* (1977).

Ludwig Feuerbach (1804–1872) made a great splash in Europe upon the publication of *The Essence of Christianity* (1841). His argument that God is merely the outward projection of man's inward essence scandalized contemporary society. Born in Bavaria, he traveled to Berlin to study under Hegel, an eminent philosopher. Although Feuerbach never managed to surpass his first work, he inspired another influential thinker: Karl Marx.

Sigmund Freud (1856–1939) refined the techniques of psychoanalysis for the treatment of psychological and emotional disorders. On March 12, 1938, Nazi troops marched into Austria and assumed power. On June 4, following numerous international interventions, Freud was allowed to emigrate to London with his wife, his youngest daughter Anna, his housekeeper, and his medical caretaker. Freud's other children also managed to escape. Four elderly and infirm sisters were forced to remain in Vienna and eventually died in concentration camps in 1941.

Bernard Mandeville (1670–1733) enjoyed a spectacular rise to fame on the strength of his verse *The Fable of the Bees*, published in England. A physician interested in ethical matters, he grew up and wrote in a country wracked by controversy over modern commerce and its moral consequences. His work influenced the philosophical doctrine of utilitarianism, the idea that acts should be evaluated on the basis of how happy they make people.

H. L. Mencken (1880–1956) opposed Prohibition openly and spoke out on a wide variety of social issues in the United States. The most prominent newspaperman and political commentator of his day, he considered religious belief a curse, a blemish on human history. His admiration for Nietzsche sat well with his frequent appeals to common sense as the way out of confusion and disagreement. A native of Baltimore, he rode far on the strength of an exceptional prose style.

Jerome Neu holds a doctorate in philosophy from Oxford University. He is Professor of Philosophy at the University of California at Santa Cruz, where he has at various times been chair of the programs in Philosophy, History of Consciousness, and Legal Studies. He is the author of *Emotion, Thought, and Therapy* (1977) and of *A Tear Is an Intellectual Thing: The Meanings of Emotion* (2000) and editor of *The Cambridge Companion to Freud* (1991).

Friedrich Nietzsche (1844–1900), a German, grew up the son of a Lutheran minister. While astonishingly young, he accepted the chair of Classical Philology at the University of Basel. He determined to give his age new values, Schopenhauer's "will to power" serving as the guiding principle. For Nietzsche the will to power held ethical primacy and properly represented the noble man's ultimate objective. Nietzsche denounced Christianity for resenting this world and for consigning all whom it hates to hell. In his major work, *Thus Spake Zarathustra* (1884), he introduces his ideal, a man he called *Uebermensch* or "superman."

Humanity should recognize, Nietzsche insisted, that certain "supermen," by virtue of their native superiority, simply cannot be expected to follow by the rules of the hoi polloi. Ultimately, he went insane and had to be cared for by his rebarbative sister Elisabeth.

David Novitz studied at Rhodes University in South Africa before finishing his doctorate in philosophy at Oxford University. He is author of *Pictures and Their Use in Communication* (1977); *Knowledge, Fiction and Imagination* (1987); and *The Boundaries of Art* (1992), as well as numerous journal articles. He has also coedited two well-known collections of essays on New Zealand society (together with sociologist Bill Willmott).

Joyce Carol Oates, Roger S. Berlind '52 Professor in the Humanities at Princeton University, is the author of numerous works, including *Blonde* (2000); *Broke Heart Blues* (1999); *My Heart Laid Bare* (1998); *The Collector of Hearts* (1998); *We Were the Mulvaneys* (1996); *Zombie* (1995); and *What I Lived For* (1994), the last of which was nominated for the Pulitzer Prize. A winner of the National Book Award (1970), she is a member of the American Academy of Arts and Letters.

John Portmann's book *When Bad Things Happen to Other People* (2000) was nominated for Phi Beta Kappa's Ralph Waldo Emerson Prize. He studied philosophy at Yale and Cambridge and now lectures at the University of Virginia.

David A. J. Richards holds a Ph.D. in Moral and Political Philosophy from Oxford University and a J.D. from Harvard. The Edwin D. Webb Professor of Law at New York University, he teaches both criminal law and constitutional law. Richards was a founder of NYU's internationally distinguished Program for the Study of Law, Philosophy, and Social Theory, of which he is currently director. He is the author of numerous books and articles, including *Conscience and the Constitution* (1993) and *Identity and the Case for Gay Rights* (1999).

Seneca (4 B.C.–65 A.D.), one of the most insightful moralists of the ancient world, outlived Jesus, his contemporary. Not long after beginning a career in politics and law in Rome about the year 31 A.D. , the emperor Caligula tried to have him killed. Next, in 41 A.D., the emperor Claudius banished Seneca to Corsica on a charge of adultery with the princess Julia Livilla, the emperor's niece. Seneca was allowed to return to Rome eight years later, thanks to the efforts of the emperor's wife. He became praetor in 50, married rich, established his power, and became tutor to the future emperor Nero. Seneca retired in 62 A.D. and proceeded to write some of his best philosophical works. When political enemies denounced him in 65 A.D., he was ordered to commit suicide and met death calmly.

Jonathan Swift (1667–1745) is widely considered one of the greatest writers of the eighteenth century and one of the most gifted satirists of all times. An Irishman, he was ordained a priest in the Anglican Church. His masterpiece, *Gulliver's Travels*, was published anonymously in 1726.

Richard Wasserstrom is Professor Emeritus of Philosophy at the University of California, Santa Cruz. He has published a number of articles in philosophy that examine the moral issues and arguments in topics such as racism and sexism, affirmative action, punishment, privacy, and war.

Oscar Wilde (1854–1900), an Irishman, was educated at Magdalene College, Oxford and served two years in prison for acts of "gross indecency." Among his celebrated works figure *The Importance of Being Earnest* (1895), *Lady Windemere's Fan* (1892), *A Woman of No Importance* (1893), and *De Profundis* (1905). He died in poverty and disgrace in a Paris hotel after having hopelessly pursued an English aristocrat, Lord Alfred Douglas, who refused to resume their romance and later converted to Roman Catholicism. Wilde himself converted to Catholicism on his deathbed.

INDEX